SCHOOL FOR CITIZENS

SCHOOL FOR CITIZENS

Theatre and Civil Society in Imperial Russia

MURRAY FRAME

YALE UNIVERSITY PRESS
NEW HAVEN AND LONDON

For my Mum and Dad

For information about this and other Yale University Press publications, please contact:

U.S. Office: sales.press@yale.edu   www.yalebooks.com
Europe Office: sales@yaleup.co.uk   www.yaleup.co.uk

Set in Minion by MATS typesetting, Southend-on-Sea
Printed in Great Britain by St Edmundsbury Press Ltd, Bury St Edmunds

Library of Congress Cataloging-in-Publication Data

Frame, Murray.
School for citizens: theatre and civil society in Imperial Russia / Murray Frame.
p. cm.
Includes bibliographical references and index.
ISBN 0-300-11101-0 (cl. : alk. paper)
1. Theater and society--Russia--History. I. Title.
PN2721.5.F73 2006
792.0947--dc22

2005034839

A catalogue record for this book is available from the British Library.

10 9 8 7 6 5 4 3 2 1

CONTENTS

ILLUSTRATIONS

1. The Free Russian Theatre on Tsaritsyn Meadow, St Petersburg (Kallash and Efros (eds.), *Istoriia russkogo teatra*).
2. Denis Fonvizin (Kallash and Efros (eds.), *Istoriia russkogo teatra*).
3. Frontispiece of the 1783 edition of *The Minor* (Kallash and Efros (eds.), *Istoriia russkogo teatra*).
4. Alexander Shakhovskoi (Vsevolodskii-Gerngross, *Teatr v Rossii v epokhu otechestvennoi voiny*).
5. Expulsion of a French actress from Moscow during the war with Napoleon (Vsevolodskii-Gerngross, *Teatr v Rossii v epokhu otechestvennoi voiny*).
6. Nikolai Sheremetev (Kallash and Efros (eds.), *Istoriia russkogo teatra*).
7. The theatre at Ostankino (Kallash and Efros (eds.), *Istoriia russkogo teatra*).
8. Mikhail Shchepkin (*Ezhegodnik imperatorskikh teatrov. Sezon 1907–1908 gg.* (St Petersburg, n.d.)).
9. Vasily Karatygin (*Ezhegodnik imperatorskikh teatrov. Sezon 1903–1904 gg.* (St Petersburg, n.d.)).
10. Pavel Mochalov (*Ezhegodnik imperatorskikh teatrov. Sezon 1896–1897 gg. Prilozheniia, book 3* (St Petersburg, 1898)).
11. Vissarion Belinsky (*Ezhegodnik imperatorskikh teatrov. Sezon 1897–1898 gg. Prilozheniia, book 1* (St Petersburg, 1899)).
12. Ivan Sosnitsky and Pyotr Karatygin (brother of Vasily) in *Woe from Wit* (*Ezhegodnik imperatorskikh teatrov. Sezon 1892–1893 gg.* (St Petersburg, 1894)).
13. Bolshoi Theatre, Moscow, during a coronation gala performance, 1856, by M. A. Zichi (*Ezhegodnik imperatorskikh teatrov. Sezon 1907–1908 gg.* (St Petersburg, n.d.)).

ACKNOWLEDGEMENTS

It is a pleasure to thank the many individuals and institutions whose support and encouragement have made this book possible. My research in archives and libraries in Britain, Finland, Russia and the United States was facilitated by generous grants from the British Academy, the Carnegie Trust for the Universities of Scotland, the University of Illinois at Urbana-Champaign, the Department of History at the University of Dundee, the Kennan Institute for Advanced Russian Studies at the Woodrow Wilson International Center for Scholars, and the Leverhulme Trust, whose award of a research fellowship during the early stages of this work enabled me to undertake sustained archival research in Moscow and St Petersburg.

I thank the staffs of the archives and libraries whither my research led me: in Britain, the National Library of Scotland, the Bodleian Library, the British Library, and the university libraries of Aberdeen, Dundee and St Andrews; in Finland, the Slavonic Library at the National Library of Finland, Helsinki; in Moscow, the Russian State Archive of Literature and Art, the manuscripts department of the State Central Theatre Museum and the Russian State Art Library; in St Petersburg, the Russian State History Archive, the Russian National Library and the St Petersburg Theatre Library; in the United States, the Library of Congress and the Slavic collection at the University of Illinois, Urbana-Champaign. I am grateful to all for their enthusiastic support. Special mention must be made of Irina Lukka at the Slavonic Library in Helsinki and Alexander Sapozhnikov at the newspaper department of the Russian National Library for their invaluable assistance. I would also like to thank Alan Grant at the University Library, Dundee, for essential help in tracking down some old books that are difficult enough to find in Russia, let alone on the east coast of Scotland.

Some of the material in three chapters of this book has appeared elsewhere in article or chapter form, and is used here with permission: chapter 3 in the *Slavonic and East European Review*, 83, no. 2 (2005); chapter 4 in Ian D. Thatcher (ed.), *Late Imperial Russia: Problems and Prospects: Essays in Honour of R. B. McKean* (Manchester, 2005); and chapter 6 in the *Historical Journal*, 48, no. 4 (2005).

Many friends and colleagues have offered advice and inspiration, provided helpful comments on draft chapters, or directed my attention to unexpected sources. For such kindnesses I thank, in particular, Cath Brennan, Liisa Byckling, Simon Dixon, Paul Dukes, Dmitry Fedosov, Bob McKean, David Moon, Lynn Sargeant, David Saunders and Elise Kimerling Wirtschafter. I am especially grateful to Richard Stites and Tony Swift, who, in addition to helping in the various ways mentioned above, read the entire manuscript and generously provided me with the benefit of their keen insights and expertise. I also thank Mary Schaeffer Conroy, Richard Stites and Lisa McIntosh Sundstrom for allowing me to read then unpublished manuscripts. It goes without saying that none of the above is responsible for any errors of fact or judgement in this book.

Most of all I thank Rachel for all her love and support, and especially for showing remarkable patience during the final stages of the writing of this book. My deepest gratitude is to my parents, for all that they have done for me over the years, and I dedicate this book to them, with much love.

NOTE ON TRANSLITERATION AND DATES

Throughout the text, Russian names are normally given in their common anglicized forms (for example, Alexander, not Aleksandr; Ostrovsky, not Ostrovskii). The titles of plays are given in English translation, the original Russian titles being listed in an appendix. Newspaper and journal titles are given in English translation in the text but the Russian original is used for references in the notes. For references and the bibliography, the Library of Congress transliteration system is used (hence, the reader will find Kugel and Ostrovsky in the text, but Kugel' and Ostrovskii in the references and bibliography). Until February 1918, Russia used the Julian (old style) calendar. In the eighteenth century, this was eleven days behind the Gregorian (new style) calendar used elsewhere in Europe; in the nineteenth century it was twelve days behind; in the twentieth century, thirteen days behind. As is customary in Russian studies, dates are given according to the style which obtained at the time (and where contemporaneous newspapers also gave a 'new style' date in parenthesis, both are included).

INTRODUCTION

During the nineteenth century, theatre became a prominent feature of public and intellectual life in Russia. By 1914, Vladimir Kallash and Nikolai Efros could proclaim with some justification, 'In no other country has theatre played such a role as in Russia.'[1] This sentiment has been echoed in many other histories of the Russian stage. The introduction to the *History of the Russian Dramatic Theatre* declared, 'In the history of Russian artistic culture, in the history of the spiritual life of Russian society, theatre has an exceptionally important place',[2] and in a more recent study one scholar has written of the 'exceptionally high position which the theatre occupied for many years in Russian society'.[3]

Statements like these are derived fundamentally from the widespread conviction among Russians that theatre was not simply a form of entertainment, but a powerful means of education. This idea was fostered initially during the second half of the eighteenth century by the state, which, under the influence of the European Enlightenment, conceived of theatre as a 'school for morals'. It was soon appropriated and adapted by members of the intelligentsia, who, partly in response to tsarist censorship, regarded the drama stage as a potential forum for the public expression of their ideas. In 1843, Alexander Herzen described theatre as a 'high tribunal for the resolution of vital issues',[4] in 1845 Nikolai Gogol spoke of it as 'a kind of pulpit from which much good can be spoken to the world',[5] and in 1899 the critic Ivan Ivanov declared, 'For us, plays and theatres are what parliamentary affairs and political speeches are for Western Europe.'[6] Kallash and Efros, moreover, emphasized that Russian audiences were attracted to theatre not only for artistic reasons, but also because it was a place where they 'looked for and found answers to other questions, including social ones'.[7]

Such observations (and dozens of others) are indicative of the extent to which theatre in imperial Russia was regarded as a meaningful – or potentially meaningful – intermediary between the state and society, and between the intelligentsia and the masses. Both the state and the intelligentsia regarded the stage as influential, but from radically different positions. The state promoted theatre as an accoutrement of civilization and respectability for the elite, but it was uneasy about extending its accessibility to a broader audience and maintained a tight grip on the patronage and supervision of theatrical entertainments, especially in St Petersburg and Moscow, where the government theatres enjoyed a monopoly until 1882. The intelligentsia, on the other hand, came to regard theatre as a forum for the exploration of a wide range of issues, particularly the nature of Russian national identity, as well as a means of raising the 'cultural level' of the masses, by which they usually meant the peasantry or, especially from the 1880s, the urban working class. The consequent tension between state supervision and intelligentsia ambition was central to the development of theatre's public profile during the nineteenth century.

This book charts the establishment of theatre as a factor in Russian public life, and shows how that role evolved from the late eighteenth to the early twentieth century in the hands of the state and the intelligentsia, as well as impresarios and stage workers themselves. It emphasizes two main aspects of that story – the rise and regulation of the theatre industry, and the idea of theatre in society. In considering the former it examines the proliferation of theatres during the nineteenth century, their organization and the extent to which they were influenced by the state and by private impresarios, encompassing such topics as theatre buildings, the administrative apparatus and state regulation. Consideration of the latter involves an elucidation of the way different people related to, and wrote about, theatre, in particular the expectations they invested in it, focusing on theatrical reportage, criticism, and social attitudes towards thespians. In relating this story, the book adopts as a loose paradigm the concept of civil society. Prior to explaining the book's structure, a few words about this concept and its relevance to imperial Russia are in order.

Civil society and imperial Russia

Civil society, broadly understood, is the public sphere of organized and mainly self-supporting associational activity that is separate from the state. It is defined by Ernest Gellner as 'institutional and ideological pluralism, which prevents the establishment of monopoly of power and truth, and counterbalances those central institutions which, though necessary, might otherwise acquire such a monopoly'. It therefore consists of 'that set of diverse non-governmental institutions which is strong enough to counterbalance the state and, while not preventing the state from fulfilling its role of keeper of the peace and arbitrator between major interests, can nevertheless prevent it from dominating and atomizing the rest of society'.[8] This definition of civil society as a set of non-governmental public organizations which counterbalance the state has enjoyed considerable popularity in academic circles since the collapse of Soviet-bloc regimes in Eastern Europe. In particular, scholars working in the field of transitional studies have found the concept useful because it provides a focus for considering how institutional pluralism might develop from the remains of monolithic regimes and set them on the path to democracy. After all, civil society emerged in Eastern Europe as a dissident phenomenon, explicitly opposed to the state, notably through the Solidarity movement in Poland.

Yet while civil society and the state are separate by definition, their relationship is not necessarily adversarial or antagonistic. Indeed, if civil society is the realm where individuals pursue their interests independently of governmental institutions (through independent organizations, associations and entities like the market), they still rely on the state to guarantee and enforce the legal codes and moral norms that underpin the functioning of the public sphere. The components of civil society therefore work within a legal order (even where they aspire to amend that order), and the definition of civil society therefore excludes uncivil groups that sanction violence or transgress the rule of law in other ways.[9] Moreover, the state and its agencies might be necessary in order to counterbalance potential excesses emanating from civil society, such as infringements of individual legal rights. Ultimately, then, while the absence of a proper civil society almost certainly entails the absence of 'institutional and ideological pluralism', the presence of civil society does not preclude collaboration with, or even reliance upon, the state. It is even possible for a civil society to exist within an autocratic political system, as the case of imperial Russia indicates, but whether both can coexist indefinitely is another matter.[10] And, of course, the state may even encourage the kind of civic activism that leads to the development of civil society, although in general the latter constitutes public activity that is initiated by citizens rather than by the state.

There is a general consensus among historians that some form of civil society was beginning to emerge in imperial Russia. It was manifested from the late eighteenth century in the proliferation of learned societies, clubs, theatres, salons and a print culture, all of which constituted, in the words of one historian, Russia's 'social sites of the public sphere'.[11] During the first half of the nineteenth century the institutions of civil society continued to develop at a steady pace.[12] For instance, at least twenty-eight independent charitable associations were established during the reign of Alexander I (1801–25), and another twenty appeared under Nicholas I (1825–55), whose reign is chiefly remembered for growing repression.[13] Civil society began to develop more rapidly during the second half of the nineteenth century. The 'great reforms' of the 1860s and 1870s, initiated by Alexander II (1855–81) in response to Russia's defeat in the Crimean War, stimulated an unprecedented degree of autonomous activity on the part of educated society, notably by creating new institutions of local government (the *zemstva*), expanding educational provision to foster the professional classes, and relaxing censorship.[14] These developments were accompanied by increasing urbanization, the rapid growth of commerce and industry, and the appearance, especially in Moscow, of a new business elite.[15] Based largely on these middling groups and sitting incongruously with Russia's traditional estate structure, this proverbially 'nascent' civil society expressed itself through an extraordinary range of voluntary associations, learned societies and charitable organizations, all closely monitored by a deeply suspicious autocracy.[16]

The issue of civil society has been seen as central to tsarist Russia's failure to evolve a liberal alternative to revolution. According to most historians of the period, Russia's civil society posed little threat to the tsarist regime because it was underdeveloped and fragmented, and lacked a coherent identity. As one observer succinctly puts it,

The emergent middle classes were politically splintered and socially fissured. The commercial and industrial middle classes never developed a common mentality, social consciousness, or political allegiance. Ethnic diversity and regional economic rivalries divided entrepreneurs and merchants. Finally, the professional middle class was numerically small, as well as being legally and economically dependent on the state.[17]

For these reasons, it is argued, civil society was ill equipped to mount an effective challenge to the autocracy, even after the 1905 revolution, when, during the period of the constitutional monarchy, there was relatively greater scope for organization in the public sphere. The implicit assumption is that a more cohesive and assertive civil society – or the coordinated mobilization of the middling groups – might have been able to appropriate substantive political influence from the tsarist regime, leading in turn to a more pluralistic and responsive political system, thereby avoiding revolutionary upheaval.[18]

One of the problems with this kind of analysis is that it tends to attribute to civil society a necessary, or preordained, historical function, namely that it counterbalances the central authority of the state and develops in proportion to the advance of liberal democracy. In the case of imperial Russia, there is arguably a sense in which this reasoning has been shaped by the 'outcome', the 1917 revolution. That is to say, because there was a violent upheaval, civil society, which is assumed to foster stability and create avenues for gradualist or evolutionary reform, must have been relatively insignificant. Yet historians are increasingly persuaded that late imperial Russia possessed a rich and vibrant civil society, and its significance cannot be dismissed by reference to certain limitations on its activity, like censorship, fragmentation or financial insufficiency. Moreover, this civil society should be explored as a pheno-menon in itself – how it emerged and functioned – and not simply as an explanatory factor in the origins of the Russian revolution. Otherwise there is a risk that the contemporaneous significance of civil society, and its contri-bution to change, will remain obscured.

In particular, the historiographical emphasis on civil society's frag-mentation and its debilitated relationship to the state has obscured an important feature of the paradigm. According to Ernest Gellner, communities that resist central authority – and therefore appear to possess a robust civil society – do not necessarily guarantee the 'institutional and ideological pluralism' associated with civil society. Strong communities, for example, have the capacity to inhibit individualism and often demand adherence to a local culture and its traditions. Civil society, on the other hand, allows individuals to choose their identities, and to move freely between them.[19] For Gellner, then, a genuine civil society 'excludes both stifling communalism and centralized authoritarianism',[20] and its *sine qua non* is 'modular man', the individual who can enter into associations and form 'alignments and opinions', yet without these being totally binding.[21] Knowledge, convictions and allegiances in civil society are fundamentally flexible, and 'modular man' can shift between them without incurring the wrath of the community or its authorities. Political heterodoxy, for instance, will not be considered treasonous, religious beliefs will not be regarded as apostasies, and so forth. Therefore, in Gellner's final analysis, 'Civil Society is a cluster of institutions and associations strong enough to prevent tyranny, but which are, none the less, entered and left freely, rather than imposed by birth or sustained by awesome ritual.'[22] Consequently, civil society must be understood in terms of its two distinct relationships, one with the state, the other with the individual. In both respects, the emphasis is on pluralism and flexibility, not only for institutions and associations, but also for ideologies and identities. The notion of a unified civil society therefore appears somewhat contradictory, because its very essence, its unique strength, lies in its resistance to unity, and therefore its resistance to monopoly and manipulation.

The major historical exception to this ostensible rule is the 'macro-community' of the nation, especially in the form it has developed since the late eighteenth century. The one thing that binds 'modular man' and the institutions of civil society together is adherence to the nation-state. This is because, if 'modular man' is to be able to communicate in a pluralistic and flexible society, some common codes and identities are still required. Literate culture provides the necessary conduit, and as communication increasingly occurs through common media (such as newspapers, a national education system, cinema), and urbanization and improved transportation make regular interaction over larger geographical spaces a characteristic of modernity, pressure is towards a common set of norms which provide a necessary balance between a plurality of identities and membership of the nation. Thus, historically, as civil society gathers strength, so does the idea of the nation and national identity. This process was evident in nineteenth-century Russia: as the institutions of civil society proliferated, so did efforts to define and assert Russian national identity as a means of binding society together.[23]

Theatre and civil society

In the process of exploring how the stage became a factor in Russian public life during the nineteenth century, this book also considers theatre within the broad realm of civil society. It examines the contribution of civil society to theatrical culture (in particular through the creation of new artistic institutions independent of the state), as well as that of theatre to civil society (non-state theatres *created* by civil society also represented the further *development* of civil society itself). The aim is neither to analyze civil society as such, nor to uncover further evidence of its existence, but rather to utilize the concept as a framework for understanding the development of theatre as public space. The broad contours of the story can be summarized as follows.

During the late eighteenth century, private (that is to say, non-state) theatres were encouraged by the authorities in St Petersburg and Moscow, the two capitals of the empire. From the early years of the nineteenth century, however, the state theatres (that is to say, the Imperial Theatres, those funded and administered by the government) began to acquire a monopoly on stage entertainments in the capitals, and the persistence of the monopoly until 1882 meant that private theatres, independent of the state, were not allowed to exist, except under special circumstances (although they proliferated in the provinces where the monopoly did not apply). Nevertheless, during the period before 1882 the *idea* that theatre was an important public forum became established among educated Russians, particularly in connection with the exploration and assertion of Russian national identity, and a growing number of people called for the monopoly to be abolished in order for civil society to build new theatres which would represent Russian identity more effectively.

After 1882, civil society began to construct a range of innovative theatrical enterprises in St Peterburg and especially Moscow. But despite the emergence of a mass-entertainment market, financial difficulties served to limit many of their achievements. Commercial considerations came to predominate, and the theatrical enterprises that survived often did so because of the intervention of powerful and wealthy patrons, not because they were supported by an instrinsically healthy market for legitimate theatre. Nevertheless, the activity of several new theatres after 1882 revealed the existence of the modular identity that accompanies a flourishing civil society. The most significant theatrical contribution to civil society was arguably made by the associational activity in which stage people began to engage in order to alleviate their dire material circumstances. In particular, from 1894 the Russian Theatre Society began to professionalize stage workers, raise occupational self-awareness and regulate conditions within the theatre industry, thereby emerging as a significant intermediary between the state and society, certainly in a more immediate, practical and identifiable manner than occurred on the stage.

The spread of theatres after 1882, as well as the associational activity of theatre people, was observed warily by the government. Although Alexander II's administration had encouraged a greater level of public activity on the part of educated society, his assassination at the hands of revolutionary terrorists in 1881 led to a political reaction under his successor, Alexander III (1881–94). From the late 1880s, various steps were taken to monitor and regulate the increasingly vibrant theatrical civil society, including the promulgation of special censorship rules and the forging of links with the Russian Theatre Society. There were even rumours that the government planned to take possession of all theatres in the provinces, although they proved unfounded. By the time of the 1905 revolution, it was evident that theatre had cultivated a sense of civil society and of citizenship among its employees. The rise of the theatre industry during the nineteenth century had unwittingly trained thousands of ordinary people in the language and practice of civil society, including aspirations to self-regulation and professional rights. This was a result not of any moral or political instruction offered by the repertoire (as envisaged by the intelligentsia) but of the organizational experience gained in the struggle against low social status and material hardship. Theatre was vaunted as a 'school for morals' and a 'school for the people', but in a sense it was more akin to a 'school for citizens', contributing to the development of civil society less from across the footlights than through the stage door, where the actors emerged from their fictional worlds to confront their often difficult social and material circumstances.

The chapters that follow elaborate these themes in a broadly chronological manner. Chapter 1 investigates how theatre became a significant factor in public life from the time of Catherine the Great to the early 1820s, largely as a result of the state's efforts to promote theatre as a fashionable accoutrement of 'civilization'. In the process, stage entertainments in the capitals were gradually centralized under the so-called directorate of Imperial Theatres, which led to friction with educated society over control of theatrical life. Chapter 2 develops these themes for the period from the 1820s to the early 1850s, showing how theatre-going was established as the epitome of refinement at the same time that the intelligentsia began to invoke the stage as a potential means of transforming social and political attitudes. Chapter 3 focuses on developments from the 1850s to the abolition of the Imperial Theatre monopoly in 1882. In particular, it examines how the monopoly was consolidated, why it was attacked, and how it came to be abrogated. It will be argued that the forces of civil society, although still relatively weak, were keen to wrest exclusive control of theatrical entertainments in the capitals from the state in order to create a national theatre and regenerate what was widely regarded as a stagnant dramatic culture. Chapter 4 explores the institutional emergence of a theatrical civil society in the capitals by focusing on the major impresarios of St Petersburg and Moscow during the 1880s and 1890s and the ventures which they founded. It asks why they established theatres, what obstacles they faced, and what contributions were made by their enterprises. Chapter 5 also deals with the 1880s and 1890s, concentrating on responses to the emergence of commercial theatres in the capitals. In particular, the chapter investigates the 'discourse of decline' that surrounded the stage during these years. It argues that a growing number of calls for state-funded people's theatres were a response to the implicit recognition that, with a few exceptions, civil society was not prepared to foster the kind of theatre advocated by the intelligentsia. Allied with the fact that the reputation of the Imperial Theatres enjoyed a temporary revival at the same time, this suggests that civil society was not unanimously viewed as the ideal means of ensuring that theatre fulfilled the educative function that both the state and the intelligentsia desired. Chapter 6 explores how the Russian Theatre Society began to professionalize theatre people from the 1890s and argues that it became a meaningful intermediary between the state and society at large, at least until the 1905 revolution, indicating that theatre people were increasingly confident members of civil society. Chapter 7 draws many of these themes together by recounting the early history of the Moscow Art Theatre and assessing what it reveals about the condition of theatre and civil society at the beginning of the twentieth century. The chapter concludes with a consideration of theatre during the 1905 revolution, a convenient point for measuring the overall contribution of theatre to civil society as Russia entered its turbulent twentieth century.

Finally, a few words about the scope of the book. In geographical terms, while the provinces regularly loom in the background, the main focus is on the two capitals, St Petersburg and Moscow. This is because the Imperial Theatre monopoly – which never applied to the provinces – made the struggle for a theatrical civil society more urgent and more politically charged than elsewhere. It was in the capitals, for example, that the issue of a national theatre was mooted. The main focus is on drama theatre, rather than opera, ballet or other forms of entertainment, although some of these are mentioned where appropriate, notably in chapter 4. This is for reasons of manageability and enhanced focus. In terms of approach (or 'methodology'), my examination of the sources has been determined by the broad concerns of the book, namely the rise of the theatre industry and the idea of theatre in society during the nineteenth century. The same sources could be examined with a view to investigating other aspects of Russian theatre, such as acting techniques, the history of *mise-en-scène*, the extent to which issues of class, gender or ethnicity inhered in the repertoire, and so forth. These themes occasionally make cameo appearances, but none are central to the book.

Chapter 1

EMBLEM OF ENLIGHTENMENT

During the late summer of 1782, as the cultural and political establishments of St Petersburg began to contemplate the forthcoming season of masquerade balls, concerts and other recreations available to the *haut monde* of the Russian empire, particular curiosity was kindled by a new comedy, Denis Fonvizin's *The Minor*. Its premiere was the most eagerly anticipated cultural event there had been in the city for many years, although rumours circulated that the government would intervene to prevent it from being staged. When the play was finally performed to a packed house on 24 September 1782, it met with rapturous applause. Prince Grigory Potemkin is reputed to have remarked to the author, 'Die now, Denis, or never write anything else! Your name will be immortal for this one play.'[1] The history of 'this one play', its composition, its inaugural performance and its immediate and longer-term aftermaths, reveals the extent to which, and why, theatre was poised by the end of the eighteenth century to establish itself as a significant feature of Russian public life. More than any other event, the premiere of *The Minor* prefigured the part theatre was to play both as a factor in the tense relationship between state and society, an arena in which different sets of interests jostled for influence, and as a forum for the discussion of Russian identity, broadly understood, until the collapse of the empire.

At the time Fonvizin was completing his masterpiece, the inhabitants of St Petersburg were served by a small but varied theatrical scene. By far the most prestigious theatre in 1782 was the small opera house inside the Winter Palace, reserved for the invited guests of the court. A short distance from the Winter Palace, eastwards along the affluent Millionaire Street – where Antonio Rinaldi's magnificent Marble Palace, a gift from Catherine the Great to her lover Grigory Orlov, was nearing completion – lay Tsaritsyn Meadow, a flat expanse of marshy land bounded by the River Neva to the north, the River Moika to the south, the Summer Garden to the east, and the site of the future Pavlovsky barracks to the west. The meadow was used primarily for military parades, but it was also the location of what were then the city's two public theatres, both accessible to anyone who could obtain a ticket. One of the theatres, a small wooden structure, stood on the south-eastern corner of the meadow, close to the Summer Garden, and was run by the French impresario I. A. Poshet. The other, known as the Free Russian Theatre, was situated at the south-western corner, close to where the Catherine (now Griboyedov) Canal runs into the Moika. It was here that *The Minor* was premiered.

The building that housed the Free Russian Theatre, which was established in 1779, was originally a wooden manege.[2] At the end of 1770, it was turned into a theatre in order to accommodate a group of touring 'English comedians' and became known for a while as the English Theatre.[3] Between 1772 and 1775 it was used by an Italian impresario, Bertolotti, for masquerades and concerts, the most popular pastimes of St Petersburg's socialites. Subsequently it was used by a German troupe, organized from 1777 by the German merchant and factory owner Karl Knipper. In 1779, while continuing to maintain the German troupe, Knipper established the Free Russian Theatre, bringing pupils all the way from the Moscow Foundling Home to work as actors. As a result, the building on Tsaritsyn Meadow became popularly known as the 'Russian and German Theatre'. As for its formal title, the theatre was 'free' (*vol'nyi*) in the sense that it was not a court institution with restricted access, but was open to the public.

Two years later, in 1781, as the rickety old wooden structure showed increasing signs of dilapidation, the St Petersburg Foundling Home – where Russia's greatest actor of the century, Ivan Dmitrevsky (1734–1821), taught the pupils the theatrical arts when he was not performing at the court theatre – agreed to subsidize the construction of a new building on the same site. Erected on a stone foundation and sporting an iron roof, the new venue was otherwise fashioned from wood and presented an unremarkable façade. Its interior, however, struck observers as something special. According to a visiting Frenchman who attended the opening of the new theatre,

The stage is very high and wide, and the hall for the audiences forms three-quarters of a circle. There is no loge, but in addition to a parquet and a parterre with benches there are three tiers of balcony, rising up one above the other and encircling the auditorium continuously. The picture is very beautiful, and the sight is very pleasing when, on entering, you see the audience sitting amphitheatrically, as in antiquity.[4]

The renovated building, still officially the Free Russian Theatre, was now also called the 'Novyi' or the 'Theatre near the Summer Palace' (on account of its proximity to Empress Elizabeth's palace, where Engineers' Castle now stands, not to be confused with Peter the Great's Summer House, which still exists). Artistic affairs were overseen by Dmitrevsky, while Knipper acted as financial impresario. By all accounts the theatre was a successful enterprise, drawing audiences away from Poshet's theatre at the other side of Tsaritsyn Meadow.[5] It would later be sequestered by the state.

The repertoires of the Tsaritsyn Meadow theatres blended comedies, tragedies, ballets and light operas. The lines between these genres were not sharply drawn, at least in terms of performance. All forms of theatrical spectacle were offered by each company, often on the same evening, individual artists being expected to alternate between tragic declamation, dancing and singing. Only in the nineteenth century did a clear distinction develop between, for instance, an opera theatre and a drama theatre, an opera troupe and a drama troupe, a singer and an actor. The works that were performed were either direct translations or adaptations from the European repertoire, notably plays by Molière, Racine, Corneille, Beaumarchais, Voltaire and Shakespeare. Foreign plays were often Russified, which meant that while the essential plot structure was maintained the characters were given Russian names and the action transposed to a Russian location. Yet such adaptations hardly amounted to a national repertoire, since by definition none of the situations represented was authentically Russian. Even Alexander Sumarokov (1718–77), generally considered Russia's first professional dramatist, modelled his plays on French classics. This state of affairs partly explains why Fonvizin's *The Minor* registered such an impact.

Born in Moscow in 1745, Denis Fonvizin became one of the leading literary figures of his time. Admitted to Moscow University as a precocious ten-year-old in 1755, the year it was founded, he quickly became acquainted with the ideas of the German Enlightenment and also found time to perform in university theatricals. When he graduated in 1762 he embarked on a career in the state service that spanned twenty years. This entailed moving to St Petersburg, where he served in the College of Foreign Affairs as an assistant (1763–9) to Ivan Elagin, another Russian statesman with a predilection for the literary arts who became, in 1766, the first director of Imperial Theatres. It was not unusual for government officials to engage in literary activity, and Fonvizin devoted much of the 1760s to translating foreign essays and dramas. The first work of any significance which he authored was the five-act comedy *The Brigadier* (1769), a biting satire on the Russian establishment's obsession with French customs. Its attention to authentic characterization and its use of local idiom made *The Brigadier* the first original Russian play, although nothing is known about its early stage history. During the 1770s, Fonvizin worked as secretary to the influential Nikita Panin, Catherine the Great's foreign minister from 1763 to 1781. He finally retired from the service in March 1782, shortly after Panin's resignation, spending most of his latter years in Moscow, where he died in 1792.[6]

The Minor, completed no later than the spring of 1782, is a five-act comedy which relates the tale of the Prostakovs, a lesser gentry family, and their son Mitrofan. The plot is simplistic and full of improbable coincidences, but it served Fonvizin as a vehicle for the expression of certain political and moral principles which, for reasons elucidated below, he wanted to air in public. The term 'minor' in the title of the play (*Nedorosl'* in Russian) denoted a nobleman's son who was still under the age of fifteen. Upon reaching fifteen, all noblemen were expected to commence their training for the civil or military service. Although compulsory service was abolished in 1762 by Tsar Peter III, members of the nobility were still expected to enter the service from a sense of duty. Mitrofan, the eponymous *nedorosl'*, is almost sixteen, a fact intended to emphasize his slow development.

The action takes place on the Prostakovs' estate near Moscow. While they are busy planning the betrothal of Sofia, an orphan residing with them, to Mrs Prostakova's brother Skotinin (an event of which Sofia herself is unaware), news arrives that Sofia's uncle, Starodum, has recently returned to Moscow after making his fortune in Siberia, and intends to make his niece his heiress. Upon hearing this news, Prostakova duly declares that Sofia will marry Mitrofan, her son, not Skotinin. Meanwhile, Pravdin, an official sent to inspect the region, arrives on the scene and immediately registers his disapproval of local conditions: 'I cannot fail to observe the presence of certain evil-minded and ignorant individuals, who make cruel and inhuman use of the absolute power that they hold over their people.' It soon becomes clear that he has the Prostakovs in mind. At this point, an army officer, Milon, whom Sofia loves, appears. Starodum also arrives suddenly and Prostakova sycophantically defers to him, deviously feigning affection for Sofia. When Starodum announces that he plans to take Sofia to Moscow to marry a man of great merit who has been suggested to him, it transpires that the man in question is none other than Milon. Starodum grants Sofia and Milon his blessing, whereupon Prostakova devises a scheme to have Sofia kidnapped and married to Mitrofan. Her servants, however, bungle the plan, and Pravdin steps in to charge Prostakova with abuse. Starodum pardons her, but when she then announces her intention to punish her servants for failing to kidnap Sofia, Pravdin declares to Mr Prostakov that, 'in consequence of the inhuman conduct of your wife, which you have shown extreme weakness of character in permitting, I am commanded by the Government to take your house and your manors into sequestration'.[7]

Why did Fonvizin compose such a play? Central to understanding his motives is that he regarded himself as a kind of enlightened *philosophe* whose duty it was to counsel monarchs. In this respect, he was very much a product of his time. As Derek Offord aptly puts it, 'Fonvizin's writings exemplify the civic and prescriptive role that was being assumed by a literary culture in which drama, satire and other artistic forms merged with social and political discourse and moral philosophy.'[8] His conception of political authority, forged by his education and his administrative experience, is important for appreciating both the genesis of *The Minor* and its broader significance. Fonvizin was not a distant and uninformed observer, but a government official, effectively a member of the ruling establishment. There is a certain symbolism in the fact that he composed *The Minor* at No. 38 English Embankment, just a few hundred yards along the River Neva from the Winter Palace.[9]

Fonvizin had four interconnected aims in writing *The Minor*, the plot of which acted as a loose structure around which certain ideas could be articulated. First of all, he wanted to assert the importance of duty and of holding government office on the basis of merit, not favour. Starodum puts it this way:

As soon as everybody sees that nobody can take a place in Society without good morals, that rewards are to be earned for services rendered, not to be won by base time-serving, nor to be purchased for any money; that men are to be chosen for offices, rather than the offices to be snatched by the men – then everyone will see that it is to his advantage to be moral, and everyone will be good.[10]

Starodum, the 'friend of honest men' as he describes himself, is concerned to demonstrate that honesty and enlightenment do not necessarily accompany rank and high office: 'there is sometimes an immeasurably wide difference between honourable men and men in favour'.[11] This was not, however, an implicit attack on Russia's rulers or its system of government. Instead, Fonvizin's purpose was to slander the political faction that had displaced his patron, Nikita Panin, a few months earlier. David Ransel has even described *The Minor* as 'the principal public expression of the Panin party's ideas',[12] namely that, in politics, merit should take precedence over favouritism. These were regarded as Petrine notions whose betrayal was allegedly evidenced by the removal of the Panin faction from positions of influence. Starodum was even modelled, in part, on Nikita Panin.[13]

In foregrounding the issues of duty and merit, Fonvizin also intended to express the view that the abolition of compulsory service in 1762 had not divested the nobility of its moral duty to serve the country. The nobility, he argued, must take a greater responsibility for the country's economic fortunes and moral health, a theme that permeated much of his work. In particular, he advocated its transformation into a 'trading nobility', one that embraced rather than scorned commerce. It was to this end that he had translated Gabriel-François Coyer's *La Noblesse commerçante* into Russian in 1766, a venture which resulted in a cooler relationship with Catherine the Great, who did not entirely approve of the idea.[14]

Another motive for writing *The Minor* was a desire to attack the abuses of serfdom. Fonvizin clearly despises the manner in which Prostakova treats her serfs, notably Yeremeyevna, Mitrofan's nanny, who declares that her remuneration amounts to 'five roubles a year, and five face-slaps a day'.[15] Skotinin is also depicted as a ruthless exploiter of his vassals. Later commentators often interpreted the play principally as an attack on serfdom. Yet Fonvizin was not opposed to serfdom as such. Indeed, he was the owner of a large number of serfs himself, having been granted in 1773 an estate in Belorussia comprising 1,180. Rather, he was concerned to highlight abuses in the system, and *The Minor* was a plea for moderation in the way people treated each other within the existing social structure, not for its radical reformation.

A third motive behind the play was Fonvizin's conviction that the political nation was quite distinct from, and ultimately more important than, the state, a possible allusion to the need for reform. David Ransel and others have refuted the idea that, during the late eighteenth century, members of the Russian nobility were engaged in a struggle to place constitutional limits on the monarchy. Although many noblemen deployed the language of political reform, they were concerned not so much with attacking the autocratic principle as with positioning themselves in a struggle between rival kinship networks for monarchical patronage. Fonvizin amalgamated both views. He was a loyal supporter of Catherine the Great, but as one observer notes, 'Where the Empress would subordinate the national principle to the interests of the Imperial state, Fonvizin defined the autonomy of the Russian "fatherland" apart from the claims of the state.'[16] This was evident in his use of Starodum to affirm his commitment to enlightened despotism in a way that hinted at the importance of law for good government:

> where the Sovereign exercises reason, where he knows what makes for his true glory, there it is that mankind's rights must surely be regained. There it is that everyone is quick to perceive that each must seek his fortune and profit only within the law, and that oppression and enslavement of fellow men is against the law.[17]

After their removal from office, Fonvizin and the Panin party collaborated on a constitutional reform project, one outcome of which was the *Discourse on Permanent State Laws*. Ultimately, however, Fonvizin's view that the 'nation' (*otechestvo*) was not synonymous with the 'state' made him slightly suspect at a court where the principles of the Enlightenment were honoured more in the breach than in the observance.

A fourth intention underlying *The Minor* was to assert the importance of native Russian customs. In *The Brigadier*, Fonvizin had lampooned the nobility's deferential aping of French culture. Some years later, during 1777–8, he travelled to France, where he met, among others, Benjamin Franklin. Fonvizin remained unimpressed by Paris and insisted that he preferred St Petersburg, although he never idealized Russia. Yet he possessed a patriotism consistent with his belief that the nation and the state were separate entities. As Charles Moser puts it, for Fonvizin 'the individual must be bound to his society, to his nation, by the bonds of patriotism'.[18] Hans Rogger has identified *The Minor* as part of Russia's developing national consciousness in the late eighteenth century (although this was explored more explicitly in *The Brigadier*).[19] Starodum, for instance, was educated in the 'old ways', which were deemed far more virtuous than the foreign education sought for Mitrofan. Furthermore, the attention to Russian manners and language lent *The Minor* a refreshing authenticity. Nevertheless, Fonvizin did not dismiss French or European culture. Speaking of the Russian 'aristocracy of education and intellect' of the end of the eighteenth century, of which Fonvizin was a leading member, Rogger has written that 'Its search for a national identity was not a rejection of Europe; it was itself another aspect of the Westernization of Russian society.'[20] That is to say, if the peoples of western European countries could celebrate their customs, language and achievements, so could – indeed should – Russians. It is also worth noting that Fonvizin's theoretical separation of the state and the nation hints at an early recognition that placing limits on monarchical authority requires a set of overarching identities that transcend government.

The Minor, then, was effectively a manifesto for a political faction at the centre of Catherinian Russia. Its attacks on the abuses of patronage, serfdom, unbridled autocracy and, more tangentially, the enduring infatuation with French culture rendered it much more than a comedy. No other play had addressed so many aspects of Russian politics and society with such calculated wit and arresting authenticity. Would the authorities allow such a play to be performed in public?

In May 1782, not long after Fonvizin had completed his play, Dmitrevsky suggested that it be staged for his benefit performance at the court theatre in the Winter Palace. Fonvizin, however, refused to make certain changes that would obviate the risk of his work offending anyone at court, and so permission was withheld. In the meantime, news of Fonvizin's new comedy spread and, as was the custom, the author was invited to several gatherings to deliver readings from the manuscript. One such reading took place during a dinner at B. N. Pestel's house in Moscow, where the response presaged the success that the play was soon to enjoy throughout the empire:

> By dinner time a great company of men of letters and connoisseurs had gathered; the curiosity of the guests was so great that the host asked the author to read at least one scene as a matter of urgency; he complied with the general desire, and when he stopped after Prostakova's discussion of Mitrofan's shortened kaftan with the tailor Trishka, those present were so interested that they requested that the reading continue.

After dinner, Dmitrevsky was persuaded by the enthusiastic audience to deliver another reading of the entire comedy.[21]

Such readings acquired for *The Minor* a certain notoriety, months before its first public performance. This hardened Dmitrevsky's resolve to stage the play for his benefit. While the court could refuse to countenance a performance in the Winter Palace, only the permission of the city police was required for a play to be staged in a public theatre.[22] Dmitrevsky therefore invited members of the court troupe to perform it at the Free Russian Theatre. It was rumoured that some of the actors were reluctant to participate in view of the court's refusal to stage the play, but as Pimen Arapov noted, the rumours were unfounded.[23] Although the premiere was announced only four days in advance, on 20 September in the *St Petersburg Gazette*, it proved to be a triumph. Fonvizin himself directed the production, and the main roles were performed by leading actors of the court: Dmitrevsky played Starodum, P. A. Plavilshchikov was Pravdin, and Ya. D. Shumsky took on the role of Yeremeyevna.[24] Fonvizin claimed that the premiere was 'a complete success', primarily due to Dmitrevsky's depiction of Starodum.[25] Other evidence suggests that the comic scenes involving Yeremeyevna, whose appearances on stage caused great merriment, were the best received.[26] Nikolai Karamzin witnessed the premiere and remarked that it captured the attention of the audience, 'which at that time adored such expatiations on the stage, especially if they were full of caustic remarks about fashionable customs and the weaknesses of the time'.[27] According to *The Dramatic Dictionary*, an inventory of plays performed in Russia that was published in 1787, the 'audience applauded the play with the throwing of purses', the customary sign of audience approbation on benefit nights.[28] A second performance of *The Minor* was staged on 30 January 1783, but there is no further information about early performances.[29] The play soon became a hit at the Moscow Petrovsky Theatre, however, where it was staged in May 1783. It was also granted permission for performance at the court, which never liked to miss out; but whereas the play had been premiered in its full version, for the court performance cuts were made to the scene where Starodum, in conversation with Sofia, rehearses his views on virtue and duty.[30] The text of the play was published in 1783, and this in turn meant that it was soon being staged across the empire. In 1791, the political exile Alexander Radishchev recorded a performance as far off as Irkutsk.[31]

Although there is no evidence that audiences were cognizant of Fonvizin's veiled attack on the faction that had replaced the Panin party at the centre of Catherinian politics, the government was alert to the success of the play and also to the capacity of theatre to function as a critical forum which it seemed to herald. In 1783, the Free Russian Theatre, beset by financial problems which left its actors unpaid, was taken over by the government in the midst of a general reorganization of the state theatrical administration. Theatre historian Sergei Danilov suggested that this was a direct result of its staging of *The Minor*,[32] while others have suggested that the authorities were increasingly aware of the competition that public theatres represented for the court theatre.[33]

If official suspicions were indeed behind the sequestration of the Free Russian Theatre, they could not have been allayed by the growing reputation of *The Minor*. Its characters quickly became recognized types, and the play spawned several thinly disguised imitations. Various writers attempted to exploit the play's success, adding 'episodes' in the lives of the characters in new though far less accomplished works, such as Plavilshchikov's one-act comedy *Kuteikin's Betrothal* (1799 and 1821) and G. N. Gorodchaninov's five-act comedy *Mitrofanushka in Retirement* (1800).[34] While such imitations were devoid of literary or dramatic distinction, it has been observed that 'their very existence demonstrates that *The Minor* cut a swath through the Russian theater for a quarter-century or more'.[35] That the play was translated into German in 1787 (under the title *Das Muttersöhnchen*) was a further sign of its emerging status as the emblem of contemporary Russian theatre.[36]

The popularity of Fonvizin's comedy is explained to some extent by the fact that it was the first play to hold up a mirror to Russian society. During one of the early performances, according to Nikolai Grech, an army major sat without emotion while the rest of the audience laughed. When he was asked by his neighbour how he was able to sit through such entertainment with indifference, he replied, 'What is there to laugh about? That's how we behave here.'[37] The Russian historian Vasily Kliuchevsky found the play realistic, using it as evidence for the manners of Catherinian Russia. 'This comedy,' he reflected, 'is an incomparable mirror.'[38] Not everyone thought the play reflected Russian reality: two critiques from the early nineteenth century claimed that Fonvizin's characters were not lifelike.[39] But the overwhelming opinion was that, at the very least, Fonvizin had shown how Russian life might be depicted on stage.

The view that *The Minor* was the first Russian play of any significance has persisted. Marc Slonim claimed that it marked 'the birth of Russian theatrical repertory',[40] and more recently it was described by the *Nevsky Times* as 'laying the cornerstone in the foundation of Russian classical dramaturgy'.[41] It is, moreover, the only Russian play written before 1800 to retain a prominent place on the Russian stage today. Nevertheless, some exaggerated claims have been made on its behalf. During the Soviet period, it was regarded as an exposé of tsarist injustice. One writer asserted that 'it was a great step forward in the democratization of Russian theatre and Russian drama',[42] while another claimed that 'The success of Starodum was the political success of a comedy among the leading section of the Petersburg nobility and the democratic audience of the theatre on Tsaritsyn Meadow.'[43] Such views were not exclusive to Soviet writers. Pushkin regarded *The Minor* as a 'monument of national satire'[44] and described Fonvizin as 'freedom's friend'.[45] It is important, however, not to exaggerate Fonvizin's radicalism. Notwithstanding his calls for an end to systemic abuses, he remained an advocate of the prevailing order in Catherinian Russia.

Yet Fonvizin produced the first authentic Russian play to achieve lasting prominence, one which deployed vernacular dialogue and paraded, with deft satirical skill, a motley of recognizable types. At the same time, he demonstrated theatre's capacity to reflect critically on the institutions and mores with which audiences were directly familiar. His play thus illuminated the potential role that theatre could perform in Russian society. It was the exemplar of the Enlightenment play, didactic and moralizing, teaching as well as entertaining. *The Minor* therefore marked several things that were new in Russian theatre, including the idea of a theatre that aspires to be politically or socially influential.

Fonvizin's celebrated comedy presented the Russian state with a dilemma that was to remain unresolved for over a century: how could it use theatre for political and educational purposes while preventing it from questioning or undermining the established order? The obvious answer was to assert governmental control over the theatre and use censorship to regulate what appeared on stage. This was to prove fairly effective while theatre remained principally a fashionable pastime of the imperial establishment. But the gradual diffusion of theatricals throughout society during the nineteenth century would make the task more difficult. In the meantime, theatre was promoted as a useful 'school for the people', but with two significant qualifications – the 'school' was carefully supervised by the authorities, and the 'people' meant, in practice, the urban elite.

Under Elizabeth (1741–61) and especially under Catherine the Great (1762–96) the Russian state had promoted theatre as a presumed force for the improvement of morals and cultural knowledge. This marked a significant break with the past, in that theatricals had for the most part been frowned upon in official circles. Like all European countries, Russia had known popular forms of theatrical spectacle from the time of the earliest written records for its history. The *skomorokhi*, or wandering minstrels, were found in Kievan Rus from at least the eleventh century, but suffered persistent opposition from the Orthodox Church and were finally outlawed in 1648 by Tsar Alexei.[46] The first literary theatricals, those based on written texts, originated in amateur school theatres organized by the Church during the seventeenth century. The Belorussian Simeon Polotsky (1629–80) was an influential figure in this development. A graduate of the Kievan Spiritual Academy, and later a teacher in the Polotsk Church school, he was the author of two scholastic dramas, the first plays to be written in the country.

The key to the development of secular theatre was held by the court. Despite his earlier ban on the *skomorokhi*, Alexei had a theatre built in the Moscow Kremlin in 1672, but it was discontinued by his successor, Fyodor. Peter the Great (1689–1725) was the first Russian ruler to experiment with the idea of a public theatre. He ordered the construction of a wooden theatre on Red Square (1702–6), but lack of interest from local inhabitants led to its demise. A small public theatre was also maintained by the Tsarevna Natalya Alekseyevna in St Petersburg between 1710 and 1716. Despite such inter-mittent interest on the part of the court, there was as yet little nurturing of native theatrical talent. The theatres established by Alexei and Peter were run by foreign impresarios and most of the actors and technicians were non-Russian. Throughout the eighteenth century foreign troupes remained a common feature at the court. They also received privileges to perform in different parts of Russia. Early examples included the troupe of I.-K. Eckenburg, which visited Russia in 1719, and an Italian troupe of entertainers of 1721.[47] The transfer of the court to St Petersburg served to intensify the elite's exposure to western culture, and during the reign of Anna (1730–40) Italian opera and ballet became the preferred forms of entertainment.[48]

The 1750s proved to be an important decade in the history of *Russian* theatre, as distinct from theatre *in* Russia. Moscow University, established in 1755, became an active centre for theatricals, notably through the efforts of Mikhail Kheraskov. It was also during the 1750s that Sumarokov emerged as Russia's first professional dramatist. Most famously, in 1752 Fyodor Volkov's company of actors from Yaroslavl (which included Ivan Dmitrevsky) was invited to perform at the Winter Palace for Elizabeth. On 30 August 1756, the empress decreed the foundation of a Russian theatre, to be located in the Golovkin Mansion in the Vasilevsky Ostrov district of St Petersburg, staffed by Volkov's troupe and others, and managed by Sumarokov.[49] This was the first permanent Russian state theatre. It was granted an annual subsidy of five thousand rubles. The amount proved insufficient, however, and when it was increased in 1759 to seven thousand rubles, the state also assumed the task of running the theatre.[50] The significance retrospectively accorded to 30 August 1756 has served the need for a defining, formative date in Russian theatre history, but it has been exaggerated. While the date marked the beginning of continuous state support for drama theatre in Russia, government patronage of the stage remained limited until the reign of Catherine the Great.

Catherine did much to build up the formal state administrative apparatus for theatre. In 1766, a directorate was created to manage the affairs of the Russian theatre in Vasilevsky Ostrov. Although it was initially established as a public theatre for ticket-buying audiences, after 1759 the Russian theatre was reserved for invited guests and remained closed to the general public for twenty years.[51] Private (i.e. non-state) theatres were, however, permitted, and were even encouraged. Most were still organized by non-Russians. For example, in 1762 Peter III granted permission to the troupe of the German Johann Neuhof to perform in St Petersburg, Moscow, Revel and Riga, and in 1770 Catherine the Great granted Poshet the 'privilege' of organizing a theatre in St Petersburg.[52] Other ventures included Knipper's Free Russian Theatre, the troupe of Italian actors organized by Antonio Kazassi (Kazachi, or Casacci) in St Petersburg, and Michael Maddox's Petrovsky Theatre (1780–1805) in Moscow. In 1783, when Catherine established a special committee for theatrical spectacles and music, it was made clear that neither the committee nor the directorate had an 'exclusive right' to administer entertainments, and that 'anyone is permitted to organize entertainments that are decent for the public, adhering only to state laws and police orders'.[53] This combination of theatrical dirigisme and *laissez faire* set the scene for a complex and shifting relationship between state regulation and free theatres that was to last until the 1920s.

In keeping with Enlightenment convention, Catherine the Great was both a keen amateur playwright and a proponent of the didactic function of theatre.[54] Nikolai Drizen speculated that she was familiar with Peter I's statement 'I love theatre in so far as it serves the general interests of the state. Outside this sphere, it is useless or harmful.' Catherine certainly advocated an instructive role for drama, famously declaring that 'Theatre is a school for the people [*shkola narodnaia*]'.[55] She elaborated as follows: 'All the enlightened world knows how useful and at the same time amusing are theatrical works, fostering the moral education of children . . . showing them in the characters on stage the gravity of wrongdoing, the temptation in weaknesses, impudence, disobedience and many other human failings.'[56] But Catherine also made clear that theatre could perform such a function only if carefully monitored by the monarch: 'It is absolutely essential that it be under my supervision, I am the teacher in charge of this school, and mine is the prime responsibility to God for the nation's morals.'[57]

The idea that theatre had a role to play in the enlightenment of the political nation permeated the cultural life of Catherinian Russia's upper echelons. The 1784 'Regulations for Members of the Court Theatres' stated that theatre 'should be a school for morals' and that members were consequently required to 'conduct themselves with a degree of propriety'.[58] The first Russian publication devoted to theatre, Princess Dashkova's compendium of plays *The Russian Theatre*, appeared in 1786 with the declaration that theatre was a sign of an 'enlightened people',[59] while the introduction to *The Dramatic Dictionary* insisted that theatre was part of a good education.[60] It seems that very few among the imperial establishment disagreed with such sentiments. A rare dissenting view was offered by Prince M. M. Shcherbatov, a critic of Catherine the Great, who associated theatre with declining morals. Writing in 1786–7 of the Convent for the Education of Young Ladies of the Nobility, he suggested that the pupils 'have emerged with neither learning nor morals, apart from what nature has provided them with, and their education has consisted in acting comedies rather than in the improvement of their hearts, morals and reason'.[61]

The state's promotion of theatre as an emblem of enlightenment, especially in the latter half of the eighteenth century, made it increasingly fashionable among the nobility and other members of the urban population. Whereas earlier official proscriptions had militated against the development of a theatrical culture among the elite, now that the ruling ideology stipulated that drama and the stage were integral features of learning and civilization, urban society came under pressure to embrace theatre. The initial response from society ranged from tentative acceptance to indifference. Noting thinly populated stalls, Elizabeth even decreed that leading merchants could attend theatricals free of charge, as long as they were suitably dressed. The evidence suggests that, at least initially, attendance was regarded as a duty rather than a pleasure. On observing another sparsely populated auditorium, Elizabeth is reputed to have 'requested that the Ladies of Honour be sent to her so as to be asked of the Imperial Personage herself, had they not forgotten there was to be a comedy that day?'[62]

Nevertheless, members of the imperial establishment and others were soon keen to demonstrate their enthusiasm for the stage, both as participants and as observers. Amateur theatricals became popular with leading members of the nobility, a phenomenon that gave rise to serf theatres.[63] In 1769 the satirical journal *All Sorts* (to which Catherine the Great was an anonymous contributor) ridiculed the growing fashion for stage entertainments:

> As a rule, our nobles and most young people are convinced that they are great enthusiasts for theatrical performances and regard themselves as experts in this affair. As soon as they hear about a new drama, crowds gather at the theatre and impatiently wait to comment, on the cast rather than the characters represented by them. They take more interest in small disputes and disagreements about actors than in the fate of those glorious heroes and heroines as whom those actors appear before us.[64]

For some, displaying a fashionable interest in theatricals appeared to be even more important than comprehending what happened on the stage. For example, in October 1770 the British ambassador to St Petersburg, Lord Cathcart, wrote that a company of English actors, led by a Mr Fisher and resident in the capital between 1770 and 1772, had been warmly received by the Russians, 'who regularly frequent and applaud them, and indeed seem much entertained though they do not understand the language'.[65] In the 1820s, the impression lingered that sections of the audience attended theatre as a social necessity. In his remarks on St Petersburg's theatrical life, Pushkin observed that 'if at half past six some people appear from the barracks and the council to occupy the first rows of the subscription stalls, it is because this is a conventional etiquette rather than a pleasant relaxation'.[66]

Lest we conclude that public theatre emerged as an important aspect of the life of educated society purely as a consequence of governmental fiat, it is worth noting here that the proliferation of serf theatres from the 1790s, to be discussed below, indicated that members of the Russian nobility were by no means reluctant theatromanes. Once the state began to promote the idea of theatre as a mark of education and refinement, it became clear that there was no shortage of individuals prepared to contribute to the creation of a broader theatrical culture in Russia. The pursuit of plain fun and entertainment was a big motive. It has also been suggested that members of the Russian nobility were enthusiastic consumers of theatricals because they were expected to resemble western Europeans. Not only was theatre-going regarded as a prestigious foreign custom, but the stage was one of the few places where the languages and mores of non-Russians could be observed and assimilated. Hence the remarkable popularity of French drama among the elites of St Petersburg and Moscow, even after 1812.[67]

As Russia's theatrical culture emerged during the late eighteenth century, its reliance on the state for encouragement, at least in the capitals, and its adoption by the elite as an accoutrement of high fashion guaranteed its deferential character. The appearance and reception of Fonvizin's *The Minor* demonstrated how this culture might in fact pose a challenge to the prevailing order by questioning aspects of politics and society. Less than a decade later, copies of Yakov Kniazhnin's *Vadim of Novgorod* (1789) were destroyed by order of Catherine the Great after Platon Zubov, amid growing trepidation over events in France, informed her that it was laced with republican sentiments.[68] Consequently, if this new theatrical culture was to be preserved, to what extent could it be trusted? Would the state seek to delimit theatre's public space? Would educated society endeavour to use theatre as an independent forum as the stage became ever more popular and playwrights ever more daring? These questions found their answers in the following century.

During the early years of the nineteenth century, the state continued to support public theatres in the capitals. By that time, St Petersburg had three public theatre buildings, all of which were owned by the government and came under the direct authority of the directorate of Imperial Theatres. The Bolshoi Kamenny, which opened in 1783, was the first permanent theatre building in the city and remained its principal imperial playhouse until the 1830s. Home to the Russian and French troupes until they acquired their own separate buildings in 1832 and 1833 respectively, it was destroyed by fire in the early hours of 1 January 1811 and reopened in 1818.[69] The Malyi Wooden Theatre in the Ekaterinsky Garden on Nevsky Prospect (1801–32), where Kazassi's Italian troupe performed, was acquired by the directorate in 1803.[70] The city's third public theatre was the Kushelevsky German Theatre (1798–1819), also known as the Novyi Theatre, situated on Palace Square where the building of the General Staff now stands. Kushelevsky was the theatre's impresario, and its artistic manager was the popular German playwright August Kotzebue. The building was rented by the directorate from September 1800, and was later used by the Russian drama troupe when the Bolshoi Kamenny was being repaired.

Moscow had only one public theatre building at the beginning of the nineteenth century, the privately owned Petrovsky, run by the English impresario Michael Maddox. Known as 'The Cardinal' because he wore a billowing scarlet cloak, Maddox had been granted a monopoly on public theatricals in Moscow in 1780, which he retained until the Petrovsky was destroyed by fire in 1805. Unable to finance the reconstruction of his theatre, in 1806 Maddox sold his troupe to the directorate of Imperial Theatres. From 1806 to 1808 the troupe performed at the Pashkov House, and then, from 1808 to 1812, at the Arbatsky Theatre (also known as the New Imperial). Designed by Rossi, the Arbatsky housed the Russian and French drama troupes, and also staged ballet performances. It was destroyed in the conflagration of 1812, after which the Russian troupe performed, from 1814 to 1818, at the Znamensky (or Apraksin) Theatre, located in the house of the merchant S. S. Apraksin on Znamenka Street. Subsequently the troupe returned to the Pashkov House, finally acquiring a permanent home in 1824 when the building of the Malyi Theatre was completed. When construction of the Bolshoi Theatre was completed in 1825 on the site of the old Petrovsky, adjacent to the Malyi, the present-day Theatre Square in the centre of Moscow began to take shape.

As the state confirmed its commitment to maintaining public theatres in St Petersburg and Moscow, it also started to build a monopoly on theatricals in the two capitals. It began by appropriating several privately owned ventures, assuming control of the Free Russian Theatre in 1783, Kazassi's Italian troupe in 1803, and of course the remnants of Maddox's theatre in 1806, the latter sequestration constituting the inauguration of the Moscow Imperial Theatres.[71] Initially, at least, the process does not appear to have been systematic or determined by a single motive. As noted earlier, Sergei Danilov claimed that the Free Russian Theatre was sequestered because it dared to stage *The Minor*,[72] while others were taken over to rescue them from financial trouble, as was clearly the case with Maddox's troupe and the directorate's decision to rebuild the Petrovsky. To some extent, this is explained by the government's wish to encourage cultural institutions, with the relative weakness of civil society compelling it to play an active role.[73]

However, under A. L. Naryshkin, director of Imperial Theatres from 1799 to 1819,[74] an impetus towards placing constraints on private theatrical enterprise became evident. The initial motive appears to have been financial. Naryshkin, who has been described as 'a Russian *barin* from head to foot' and was, according to Stepan Zhikharev, 'the greatest gourmet of his era',[75] presided over a burgeoning deficit in state theatre finances. To address this problem, in 1803 he secured the 'exclusive right' for the state theatres 'henceforth forever' to organize 'public masquerades'.[76] Since there was no reference to drama, opera or ballet (and the word *maskarad* was not used as a general designation for all theatricals, but specifically for balls and dances),[77] the measure was clearly designed to ensure that the directorate reaped all the financial benefits from a popular pastime that would otherwise be organized by independent societies. One account claims that this measure marked the beginning of the Imperial Theatre monopoly, but inasmuch as it did not prohibit private theatricals in general, the assertion is unwarranted. At most, the 1803 regulation might be regarded as one of the earliest signs of a monopolistic *tendency* on the part of the directorate.[78]

This tendency was manifested in other measures. In 1804 the directorate was granted a monopoly on the printing of playbills, thereby ensuring that any non-state theatrical ventures, such as visiting troupes, would be unable to publicize their performances without paying a fee to the state theatrical administration. In Danilov's estimation this 'concentrated control over virtually all the theatrical life of the capital in the hands of the directorate'.[79] Yet this too is an exaggerated assessment, in that, at least in theory, private theatres could still be established without the directorate's sanction. Then in 1808 state theatre performers were prohibited from joining private troupes,[80] so that if audiences wanted to marvel at the latest celebrities they would have to purchase tickets for the Imperial Theatres.

Creeping monopolization of theatrical entertainments in the capitals was accompanied by a reorganization of censorship arrangements. Formal institutional censorship of theatre did not exist in Russia until the nineteenth century. A decree of 1782 had granted the police the authority to carry out surveillance and supervision of any theatrical activity in the empire, with the sole exception of court theatricals. Between 1766 and 1804, responsibility for monitoring the repertoire in St Petersburg belonged to the directorate, while in Moscow this was the province of the police. These arrangements were replaced by a censorship law of 1804, which instituted preliminary censorship for all publications, including collections of plays, a task undertaken by the Ministry of Education. Censorship of plays intended for performance was carried out from 1811 by the Ministry of Police, and from 1819 by the new Ministry of Internal Affairs.[81] Viewed together, the drift towards a monopoly for the Imperial Theatres and the new censorship regulations create the impression that the state was carefully tightening its grip on theatrical life. While this seems undeniable, it is important to make a distinction between the motives for each development. The tendency towards a monopoly arose for economic reasons, while the new censorship statute was concerned primarily with the control of opinion. The net effect, or course, was that civil society, then still in its infancy, would find it well nigh impossible to manifest itself in the form of theatrical ventures, at least in the capitals.

The Enlightenment idea of theatre as a school for morals, proclaimed for Russia by Catherine the Great, became a regular refrain of nineteenth-century theatrical commentary. Alexander Shakhovskoi, the doyen of Russian theatre during the first third of the nineteenth century, believed that theatre's role was 'To strive to refine taste, to soften manners, to eradicate vices, to rouse the spirit and a sense of patriotism'.[82] In 1804, the dramatist Fyodor Ivanov defended the vocation of acting by suggesting that 'an actor does not entertain but teaches, in exchange for money but not for the sake of money, just as a professor gives classes for money and an author publishes his works'.[83]

There was, however, little unanimity about the value of theatre. Some regarded it as a pernicious influence, and society generally held the vocation of acting in 'contempt'.[84] As in the rest of Europe, acting was regarded as an especially debased pursuit for women. The great actor Mikhail Shchepkin recalled that the parents of schoolgirls, upon hearing that they had been offered parts in a school production, expressed utter horror at the prospect of their becoming actresses.[85] In addition to the social disrepute that commonly accompanied a stage career, young actresses were forced to endure years of ruthless exploitation at the hands of managers, and the Imperial Theatre School was notorious for attracting the attentions of libidinous theatromanes and acolytes of the administration.[86]

The extent to which the value of theatre was a contested issue during the early years of the nineteenth century can be inferred from an article published in 1811 by Vladimir Yushkov entitled 'Thoughts on the Harm and Benefit of Theatres'. It provides one of the few extended considerations of the subject for that period, and indicates quite clearly that Russian society was divided over theatre. According to Yushkov, some people regarded drama as a 'strict judge of vice and a zealous defender of good morals' – the standard Enlightenment refrain – while others viewed it as a 'school of waywardness' in which the dramatis personae, concealed under masks of virtue, can instil a 'venom of the most pernicious depravity' in the heart of the audience. 'There is still no established agreement,' Yushkov asserted, 'on the harm or benefit of the performance of theatrical spectacles.'

Yushkov argued for the advantages of theatre. Good comedies which censured vices were capable of rectifying the 'corrupt morals' of citizens. Tragedies which depicted the exploits and magnanimous feats of heroes were capable of inspiring audiences to noble imitations of them. This, he insisted, was the 'sacred duty' of the Dramatic Muse. Like philosophy, drama existed to teach people about duty and the path to virtue. But if theatres were so useful, he asked, why did some people blame them for the corruption of morals? His answer was that 'The harm that comes from theatres is attributable to the poets, actors and audiences who abuse the divine gift of Melpomene.' Poets have neglected their duty to correct morals. They have lost the example of ancients such as Aeschylus, Sophocles and Euripides. 'It follows that theatre in itself cannot be the cause of human depravities and calamities – its whole aim is to instil virtue, to eradicate vice, to rectify corrupt morals.' The culprits included 'corrupt poets', 'base and self-interested actors' and 'reckless and stupid theatre bosses'. 'If we eradicate the abuse brought about by them,' he insisted, 'theatre will be transformed into the most useful school of virtue, into a school of good morals, worthy of the honest and virtuous citizen.'[87] Thus, while acknowledging the shortcomings of contemporary theatre, Yushkov nevertheless refused to abandon his belief that its ideal function was attainable.

How did audiences regard theatre? Did they share the high idealism attributed to the dramatic stage by the authorities and various writers? Evidence for the second half of the eighteenth century suggests that audiences treated the theatre less as a sacred temple of enlightenment than as a general gathering place for entertainment and social intercourse. While the St Petersburg public was gradually compelled by official prompting to embrace theatre as an accoutrement of respectability, in Moscow there remained a suspicion and distaste for drama. Instead, the Muscovite establishment considered balls and masquerades to be the mark of civilization. This was partly because there was no state-sponsored public theatre in Moscow until 1806, and no permanent court to encourage theatre-going and impart the conventional etiquette.[88] Hence, when the Italian impresario Giovanni Locatelli took his troupe to Moscow in 1760, he was confronted by unruly and violent behaviour in the auditorium.[89] The playwright Sumarokov fulminated against Moscow audiences, accusing them of munching nuts and quarrelling 'when the performance is at its fullest height'. The situation in Moscow was so bad that Sumarokov even issued an appeal to the audience before a performance of his tragedy *Semira* in December 1769:

> The author of this drama respectfully craves polite attention, so that he may present his dramas henceforward for the spectators' pleasure. He would

indeed be giving his compositions for performance to no purpose, if he anticipated that people came to the theatre, not for the sake of hearing his plays, but solely for talk and conversation; because his scenes, so industriously written for their benefit, would disturb such people gathered there for gossip.[90]

Audiences in St Petersburg, although composed of more members of the imperial establishment, were no less inclined to use the auditorium as a place for socializing and gossiping. Indeed, as Malcolm Burgess aptly put it, the beau monde 'regarded the theatre as a coffee house or large assembly-room', and he cited the comments of a German visitor to the city in the 1770s: 'In general it may be said that representations have been seen at St Petersburg, but never heard. The young officers and junior Guards officers . . . talk so loud and make so much noise that it often happens that I am unable to hear a word of the piece being played.'[91]

From the 1780s onwards, however, audience behaviour seems to have improved. One foreign visitor remarked in 1804 that 'The silence and decorum of the audience cannot but impress the mind of anyone, who has witnessed the boisterous clamours of an English audience.'[92] Burgess attributed this new-found decorum to the sheer scale of the new public theatres in St Petersburg and Moscow, respectively the Bolshoi Kamenny and the Petrovsky. Both theatres were colossal, especially for that time, and the intimacy between actors and audience afforded by smaller venues was lost. The towering and expansive architecture of the new buildings bestowed upon the auditoriums a more formal atmosphere. As Burgess put it, 'The audience was condemned to listen from afar and more than half the people seated there were unacquainted with each other. In such circumstances correct deportment and gracious bearing became the onlooker better than loud and hearty vociferation.'[93] The scale of the new auditoriums also explains contemporaneous comments about relatively empty theatres. The time when the review columns regularly printed the phrase 'teatr byl polon' (the theatre was full) had not yet arrived.[94]

Russian theatre interiors were based on the style developed by Italian Renaissance architects. According to Leonid Grossman, in St Petersburg the 'formula of a "theatre of ranks with loges" was adopted and fully corresponded to the caste requirements of the epoch'. This meant that there were 'armchairs [*kresla*] for high officials and members of the court, a standing parterre for middling bureaucrats and "bourgeois", a gallery for the crowd, loges for ladies and their companions'.[95] The parterre tended to include the intelligentsia, journalists, Guards officers and a variety of younger people.[96] The younger generation tended to congregate on the left-hand side of the parterre and consequently became known as the 'left flank'. It was here, for example, that members of Nikita Vsevolozhsky's Green Lamp literary-theatrical circle, established in 1819 in St Petersburg, would gather. The circle often discussed performances at its fortnightly meetings.[97]

The fact that audiences were generally conducting themselves more respectably by the early nineteenth century was occasionally underlined by incidents which appeared to challenge the prevailing etiquette of the auditorium. The three most famous examples all involved Pushkin, which tends to suggest that they were more typical of the young poet than of the audience. On one occasion at the Bolshoi Kamenny, he paid a visit to the box of the Kolosov family. Alexandra Kolosova, the actress with whom Pushkin had a relationship, recorded the event:

> In the middle of the most tragic scene of the play, Pushkin began to complain of the heat, took off his wig, and started fanning his face with it. The people in the nearby boxes were spluttering with laughter and those in the orchestra kept turning to look at us. We tried to make him behave, but then he slid off his chair onto the floor and settled himself at our feet, hidden by the front of the box. Then he plunked his wig onto his head like a hat. You couldn't look at him without laughing. And there he sat, on the floor, throughout the entire performance, poking fun at the play and the actors.[98]

A second incident, in December 1818, involved the St Petersburg police commissioner, who complained to Pushkin's superior in the foreign ministry:

> On the twentieth of this month ministerial undersecretary and translator Pushkin, attached to the ministry of foreign affairs, attended the theater and sat in a box at the back of the orchestra; during the intermission he went into the orchestra and, passing between the rows, stopped in front of the seats occupied by Councilor Perevoshikov and his wife. Mr. Perevoshikov asked him to move, but Pushkin, interpreting the request as an insult, spoke indecently to him and insulted him in obscene terms.[99]

The incident had arisen after Pushkin hissed one of the actresses who was the subject of admiration from another member of the audience. The poet allegedly retorted to the police commissioner, with regard to the man he had offended, 'I would have slapped his face, and only refrained lest the actors should take it for applause!'[100] A third incident was more political. In 1820 Pushkin displayed in the stalls of a St Petersburg theatre a portrait of the Duc de Berry's assassin with the words 'A Lesson to the Tsars'.[101]

These incidents demonstrate that, as theatre developed into a locus of respectability, it also provided a public space where the rules of polite society and its etiquette could be deliberately defied. One historian has suggested that it constituted 'a space in which the usual conventions of behaviour for nobles and aristocrats were suspended'.[102] Yet it could also be argued that the kind of evidence which supports this conclusion is remarkable for being atypical, suggesting rather that behavioural norms in the theatre were episodically challenged rather than entirely suspended.

Challenges to auditorium conventions during the early nineteenth century could also be interpreted as an affront to the authorities, given that the St Petersburg and Moscow theatres were state institutions. Indeed, the Imperial Theatres constituted one of the few government-funded public institutions that could be implicitly attacked, for example through the criticism of artists, who were employees of the tsar. The government was aware of this potential indignity, and in 1815 the Ministry of Police took measures to prohibit the publication of articles which criticized the Imperial Theatres and their artists. Until the ban was lifted in 1828, theatrical reviews or articles about the stage in the periodical press were few and far between.[103] A similar ban also existed between 1858 and 1863, when it was forbidden to discuss the activities of the directorate in the press.[104]

If one individual personified the world of Russian theatre in the early nineteenth century, it was unquestionably Prince Alexander Shakhovskoi (1777–1846), dramatist, translator, administrator, stage director and teacher.[105] Mercilessly lampooned for his ungainly appearance – he was tall and corpulent, with an unusually large nose – and his odd voice – characterized by a lisp and a squeak – he became the pre-eminent theatrical figure of his age, a 'living legend of theatrical Petersburg'.[106] The actor Pavel Karatygin described him as a 'fanatic for his profession',[107] and the journalist Faddei Bulgarin, in a panegyric to Shakhovskoi, claimed that no one had ever 'surpassed [him] in affection for theatre and in unselfish work for it'.[108]

Born to a landed family in Smolensk province, Shakhovskoi initially pursued a career in the army, but soon turned to theatre. He was promoted at the court in St Petersburg following the success of his first play, *A Woman's Jest*, at the Hermitage Theatre in 1795. In 1802 Naryshkin made him superintendent of the repertoire, and he effectively ran St Petersburg's theatres until he was called away for military duty in 1812. Upon his return, however, he fell out with Naryshkin's deputy, Pyotr Tyufyakin, and finally resigned in 1818. Since Tyufyakin succeeded Naryshkin as director of Imperial Theatres, a post which he held between 1819 and 1822, Shakhovskoi had to spend a few years in the theatrical wilderness, but under Tyufyakin's successor, A. A. Maikov, director from 1822 to 1825, he was readmitted to the administrative fold, this time as a teacher at the Theatre School. In 1824 the governor-general of St Petersburg, Mikhail Miloradovich, appointed him to the committee charged with drawing up new regulations for the Imperial Theatre administration, which were finally published in 1825. Miloradovich perished during the Decembrist revolt, and Shakhovskoi was again sidelined. From 1825 to 1830, he worked in the Moscow Imperial Theatre administration, and then returned to St Petersburg.

Shakhovskoi was an important figure for many reasons, all of which reflected his energetic dedication to the theatre. He was the first person of any import to acknowledge that poor remuneration for authors was a fundamental reason for the dearth of good dramatists in Russia. He established two of the earliest theatrical journals in Russia, the *Dramatic Herald* (1808) and *Repertoire of the Russian Theatre* (1839–41). He discovered and trained many of the leading actors and actresses of the time. He was also a remarkably prolific writer, producing over one hundred plays, although many were loose adaptations from foreign works. Among his more notable plays were *The New Sterne* (1805) and *A Lesson to Coquettes, or The Lipetsk Spa* (1815).

As Bertha Malnick aptly concluded, 'The true value of Shakhovskoy's contribution to the Russian theatre was his passionate and disinterested professionalism.'[109] If one goal underlay his wide range of activities, it was to make Russian theatre more Russian. Although he was an ardent partisan of vaudeville, he did not regard it as incompatible with efforts to reflect Russian life and customs on the stage. Vaudeville could be Russian as well as French, and in developing the genre in his homeland Shakhovskoi endeavoured to imbue it with native rather than imported characteristics.[110] Shakhovskoi was fundamentally a cultural nationalist, and was even a member of Alexander Shishkov's conservative Symposium of the Lovers of the Russian Word. He spoke about the idea of a 'national theatre',[111] and his plays often deployed colloquial language, for which the critics attacked him, calling it 'the prose language of coachmen'.[112] Others supported what Shakhovskoi was trying to achieve, and Sergei Aksakov remarked approvingly that, until then, there had been no such thing as 'conversation on the stage, i.e. colloquialism of language [*razgovornost' iazyka*], in conformity with the description of the dramatis personae'.[113]

In St Petersburg at the end of the eighteenth century, performances by the French and Italian troupes were the most fashionable entertainments for the theatre-going public. The German theatre in the city was patronized mainly by the city's German speakers,[114] while the Russian theatre attracted relatively few spectators. But the question of Russian national identity and the extent to which it was reflected in the repertoire was starting to occupy a growing, if yet small, number of people, as national consciousness became more pronounced within the westernized elites. Fonvizin had directed attention to the issue in his plays, and one of the leading actors of the time, P. A. Plavilshchikov (1760–1812), had also called on theatre to depict Russian life and history (his own plays on Russian historical themes included *Riurik* and *Ermak*) instead of slavishly imitating French models. This was part of Plavilshchikov's more general call for theatre to reflect the truth of life.[115]

The administration of the Imperial Theatres, however, continued to lavish the bulk of its resources on non-Russian theatre. The directorate's income in 1809 amounted to 1,388,470 rubles. The money came from four sources: the Cabinet (634,470 r.), the Exchequer (206,000 r.), St Petersburg box-office receipts (359,000 r.) and Moscow box-office receipts (189,000 r.). It was spent as follows:

St Petersburg theatres (excluding German troupe)	855,079 r. 65 k.
St Petersburg German troupe	138,390 r. 35 k.
Moscow theatres	365,000 r.

From the recorded expenditures, only the following amounts were spent on the Russian troupes:

St Petersburg Russian troupe	54,600 r.
Moscow Russian troupe	35,000 r.

Other expenditures were as follows:

St Petersburg French troupe	175,648 r.
Moscow French troupe	66,340 r.

St Petersburg ballet troupe	85,620 r.
Moscow ballet troupe	32,093 r.
St Petersburg orchestras	148,930 r.
Moscow orchestras	37,690 r.
St Petersburg wardrobes (*garderob*)	36,402 r. 33 k.
Moscow wardrobes	26,292 r.
St Petersburg scenery section	45,706 r. 67 k.
Moscow scenery section	26,292 r.
St Petersburg theatre school	49,956 r.
Moscow theatre school	16,660 r.[116]

Russia's participation in the wars against Napoleon drew closer attention to the marked imbalance between indigenous and imported theatrical works, and led to an increase in the number of plays with patriotic themes. During the 1805–6 season, the following plays appeared on the St Petersburg stage: S. N. Glinka's *Natalya the Boyar's Daughter*, based on Karamzin's tale and remaining in the repertoire until 1823; Mikhail Kheraskov's tragedy *Liberated Moscow*; and I. A. Krylov's comedy *The Fashion Shop* and magical opera *Ilya the Bogatyr*. The following year, 1807, saw the production of Ozerov's tragedy *Dmitry Donskoi*, S. N. Glinka's *Sumbeka, or The Decline of the Kazan Kingdom* and M. V. Kryukovsky's *Pozharsky*. Even after the Treaty of Tilsit in 1807, which temporarily ended the conflict with Napoleonic France, patriotic plays remained popular, at least in St Petersburg. This was partly due to the influence of Shakhovskoi. In 1815, for instance, he wrote the scenario for a patriotic opera, *Ivan Susanin*, with music by K. A. Cavos, some years before M. I. Glinka's more famous operatic treatment of the same subject.[117]

The fortunes of French theatre understandably declined during 1812, when Napoleon's Grande Armée invaded Russia. The French troupe in Moscow, originally established in 1806, continued to perform until the great fire in September 1812 made it impossible,[118] even though, as Vigel recalled, audiences began to abandon it as Napoleon's forces approached the city.[119] Another observer recalled an incident at the French theatre as the 1812 campaign was getting under way. An actor appeared on the stage between the plays to announce the next performance. Bowing three times, he approached the footlights and began, 'Messieurs!', only to realise that there was only one person in the stalls. So he started again: 'Monsieur! Demain Mardi nous aurons l'honneur de vous donner . . .'[120] As Napoleon approached, the Moscow administration removed the city's entire theatrical apparatus – with the exception of the properties of the French stage – to Vladimir, eventually settling in Kostroma. Napoleon reached Moscow on 2 September and abandoned it on 17 October. The remaining French actors performed for him in the Kremlin, and a temporary theatre on Nikitskaya Street, the Pozdnyakov Theatre, also staged performances during the occupation.[121] Not surprisingly, Naryshkin formally dissolved the French troupes in November 1812.[122]

By 1816 the French theatre had been restored to St Petersburg,[123] although its budget was affected by the rising patriotism created by the war. By 1825, expenditure on the St Petersburg Russian troupe had increased markedly to 186,000 rubles, whereas the French troupe's budget had been reduced to 100,000 rubles.[124] This was an aberration, however, and the earlier imbalance in favour of the French troupe was soon restored (see chapter 3). In Moscow, theatrical life had begun to return to normal by the middle of 1813, but it was not until the late 1820s that a French troupe was reinstated in the city.[125]

Although few of the patriotic plays produced in Russia during the conflict with France remained in the repertoire for long, they demonstrated the theatrical world's willingness and ability to adapt to circumstances, reflect the popular mood and strive to overcome long-standing prejudices about suitable themes for the stage. The question of the national character of Russian theatre, however, would remain contentious well into the nineteenth century.

The growing prestige of theatre in Russian society from the late eighteenth century onwards was demonstrated most clearly by the phenomenon of serf theatres. Established by members of the serf-owning nobility who commanded their vassals to perform as artists in dramatic and musical spectacles, serf theatres initially appeared in Moscow and St Petersburg in the 1770s, spreading gradually to manorial estates and experiencing their most rapid period of growth in the 1790s. As non-governmental organizations, the serf theatres that were not purely domestic amusements but had some form of public access constituted the most significant contribution of Russia's theatrical culture to the development of civil society in the late eighteenth and early nineteenth centuries, especially now that the state was beginning to take possession of public entertainments in the capitals.

It has been estimated that by the early nineteenth century there were 173 serf theatres (the location of eighteen is unknown).[126] The majority (103) were in urban areas, mostly Moscow and its environs. Moscow had fifty-three serf theatres, St Petersburg twenty-seven, other towns twenty-three.[127] This means that seventy were on manorial estates in the country. Most were small-scale private domestic theatres organized for special events, such as holidays, and for the private delectation of the serf owner and his invited guests. A few were open to the public, notably the Sheremetev theatre in the village of Kuskovo, now part of suburban Moscow, which was open to local residents free of charge (Maddox complained that it drew audiences away from the Petrovsky).[128] Some were practically professional enterprises for ticket-buying audiences. Most, however, were not dependent on box-office revenues but instead relied on the largesse of their baronial managers and, of course, the exploitation of bonded labour. As one commentator put it, 'Money was squandered rather than made.'[129] In this sense, most serf theatres were not strictly commercial.[130]

The preconditions for the development of serf theatre were established by two political acts. The first was the emancipation of the nobility from compulsory civil and military service in 1762. Nobles were still expected to serve from a sense of duty, but many of the wealthier ones took advantage of the new rules to retire to their estates, where they devoted themselves to a variety of cultural pastimes. Secondly, following the Pugachev uprising Catherine the Great set about strengthening administrative rule in the provinces of the empire, notably via the provincial government reform of 1775. The result was a steady exodus of serf-owning grandees and officials from centre to periphery, where, in their relative isolation, they pursued theatricals.

How do we explain this phenomenon? Initially the nobility simply followed instructions from the centre. After the legislation of 1762 and 1775, it was expected to lead the way in enlightening the provinces, in part by organizing theatricals. For example, in 1776 the new viceroy of Kaluga province, M. N. Krechetnikov, was instructed to build a theatre to 'bring people together, for the spread of social life and politesse'. Similar instructions led to the creation of theatres in Tula, Kharkov and Penza.[131] It has also been argued by one historian that 'In supporting provincial theater the noble was both emulating the autocracy and discovering a means of asserting his own power.'[132] Theatricalized display on the manorial estate, of which theatre was a part, helped the nobility to identify with the political centre and its rituals. At the same time, display allowed the nobility to articulate and reinforce local hierarchies.

Persuasive though such arguments are, it is unlikely that they account for all serf theatres. It has also been suggested that the promotion of theatricals by the nobility was a direct imitation of French customs in the wake of foreign travel.[133] Moreover, the idea that theatre brought enlightenment became so entrenched amongst the nobility that, by the early nineteenth century, it was invoked by those wishing to establish theatres on their own initiative rather than the state's. Writing to the governor of Penza in 1806 for permission to set up a theatre, Grigory Gladkov pointed to the presumed benefits of theatre, noting that theatrical performances were considered useful because they had 'some influence on morals'.[134]

Historians of Russian theatre often suggest that a few serf theatres rivalled the achievements of the state-supported imperial troupes in St Petersburg and Moscow. One pointed out that while there 'can be no *apologia* for a serf theatre ... indignation at serfdom must not blind one to the fact that some Russian serf theatres made theatrical history'.[135] Yet the Imperial Theatres had their detractors and artistic shortcomings, so it is unclear what this says about the standards of serf theatres. The extravagant bestowal of prodigious resources did not necessarily entail commensurate artistic quality. Arguably more significant than the relative artistic accomplishments of the theatres of the state and those of the nobility were the relative levels of cultural leadership. The high status of certain serf theatres testified to the fact that not all theatrical standards were set by the stages of the state.

One of the first and most significant serf theatres was that of the Sheremetev family. It was created at the end of the 1760s by Pyotr Sheremetev (1713–88) and developed by his son Nikolai (1751–1809). The family possessed eight serf theatres altogether, located in Moscow, St Petersburg, Kuskovo, Markovo and Ostankino. Members of the troupe, which numbered more than two hundred serfs, often studied with leading stage experts in Russia and abroad. Dmitrevsky, for example, worked for Sheremetev as a theatrical advisor, and the latest theatrical equipment was imported from western Europe. Prominent architects who helped Catherine the Great to develop St Petersburg, including Quarenghi, the designer of the Hermitage Theatre, worked at Ostankino. Spectacles at the Sheremetev theatres, especially Ostankino, were celebrated for their extravagance and their use of the era's leading designers. Catherine herself even attended some performances.[136]

There were other prominent serf theatres, though none matched the opulence or status of Sheremetev's. Prince Nikolai Yusupov's ventures in Moscow and at his estate of Arkhangelskoe near the city gained solid reputations. The Arkhangelskoe theatre was built in 1818 and possessed a troupe of twenty to twenty-five dancers, ten singers and twenty-five musicians. Yusupov's actresses studied both French and Italian.[137] A. R. Vorontsov's serf theatre (1792–1805) also achieved a certain renown. Its owner was a progressive man for his time, and his actors received an education and a salary.[138]

What was staged in serf theatres? The repertoire tended to consist of French *opéras comiques* and ballets. Sheremetev had a notable predilection for musical spectacles. Information survives for 116 of his productions, of which seventy-three were operas, twenty-five comedies and eighteen ballets.[139] Vorontsov favoured drama, staging the works of Kniazhnin, Sumarokov, Krylov and others. His serf theatre was the only one to perform *The Minor*; elsewhere it was banished from the repertoire.[140]

Serf artists were often brutally treated by their owners. It is a tragic irony that, while theatre was pursued as an accoutrement of culture and a mark of enlightenment, many of its noble patrons behaved in a despicable manner towards their serf artists, contradicting all that their theatres were presumed to represent. Malcolm Burgess wrote that 'the emancipation of the serf artiste from dependence upon the landowner was one of the cardinal problems of reform in the theatre at the beginning of the nineteenth century'.[141] The degradation of serf artists was the lowest point on a scale of hardship and humiliation suffered by the majority of thespians that was not confronted until later in the nineteenth century.

Count Sergei Kamensky's public ticket-buying theatre at Orel was one of the worst for actors, Kamensky himself taking a whip to members of his troupe who made mistakes. I. D. Shepelev was similarly inclined to beat the female singers who trained at his estate theatres in Vladimir province.[142] Gladkov, despite the high ideals to which he professed to subscribe, was known to 'rush on stage, where he doled out slaps and blows to the actors and actresses, after which they came on stage with flushed cheeks and tearful eyes ... some spectators even said that you could sometimes see the bruises on their faces beneath the rouge and powder'.[143] According to one historian, suicides among serf artists were not uncommon.[144]

Female serf artists were treated particularly cruelly. Actress harems were not unheard of, and there are reports of serf theatre owners forcing actresses to dance naked, or to strip naked and pose as statues.[145] Discussing the apparent prevalence of such 'coercive sexuality', Laurence Senelick concludes that 'serf theatricals must be seen as something other than the school of national art praised by Soviet historians . . . They were also a playground for sexual power relationships.'[146]

The poignant contrast between the fictional worlds that serf artists inhabited when on stage and the non-fictional world they inhabited as bonded labour is often noted. Martha Wilmot, an Irish traveller, witnessed a performance at Princess Dashkova's Troitskoe estate theatre near Serpukhov, south of Moscow, in 1803, which she mentioned in a letter to her mother:

> We have a little Theatre here, and our labourers, our Cooks, our footmen, and *femmes de Chambres* turn into Princes, Princesses, Shepherds and Sheperdesses &c. &c. and perform with a degree of spirit that is astonishing. 'tis droll eneough [*sic*] to be attended at Supper by the Herd of the piece who has been strutting before your Eyes in Gilded robes &c. &c. for half the Evening.[147]

Nevertheless, there is some evidence that a few serf owners treated the members of their theatrical troupes with compassion and respect. Sheremetev and Vorontsov provided their artists with salaries and allowances, rendering their material situation better than that of the majority of bondsmen. For a handful, the stage even proved to be a vehicle for social mobility, as talent and fame finally delivered them from the ignominy of bondage. The directorate of Imperial Theatres occasionally purchased whole serf troupes in order to replenish or augment its pool of performers, and since it was deemed inconsistent with the dignity and status of the Imperial Theatres to employ serfs, they were granted their freedom. This was the case, for example, when the directorate acquired the serf ballet troupe of S. G. Zorich in 1800, Maddox's troupe in 1806 – the serf actors of A. Stolypin had been leased to 'The Cardinal' – and the serf orchestra of Count Chernyshev in 1828.[148]

That individual serf actors might occasionally extricate themselves from bondage as a result of their celebrity is illustrated by the career of Russia's greatest actor of the nineteenth century, Mikhail Shchepkin.[149] Born in 1788 in the small village of Krasnoe in Kursk province, Ukraine, Shchepkin is generally regarded as the founder of realistic or natural acting in the Russian theatre. His serf parents belonged to Count G. S. Volkenstein, in whose theatre Mikhail performed when he was still a child. In 1800 he debuted in an amateur production staged by the students of the Sudzha regional school, where he was a pupil, and during the summer months he performed at Volkenstein's theatre. In 1801 Shchepkin transferred to the Kursk provincial school. In Kursk he visited the theatre of the Barsov brothers – Mikhailo, Nikolai and Pyotr – where, in 1804, he worked as a prompter. Although the Barsovs were serfs, Shchepkin was so impressed by the relative respect they were accorded as actors that he determined upon a theatrical career. After standing in for one of the actors in 1805, he became a permanent actor at the Barsovs' theatre, although he still had to work as a secretary for Volkenstein.

In 1816, while remaining a serf of Volkenstein, Shchepkin was transferred to the Kharkov troupe managed by the German I. F. Stein and the Pole O. I. Kalinovsky. Two years later, in 1818, a group of leading actors from the Kharkov troupe, including Shchepkin, founded the Free Theatre (*vol'nyi teatr*) in Poltava, owned by Prince N. G. Repnin and managed by I. P. Kotliarevsky. By this time, Shchepkin's rich acting talent had acquired him a solid reputation, and a bidding war began between regional impresarios for his services. In 1818 Repnin purchased him from Volkenstein for 8,000 rubles. Kamensky, who wanted the actor for his serf theatre at Orel, offered to buy him for 20,000 rubles, but he was no longer for sale. At the end of 1821, the Poltava theatre closed and Shchepkin moved to Tula, where Stein now ran a venture. The actor was readily admitted to Stein's new troupe, receiving a salary of 5,000 rubles.

The question of Shchepkin's freedom had been broached in 1818. Several individuals, including Sergei Volkonsky, the future Decembrist, and Kotliarevsky, campaigned for his freedom, and a subscription was organized to raise the sum required. Eventually, in 1822, Shchepkin and his family were liberated from Repnin. The price was 4,000 rubles, guaranteed by one of the original subscribers for the actor's freedom. Shchepkin now had to find the money to reimburse his former owner. A move to Moscow, where the pecuniary rewards for actors were greater than in the regions, seemed appropriate. By coincidence, an official from the Moscow Imperial Theatre administration was talent-scouting in the regions, and he invited Shchepkin to perform in the city. He made his Moscow debut in September 1822, formally joined the Moscow Imperial Theatre troupe in March 1823, and proceeded to establish himself as Russia's leading actor. Shchepkin's experience, however, was a prominent exception. The vast majority of serf artists remained the property of their owners, often living in pitiable circumstances and deprived of any rights.

By the early 1820s the heyday of serf theatres had passed. Their decline dated from 1797, when Paul I introduced temporary measures designed to make the organization of theatricals more difficult. For example, plays which had not been approved by the authorities could not be performed in domestic theatres.[150] Many serf theatres soon began to transform themselves into commercial enterprises. Examples included Kamensky's theatre at Orel, Gladkov's at Penza (1806–29), P. P. Esipov's at Kazan and, most notably, N. G. Shakhovskoi's at Nizhny Novgorod.[151] Consequently, during the first quarter of the nineteenth century, 'there took place a mass sale and transfer to quit-rent of serf actors'.[152] When Shakhovskoi died in 1827, his company of over one hundred serfs was sold for 100,000 rubles – an indication of its success – and all were granted their freedom.[153] By the time serfdom was abolished in 1861, most serf theatres had long since closed, as they were faced with competition from 'free enterprises'.[154]

Commercial theatre had been slow to develop in regional Russia because the material conditions to support permanent enterprises were still limited. Potential audiences were small, notably because merchants, the primary stratum of the regional population with a modicum of expendable wealth, were not yet interested in theatre as a fashionable pastime.[155] For these reasons, until the early nineteenth century commercial theatre outside St Petersburg and Moscow took the form of episodic and casual ventures. These were usually organized by local governors who were either implementing the centre's mission to enlighten and/or pacify the regions, especially in the wake of the Pugachev rebellion, or aiming to recreate the culture of the court and nobility for their own self-glorification. Towards the end of the eighteenth century, examples could be found in Yaroslavl, Penza, Voronezh, Kaluga, Kharkov and Irkutsk. Their repertoires generally imitated that of the Imperial Theatres, and entry was often gratis for the local population.[156]

The repressive policies of Paul I's reign inhibited the further development of regional theatres, but soon after the accession of Alexander I their numbers started to grow.[157] It has been estimated that between 1813 and 1825 there were at least fifteen large permanent theatres in regional towns (six of which were serf).[158] Two of the largest non-serf commercial theatres of the period were O. Lenkavsky's Kiev-based troupe (1811–30) and the Kharkov-based enterprise of Stein and Kalinovsky where Shchepkin spent two years of his acting career. While such enterprises were not technically serf theatres, they often employed serfs: Shchepkin, for instance, had not yet gained his freedom when he worked for Stein and Kalinovsky. Notwithstanding the fact that certain superlative talents like Shchepkin were fostered on the regional circuit, the quality of such theatres was generally undistinguished. An adjunct of Kharkov University, E. M. Filomafitsky, claimed of Stein's troupe in 1816, 'Our actors and actresses are sometimes so disorganized that, without the playbill, you cannot tell who the master is, who the servant, who the mother or who the daughter.'[159]

In addition to serf and commercial theatres, regional Russia was home to troupes of itinerant players. The first strolling companies appeared in southern Russia and Ukraine, where serfdom was less entrenched and mobility easier.[160] Other groups of wandering players emerged from the remnants of serf theatres: lacking a permanent base, they took to wandering the provinces in search of audiences. In Richard Stites' vivid description, they 'criss-crossed the country in a permanent caravan of troikas and carriages, rattling with musical instruments, sets, machines, and costumes'.[161] The number of people who lived as itinerant players is unknown. In general, however, such ventures represented the tentative emergence from serf theatricals of a commercial theatre culture in the regions.[162]

During the late eighteenth century, the state adopted an increasingly interventionist stance towards theatre in the belief that it was both a mark of enlightened sophistication and a 'school for morals' that could benefit educated society as a whole. In the process, it gradually centralized the organization of all theatrical spectacles in St Petersburg and Moscow under the auspices of the directorate of Imperial Theatres, a development that, within a few years, would result in a formal monopoly of state theatres in the capitals. This eventually caused friction between the state and educated society over the control of Russian theatrical life and resulted in a campaign for the liberalization of entertainment legislation. For the moment, however, the theatrical public remained relatively small and society generally quiescent.

In promoting a culture of theatre-going, the state also helped to lay the foundations for the sanctification and veneration of the stage during the early decades of the nineteenth century. This was evidenced most clearly in the phenomenon of serf theatres and in the growing respectability that attached to theatre-going. The question of the national character of the repertoire had arisen tentatively in the minds and works of a few figures, such as Plavilshchikov and Shakhovskoi, and briefly assumed a certain urgency during the wars against Napoleon, but by the early 1820s the repertoire still remained overwhelmingly dominated by translations and adaptations from foreign plays.

All of these developments took place in the shadow of Fonvizin's *The Minor*, the benchmark comedy that had demonstrated the potential for an indigenous repertoire, but had also revealed the extent to which the 'school for morals' could prove a troublesome institution for the state that patronized it.

Chapter 2

MIRRORS OF SOCIETY

During the second quarter of the nineteenth century, as Tsar Nicholas I increased the state's surveillance of society, the Russian theatre industry continued to expand slowly but steadily. The most immediate manifestation of this was the appearance of grandiose new theatre buildings in the capitals. In St Petersburg, the Bolshoi Kamenny was joined by the Alexandrinsky (1832), which replaced the Malyi Wooden Theatre and became the permanent residence of the imperial Russian drama troupe, and by the Mikhailovsky (1833), where the imperial French company would now perform. On New Year's Day in 1825, a new wooden theatre opened beside the Chernyshev (now Lomonosov) bridge, but it was destroyed by fire two months later.[1] In 1827, the Kamenny Ostrov summer theatre was constructed, as was the Theatre-Circus, where drama was occasionally staged. In Moscow, the Malyi Theatre opened in 1824 as the permanent home of the city's imperial Russian drama troupe, and in 1825 the Bolshoi Theatre, for opera and ballet, opened on the site of the old Petrovsky. Regional theatres developed more quickly because their numbers were not restricted by the monopoly on public performances that was starting to take shape for the Imperial Theatres in the capitals. In 1829 there were seventeen permanent theatres in the regions, and by the late 1850s there were approximately forty-three.[2]

The growing fashion for theatre was evident in a variety of other ways. Regular reviews of performances began to appear for the first time in 1825, in Faddei Bulgarin's semi-official newspaper the *Northern Bee*.[3] Specialist theatrical journals began to survive for longer periods. Princess Dashkova's *The Russian Theatre* had appeared in 1786 and lasted until 1794. Subsequent theatrical periodicals, however, had not lasted as long: *Thalia* lasted only from 1810 to 1812, while the *Dramatic Herald, Satirical Theatre*, the *Dramatic*

Journal and the *Russian Thalia* did not survive beyond the year of their first appearance (respectively 1808, 1808, 1811 and 1825). From the late 1830s, the market for such publications was healthier, if not entirely reliable. In 1839, the monthly *Repertoire of the Russian Theatre* began to appear, followed in 1840 by the monthly *Pantheon of Russian and All European Theatres*. Both were published in St Petersburg. In 1842, they merged to form a single monthly publication entitled *Repertoire of Russian and Pantheon of All European Theatres*. It was published until 1856 under various guises – *Repertoire and Pantheon* (1844–7), *Pantheon and Repertoire of the Russian Stage* (1848–51) and *Pantheon* (1852–6) – and was accompanied by two supplements: *Theatrical Chronicle* (1844–5) and *Repertoire of the Russian Stage* (1852–6). And, of course, new journals which were not devoted exclusively to the theatre, for instance the *Contemporary* and the *Literary Gazette*, also devoted space to the discussion of drama and related issues. Such publications presided over the emergence of Russia's rich tradition of theatrical criticism.

The rise of the critic, in turn, meant that performers were soon exposed to greater public scrutiny. Formidable thespian reputations were established, notably by Shchepkin, Mochalov and Karatygin, the status of the actor as a prominent figure in public life dating from this period. There was greater incentive for writers to apply their talents to drama, and the period witnessed further attempts to create a national repertoire, evidenced most famously in Pushkin's *Boris Godunov*, Griboyedov's *Woe from Wit* and Gogol's *The Government Inspector*. Moreover, amateur domestic theatricals, associated in the early nineteenth century primarily with non-commercial serf theatres, survived the gradual eclipse of the latter from the 1820s onwards, and the evidence, while largely impressionistic, points to their persistent popularity throughout the nineteenth century. In 1842, one journal even published an article on how to construct a little temporary stage in a house.[4] In 1854, another wrote of the 'fashion or passion for domestic performances', especially in Moscow, but noted that most of these amateur efforts were staged 'more for the pleasure of the actors than that of their audiences'.[5]

In Russian theatre historiography, the period from the 1820s to the 1850s is associated predominantly with the nascent intelligentsia's conviction that theatre was a potentially significant force for the social and political reformation of the country. The educational importance of theatre had been insisted upon by the tsarist authorities from the eighteenth century, but some individuals now looked upon the stage as a forum for debating public issues and perhaps even questioning the established order, a role that might be termed the radical idea of theatre. This significant development has been summed up succinctly by Victor Borovsky:

> A belief in theatre as a powerful instrument of education had been inherited from the past. In the nineteenth century, with increasing urgency, attention was focused not on lessons in correct, fashionable behaviour being taught from the stage, but on an awareness of social ideals. . . . In theatre notices and press reviews, in critical articles by Vissarion Belinsky, and in the reminiscences of Aleksandr Herzen, theatre stood out as a vital necessity of life. It seemed that answers to the most serious and difficult questions of the time were expected of it.[6]

The conventional explanation for this development is that, in a period characterized by the absence of political pluralism and harsh censorship, theatre was regarded as one of the few arenas where the question of social ideals could be broached. Indeed, although Russian theatre is historically important for a range of artistic reasons, not least the international influence of the Moscow Art Theatre and the Ballets Russes, when contemporaries and historians write of its special role they are usually alluding to its presumed capacity to articulate social, political and other ideas that could not otherwise be expressed.

The importance of this development cannot be denied, but the emphasis on the radical idea of theatre has tended to obscure much of the mainstream discourse about the dramatic stage during the reign of Nicholas I. Theatre certainly attracted more attention from educated society, yet the predominant issues were not always identical to those which preoccupied Belinsky, Herzen and other radical critics, who remained a small, if vocal, minority. Sources for the period, including newspapers and journals, indicate a complex array of developments and discourses surrounding theatre. Three stand out in particular: firstly, the state conspicuously intensified its efforts to regulate public entertainments, especially in the capitals, where it began to consolidate the Imperial Theatre monopoly and to promote theatre as an agency of conformism; secondly, conflicting attitudes to audiences reflected implicit disagreement about the extent to which theatre should be democratic; thirdly, calls for the repertoire to reflect the characteristics of Russian life – although there was little agreement about what these were – indicated the extent to which theatre was increasingly regarded as a forum for the expression of national identity. These three areas will be elaborated below.

During the period in question, the theatres of St Petersburg and Moscow remained separate from civil society because they were state institutions, administered and financed by the government. In the regions, existing theatres remained under the watchful eyes of governors and local police, and there was little expansion of the industry until mid century. In some discussions about theatre, however, there was an evident aspiration for theatre to become a tribune that could play an important – and possibly independent – role in public life. This represented a growing demand on the part of educated society for a greater say in the cultural and public affairs of the country, and at least in this sense the history of theatre under Nicholas I was significant for the development of civil society.

From the 1820s onwards, the state began to tighten its administrative grip on theatrical entertainments in St Petersburg and Moscow. The overall authority of the directorate in St Petersburg was further reinforced, still mainly for economic reasons, although between 1822 and 1842 the Moscow Imperial Theatres were run separately by the city's governor-general.[7] When the Ministry of the Imperial Court was formed in 1826, the directorate became one of its departments. In 1827 a 'Statute on the Administration of the Imperial St Petersburg Theatres' established a special committee under the aegis of the directorate to run the city's state theatres. The statute was concerned mainly with regulating the internal work of the administration, but it also extended the provisions of the 1803 regulation (with which Naryshkin had secured the 'exclusive right' of the state theatres to organize masquerades) by granting the management of the Imperial Theatres the authority to stipulate the days and even the hours when other theatricals could take place, particularly the masquerades and concerts still organized by clubs and noble assemblies. This suggests that the directorate had used its 'exclusive right' from 1803 to regulate the times of such events, not to prohibit them entirely. The point was contained in paragraph 2 of the statute, which required the police to consult the committee before approving the times of 'any public performances or spectacles' so as to ensure, by implication, that they would not clash with peformances at the Imperial Theatres.[8] Yet the 1827 statute did not create a state theatre monopoly because the directorate did not yet have the authority to prohibit private theatres. It is unlikely that prohibition was even considered. In 1827 there were no private (i.e. non-state) theatres in St Petersburg, and the small size of the audience probably meant that such ventures were commercially unviable. The evidence therefore suggests that the creeping restrictions on private theatricals were designed to protect Imperial Theatre revenues from masquerades and concerts.

During the 1840s, economic motives remained to the fore. In 1843 Nicholas I decreed that societies and institutions in the capitals (with the exception of the St Petersburg Noble Assembly) should not be permitted to organize masquerades. If that were allowed, reasoned the Minister of the Imperial Court when informing the director of this decree, such organizations would cause 'damage to the revenues of the theatrical directorate'. The decree, however, was superseded in little more than a decade.[9]

Sergei Danilov suggested that 'police-protective' considerations were also behind the impulse towards regulation, although there is little direct evidence for this. In fact, all the evidence adduced by Danilov for the period up to the 1850s pertains unambiguously to financial matters.[10] It is true, of course, that theatrical censorship intensified during the reign of Nicholas I. Under the censorship regulation of 1828, the infamous Third Section (the new tsar's secret police department, established in 1826) vetted works that were intended for performance and scrutinized reviews for the *Northern Bee* before they appeared in print, while the Ministry of Education had to grant its permission before any play could be published.[11] It has been argued that censorship was used to subjugate theatre to the 'ideological tasks of the government'.[12] Certainly, some plays were banned from performance because of their political undertones. Pushkin's *Boris Godunov* and Pogodin's *Marfa-Posadnitsa* were prohibited because they depicted 'the masses' as an active force, a subversive notion in an absolutist state.[13] Yet the extent to which such interventions transformed theatre into an ideological advocate of the state should not be exaggerated. The censors were largely concerned to prevent theatrical depictions of the tsars or the Orthodox clergy, and to ensure that nothing 'morally indecent' was shown on stage. Although the government monitored literary and theatrical activity, it does not necessarily follow that the record of what was published and performed constitutes a gross distortion of what dramatists and actors wanted to accomplish. The vogue for vaudeville and melodrama was such that, in all likelihood, they would have continued to dominate the repertoire in less censorial circumstances.

The directorate finally gained complete statutory control over all aspects of theatrical life in the capitals (its monopoly) in 1843, when the 'Statute on the Prevention and Suppression of Crimes' gave it the right to prohibit 'private entertainments' altogether.[14] The monopoly was further clarified and strengthened on 7 March 1854 by the new Minister of the Imperial Court,

V. F. Adlerberg, in his regulation 'On Public Masquerades, Concerts and Balls with Lotteries in the Capitals'. This provided details of the assemblies and philanthropic organizations that were allowed to organize such events, set out the rules regarding permission to organize other popular entertainments, and bolstered the directorate's right to protect its financial position by declaring that it was now entitled to levy up to 25 per cent of the takings from all other forms of entertainment that it permitted.[15]

The development of private, non-governmental theatres in the capitals was thus effectively stifled for economic reasons. This does not mean, however, that the government was unaware of the political advantages of maintaining close supervision over theatrical affairs. In some respects the state was beginning to utilize theatre to bolster the perquisites and paraphernalia of the imperial establishment, to project and display its authority, as well as to provide it with entertainment. The new theatres that appeared in the capitals during the 1820s and 1830s were all financed by the state. These generated a certain national pride. An article in the *Northern Bee* insisted that the new Bolshoi Theatre in Moscow was, in terms of its vastness and its structure, the premier theatre in Europe, even when compared to the Opéra in Paris or La Scala in Milan.[16] The government was portrayed as an ardent patron of theatre, and the 1827 statute was cited as evidence of Nicholas I's concern for 'the success of fine arts and letters in the fatherland'.[17] The reinstatement of the French troupe in Moscow in 1828 was similarly described as 'a new sign of the monarch's attention to the pleasure of the city's inhabitants'.[18]

Theatre was also viewed as something which could play an important role in cultivating and maintaining popular loyalty to the government. In 1830, Fyodor Kokoshkin, the manager of the Moscow Imperial Theatres, sought permission for a summer theatre for ordinary people in the city's Neskuchny Gardens. This, he suggested, would achieve three things. Firstly, it would acquaint ordinary people 'with patriotic history, secondly it would maintain ordinary people in their characteristic devotion to the throne and obedience to the authorities, and thirdly it would display to it all the shame and ruinous consequences of its all too common vices, such as drunkenness, indolence and others'.[19] Permission was granted for the theatre, but it had a short existence. In view of theatre's presumed capacity to influence people, Faddei Bulgarin argued that it must be closely monitored by the authorities. 'This is because theatrical plays and journals, having an extensive circle of spectators and readers, all the more quickly and powerfully affect minds and general opinion,' argued the notorious editor of the *Northern Bee* and Third Section informer.

'And since the higher police must know general opinion and direct minds according to the arbitrary rule of the government,' he continued, 'it must have in its hands the instruments that serve this aim.'[20]

If theatre actually functioned as something which encouraged 'devotion to the throne and obedience to the authorities', this was most evident with regard to the patronage of the French theatre by the elites of St Petersburg. Attendance at the Mikhailovsky constituted the height of social respectability, and the composition of the audience served to reinforce the impression that here were gathered the ruling classes of the empire, reaffirming their group identity and status. The Mikhailovsky Theatre, completed in 1833 to house the imperial French company, was undoubtedly the most prestigious entertainment venue in St Petersburg during the Nicolaevan era. It was described by one writer as 'the permanent gathering place of the best of Petersburg society', a place that looked like an 'aristocratic salon'. 'In the intervals,' continued the same writer, 'the dress-circle loges of this theatre are reminiscent of Italian theatre loges, and are transformed into small drawing rooms in which ladies receive their gentlemen acquaintances, and this imparts to the theatre a kind of life which neither the Alexandrinsky nor the Bolshoi Theatre has.'[21] The German actor Eduard Jerrmann likewise observed that 'The French theatre enjoyed the highest patronage; it had become the fashion, it was considered *bon ton* to frequent it, and its performances were subject of conversation in the most aristocratic drawing rooms; the management did all in their power to keep up its brilliancy and vogue.'[22] Jerrmann provided a description of the Mikhailovsky auditorium which conveys a sense of its official opulence and formality:

The whole house, both before and behind the curtain, is lighted – such at least was still the case in 1844 – with oil, but so well lighted that there was not a corner where one could not easily read the smallest writing. And there is no lack of brilliant dresses, which at once benefit and are benefited by the good lighting. The internal arrangement of the house is capital. The stalls are roomy and comfortable as arm-chairs, which is the name by which they go; boxes and pit are apportioned into a fixed number of places, and beyond that number no tickets are issued. Although there are broad passages through the pit and to the orchestra, no one, except the officer on duty, is allowed to stand up in the house; at the entrance, door-keepers, in rich liveries, receive the tickets and open the doors and seats; the servants who have charge of the refreshments are also in handsome liveries; everything, in short, is arranged with the utmost regard to comfort and convenience, with a sort of modest sumptuosity, and without consideration of expense. An even steady light is thrown upon the stage, which leaves nothing to be desired with respect to decorations, properties, and costumes.[23]

The attraction of the French theatre was enhanced by Nicholas I's patronage. According to Jerrmann, the tsar 'visits the theatres almost daily', in particular the Mikhailovsky. He reputedly enjoyed opera and ballet, but was especially fond of plays, and above all vaudevilles. During intervals, he liked to convey his impressions to the artists in person.[24] The occasional presence of the tsar in the Moscow Imperial Theatres likewise bestowed upon them an intermittent prestige among high society. Noting the presence of 'the best of Moscow society' and 'distinguished foreigners' in the auditorium during a performance at the Bolshoi in September 1826, one observer insisted that 'This time it was not the choice of play or the beauty of the magnificent building that attracted so many spectators: everyone knew that the emperor and empress would confer their presence on the performance.' When they appeared they were greeted with cries of 'Hurrah!' and loud applause.[25]

The popularity of the French theatre among the *haut monde* of the capital thus survived the war of 1812, although the conflict remained fresh in the collective Russian memory. Even the government's adoption of 'Official Nationality' during the 1830s – which, at least in part, was intended to emphasize native Russian culture (*narodnost'*) – did little to deflect the interest of educated society from west European theatrical models. In a sense, the enduring fascination of the St Petersburg establishment for French theatre represented its enduring alienation from ordinary Russian people, and this, in turn, invested the growing number of calls for Russification of the repertoire with an implicit political significance: attacks on the domination of French theatre, and the plays which resulted from such attacks, implied criticism of the establishment's cultural habits. We will return to this theme below.

As the state stepped up its regulation of theatrical life and high society used it as a venue for self-affirmation, a few writers and critics from among the intelligentsia responded by using theatre as a focus for the discussion of several issues, some of which implicitly questioned the prevailing theatrical order. The historiography of Russian theatre has traditionally placed emphasis on this development, privileging the comments and impressions of a relatively small number of progressive thinkers. Particular attention was paid by Soviet theatre scholars to the Decembrists, the noblemen and Guards officers who wanted to abolish serfdom and autocracy. The principal historian of this subject writes that 'Having subordinated their literary works to the tasks of political agitation, the Decembrists treated theatre first and foremost as an effective means of struggle and public education based on positive examples: the triumph of virtue and good, the punishment of evil and so forth.'[26]

Yet, in truth, theatre played only a small role in the formation and development of the Decembrists' political consciousness. M. P. Bestuzhev-Riumin claimed that his 'first liberal thoughts were picked up in the tragedies of Voltaire', while other Decembrists noted the influence of Kniazhnin's *Vadim of Novgorod* and Vasily Kapnist's *Chicanery* (alternatively rendered as *The Slanderer*).[27] The Decembrists counted a few playwrights and translators among their number. F. N. Glinka wrote *Velzen, or The Liberation of Holland* in 1808, depicting a struggle against tyranny, while the Life Guards officer of the Izmailovsky regiment P. N. Semenov was also a dramatist and author of 'popular comic operas'.[28] These examples, however, are hardly representative of either the Decembrists or the theatre of that time. One historian has written that 'The ideas of historicism, *narodnost'*, patriotism, the heroic individual dedicating himself to the service of the *narod* and the struggle for its liberation are characteristic traits of Decembrist ideology, manifest, in particular, in the development of drama and theatre.'[29] But the general mainstream repertoire of the period of Decembrism, the decade before 1825, cannot be said to have provided a critique of issues such as serfdom or autocracy.

For the period after the Decembrist uprising, the historiography has tended to accord prominence to the views of Alexander Herzen and Vissarion Belinsky, even though neither wrote primarily for, or about, the stage. In one survey of the Russian dramatic theatre during the nineteenth century, there are separate chapters on 'Belinsky and the Formation of Revolutionary-Democratic Thinking about Theatre' and 'Herzen and the Theatre'.[30] The Soviet theatre encyclopedia contains relatively substantial entries on both, which are indicative of the way the theatrical history of the period is depicted. Herzen is described as someone who regarded 'literature and theatre as a political platform for the promotion of advanced ideas', and who worked on two unfinished and unperformed plays. His friendship with the actor Shchepkin is noted, along with the short story *The Thieving Magpie*, which he wrote in 1846 on the basis of Shchepkin's reminiscences of the exploitation of a serf actress, Kuzmina, at Kamensky's theatre in Orel. The entry concludes with the exaggerated assertion that 'Herzen's legacy was of great importance for the further history of Russian stage art. His ideas exerted an extremely fruitful influence on the development of democratic tendencies in Russian art, including Russian theatre.'[31]

Belinsky, whose involvement in theatrical affairs was rather more substantial – he penned approximately 180 articles and reviews on drama[32] – is depicted as an 'ideologist of the democratic tendency in literature and theatre in the 1830s and 1840s'. His only play, a tragedy entitled *Dmitry Kalinin*, about an abusive serf owner, was banned and resulted in his exclusion from Moscow University. Like Herzen, he was a close friend of Shchepkin, and in 1846 accompanied him on a tour of southern Russia. Belinsky's ideal theatre was one that was faithful to reality. He is identified with progressive tendencies and portrayed as a crucial link between, on the one hand, Radishchev, Fonvizin and the Decembrists, and, on the other, the revolutionary-democratic criticism of the 1850s and 1860s.[33]

The radical idea of theatre and its advocates were undoubtedly important, not least for the development of criticism in Russia. The problem is that the conventional foregrounding of this theme in much, if by no means all, writing on the Russian stage has tended to obscure the wider mainstream discourse about theatre during the second quarter of the nineteenth century. It is striking that the Soviet theatre encyclopedia contains nothing on Faddei Bulgarin, arguably one of the leading commentators on the theatre of the time. The explanation for this lopsidedness is quite obvious: Herzen and Belinsky were progressive writers, critical of the prevailing order, while Bulgarin was a reactionary acolyte of the tsarist state. Some non-Soviet works on Russian theatre have tended to replicate this narrative without really subjecting it to scrutiny. It is worth noting, however, that in a recent dramatic encyclopedia, published in Moscow in 2001, there is a short entry on Bulgarin – which acknowledges his 'odious reputation' – but none on Herzen or Belinsky.[34]

Having noted this characteristic of the historiography, let us now turn to the other two issues surrounding theatre during the second quarter of the nineteenth century which stand out alongside growing state intervention, namely attitudes to audiences and demands for Russification of the repertoire. While the comments of Herzen and Belinsky cannot – indeed should not – be ignored, the aim here is to draw a broader picture of what was being written about theatre during this period. There is, of course, nothing extraordinary about the fact that topics such as audiences and the nature of the repertoire were regularly mentioned. In the context of Nicolaevan Russia, however, they were indicative of the way theatre was becoming a focal point for the expression of ideas and opinions with potentially wider implications.

It is often argued that by the mid nineteenth century Russian theatre audiences were becoming more democratic, in the sense that they comprised a broader and less exclusive section of the population.[35] This reflected changes in the population profiles of both capitals that were in turn the result of economic change. It has been estimated that between 1800 and 1860 the total population of the Russian empire more than doubled, from 35.5 millions to 74.1 millions, and that between 1811 and 1863 the urban population 'more than doubled'. In European Russia, this meant that the urban population grew from 6.6 per cent to 10 per cent of the total population. The two capitals remained the largest urban centres, and also experienced some of the sharpest population increases. St Petersburg's population grew from 335,600 in 1811 to 539,500 in 1863, while Moscow's grew from 270,200 to 462,500 during the same period. The pace of economic development quickened from the 1830s, particularly as a result of the beginning of railway construction. Cotton textiles were the most important industry, and its main centres were St Petersburg and Moscow.[36]

The picture of the theatrical public that emerges from the available evidence suggests a fair amount of diversity, although the pattern varied between theatres. The Mikhailovsky Theatre in St Petersburg, home of the imperial French troupe, was patronized by the city's establishment well into the nineteenth century and remained an exclusive venue. The audience profile of the Alexandrinsky Theatre, home of the imperial Russian drama troupe, was more variegated. The radical writer and dramatist Nikolai Nekrasov (1821–77) identified 'two publics' there. 'The first – for the most part educated, certainly decent – looked to the theatre for intelligent entertainment, expressed its approval or censure temperately', while 'The second – noisy, numerous, disorderly – visited the theatre for the sake of making a bit of noise and clapping a few times. It consisted of so many heterogeneous elements of the multinational Petersburg population that it was hardly possible to subsume it under a common standard, to detect in it a common fixed character.'[37] Nekrasov also described his glimpses of the Alexandrinsky's upper gallery:

The collar of a caretaker, the beard of an illiterate bricklayer, the red nose of a household servant, the green eyes of your cook, the unshaven chin of a sacked clerk . . . red, growing fat from grease, soggy from perspiration, the head of a stout chief cook; the pretty little face of a shop assistant, whom you often meet on Nevsky Prospect; next to her the face of a retired soldier.[38]

Belinsky painted a picture of a less diversified audience at the Alexandrinsky, contrasting it with the theatrical public in Moscow:

> In Moscow there is no specific theatrical public. To the Petrovsky [i.e. Bolshoi] theatre in Moscow come people of different classes, different degrees of education, different tastes and demands. . . . In the Moscow theatrical public there are almost as many tastes and judgments as people, and it is not rare to find there the most educated and subtle, the most elegant taste side by side with the most coarse and vulgar. . . . Not so the public of the Aleksandrinsky Theatre. This is an audience in the real, exact meaning of the word; there is no difference of class in it, it is all composed of officials of established rank; it has no different inclinations, demands, tastes; it asks for one thing and is satisfied by it; it never contradicts itself, is always true to itself. It is an individual, a person, not a multitude of people, but one man, decently dressed, solid, not too exacting, not too yielding, a man who fears every extreme, who constantly adheres to the sensible mean, finally a man of most respectable and well-meaning appearance. It is exactly the same as the most respectable classes in France and Germany, the bourgeoisie and the Philistines.[39]

These comments appear to contradict the observations of Nekrasov, yet the two audience profiles are not necessarily incompatible with one another. Belinsky's aim was to emphasize the differences between the theatrical publics of St Petersburg and Moscow, and in the process he exaggerated the uniformity of the Alexandrinsky audience. Even if Nekrasov exaggerated its diversity, when taken together the two accounts indicate that, at least across the two capitals as a whole, the audience was becoming more democratic, or socially variegated.

This was further revealed by two incidents, both of which also suggested the potential for Russian theatre auditoriums to become transformed into sites for demonstrations of sympathy for the *narod*. In April 1848, at the end of a performance of I. E. Velikopolsky's 'patriotic drama' *Recollections of the Battle of Borodino* at the Alexandrinsky, the audience remained completely silent as the curtain was lowered. The tsar demanded an explanation, and the administration put it down to elements hostile to Karatygin, who had delivered the closing monologue. Efim Kholodov, however, suggests that this was a demonstration of support for the revolutionary events then unfolding in France.[40] The second incident took place in December 1850 during the premiere of Konstantin Aksakov's *The Liberation of Moscow in 1612* at the Moscow Malyi. It was reported that, when the characters in the play criticized the boyars, there were cries of 'That's the truth!' from the gallery, and when the line 'the voice of the people is God's voice' was spoken, loud applause and expressions of approval emanated from the same area. As a result of this demonstration, the play was banned.[41]

Such incidents helped to reinforce the view of some critics and theatrical commentators that the cultural level of audiences was relatively low, that the public lacked taste and artistic acumen, and that audiences were becoming too democratic. From the 1820s, expressions of contempt – implied or otherwise – for audiences grew notably. In 1828, an anonymous critic wrote that 'the theatrical repertoires have filled up with terrible works', but nothing can be done because 'Theatre is established for the public and must present what it likes.'[42] One journalist decided to sit in the gallery of an unspecified St Petersburg theatre to gain an impression of the auditorium from that elevated perspective. He concluded that, in order for tastes to become more advanced, 'It is necessary to oblige the demands of the educated public, and the public in the gallery must be its student and not make its own judgements.'[43]

Other writers implicitly ascribed a greater level of critical competence to audiences. One reviewer commented that the public was quite right to ignore contemporary criticism because, while it shows the personal view of a writer and might command a modicum of interest for that reason, in general it has 'lost its value' and might not even be 'sincere'.[44] Another emphasized that the theatre was meant to have mass appeal:

If only theatre reviewers would bear in mind that literature exists not for the masses, but that theatre on the contrary is *for all*, then they would not expect ancient virtue and literary perfection from dramatic performances. Since it exists for everyone, theatre must speak a language that is comprehensible to everyone, portray events that are interesting for everyone. Affecting the spirit, morals, demands of its age, at the same time it must itself be a faithful echo of its spirit, morals, demands. The motto of the stage is contemporaneity.

Furthermore, the relative success of a play should be measured by its popularity rather than by esoteric critical criteria. Reviewers were judging plays the wrong way: 'If a play is liked, that means that it has achieved its aim, that it is good, and is good only because it is liked, not that it is liked because it is good.' Moreover, reviewers should bear in mind that the theatre exists not for them, but for 'the masses'. Indeed, 'the theatre is a necessity, a requirement for the *narod*.[45] Whereas the view that audiences lacked sophistication implied an elitist attitude towards the stage, the view that theatre was, by its very nature, a form of entertainment for the masses had undertones of a populist concern to insist on the accessibility of theatre to all.

From the 1820s onwards, theatre became a focal point for a wider discourse about national identity. Writers and critics increasingly demanded original plays which reflected native life, culture and mores, and pressure was thus exerted on the theatrical world to spearhead a revolution in the artistic expression of what it meant to be Russian. In many respects, theatre was the obvious arena for this development. The ubiquity of foreign, particularly French, plays in the repertoire was a constant reminder of the degree to which the reliance on non-indigenous works – including imitations of them – had become entrenched, notwithstanding the efforts of some Russian playwrights such as Shakhovskoi.

Demands for the Russification of the repertoire could be interpreted, in some instances, as implicit attacks on the tsarist authorities, since the state and the Imperial Theatres were the chief patrons of the French and other non-Russian repertoires. The issue was more complicated, however, because several of the autocracy's supporters made similar demands. This reinforces the impression that theatre was becoming a public arena through which ideas were expressed and explored, often by different groups with conflicting sets of interests – in this case the meaning of *narodnost'*, or, broadly, national identity. The fundamental difference between the two camps in the 'Russification of the repertoire' campaign consisted, firstly, in what they assumed was signified by the term, and secondly, what they expected an emphasis on *narodnost'* to achieve in the wider social and political sphere.

The term *narodnost'*, in the sense first used by P. A. Viazemsky in 1819, meant nationality. But the word from which it derives, *narod*, can mean several things, notably 'nation' or 'the people'. The crucial *connotation* of *narod*, however, is ordinary people, especially the peasantry, as opposed to the (westernized) urban elite. Consequently *narodnost'* equated nationality with the values and customs of the peasantry or common people. In this understanding of the term, the elites were less authentically national or authentically Russian than the masses. It was, of course, segments of the elite

– the government and intelligentsia – which used these concepts. For the government, the promotion of the idea of *narodnost'* – through Sergei Uvarov's trinity of 'Orthodoxy, Autocracy, Nationality' – was an attempt to assert the notion of a common bond between tsar and people. It referred to all the peoples of the tsarist empire, theoretically united under the Romanov dynasty. For the intelligentsia, on the other hand, in particular its Slavophile branch, *narodnost'* was an anti-statist, anti-westernist – essentially anti-Petrine – concept, and referred not to all the peoples of the empire but more specifically to ethnic Russians.[46] These distinctions also applied to the question of *narodnost'* and the repertoire. When issues of national identity and indigenous customs were addressed in plays and theatrical reportage, they could imply either support for the established order, or criticism of it.

The principal conservative partisan of Russian nationalism in the theatre was Faddei Bulgarin (1789–1859), the Polish journalist and novelist who lived in St Petersburg from 1819, denounced Pushkin, and spied on his acquaintances for the authorities. In 1836 he wrote that, all across the country, people attended the theatre but always complained about the artists and the plays. Any deficiences in the theatre, however, could not, in Bulgarin's view, be attributed to the artists. Rather, the fault lay with the repertoire, in particular with its foreign character. Leading theatrical cities like Paris, London, Berlin and Venice could not match spectacles like A. O. Ablesimov's comic opera *The Miller, the Sorcerer, the Deceiver and the Matchmaker*, or Kniazhnin's comic operas *The Drinks Vendor* and *Misfortune from a Carriage*, which he described as 'national plays' (*narodnye p'esy*) because they involved native actors performing in authentically Russian works. Similarly, roles like Mitrofan, Yeremeyevna and the Prostakovs in *The Minor* had been brought to 'perfection' by Russian actors. These were among the best works on stage because they were 'national' (*natsional'nyi*).

If only Ablesimov (the author of *The Miller*) had become more absorbed in his subject and continued along the path that Nature pointed out to him; if only Kniazhnin had not blindly imitated the French; if only Fonvizin had been more sparing with moral talks, and had not stopped so soon; if only Prince A. A. Shakhovskoi (our contemporary) had not exhausted his *true* talent for comedy in hasty work for benefit nights; if only Griboyedov lived and continued to work for the stage; if only Zagoskin took subjects from our daily life, and cast off the French yoke; if only Ozerov had studied German, English and Spanish letters and had not slavishly adhered to the French school; in a word, if only there were *no if onlys*, then we would already have a *national dramatic literature.*

For a while it seemed that, as people realized the 'old French forms' were 'unpleasing for us', plays started to resound with Russian phrases and the names of historical figures. For Bulgarin, however, this did not amount to the creation of a national dramatic literature but was an 'optical illusion, only a phantasmagoria'. There was no national drama in Russia 'that could endure the investigation of impartial and scholarly criticism'. Pushkin's *Boris Godunov* did not count because it was written to be read, not staged. Russian comedy was also devoid of accomplished national works, with the exception of Griboyedov's *Woe from Wit*, which, for its 'language, characters and wit', Bulgarin considered to be 'truly *narodnyi*'.[47]

In 1840, Bulgarin reflected on Shakhovskoi's earlier efforts to Russify vaudeville, imploring, 'Vaudeville writers, give us something like this! Look to the past, gaze at the present. You will find subjects galore! Can you find nothing worthy of interest in Russian life that you must resort to the adaptation of French vaudevilles to our Russian manners?'[48] Developing his themes a few years later, Bulgarin suggested that the contemporary thirst for *narodnost'* was occasionally slaked only by drama, pointing to Gogol's *The Government Inspector* (which he did not yet know about when he was writing in early 1836) as the best example. He called for dramatists to write *narodnyi* drama.[49]

The two plays which gave the advocates of a national repertoire cause for optimism were Griboyedov's *Woe from Wit* and Gogol's *The Government Inspector*. Together with Pushkin's *Boris Godunov*, they appeared to demonstrate the rich potential for a national Russian repertoire, and to continue a tradition inaugurated by Fonvizin. These were national plays in the sense that they depicted authentic Russian characters in recognizably Russian milieux. What made them stand out from other efforts to create a national repertoire during the early nineteenth century was their accomplished style, effective structure and witty dialogue. As Bertha Malnick explained, 'all three writers broke the barriers that then existed between literary language and living speech, thrusting into striking prominence the vernacular so many of their countrymen ignored'.[50] Furthermore, *Woe from Wit* and *The Government Inspector* both demonstrated how the pursuit of a national repertoire could have subversive implications.

Alexander Griboyedov (1795–1829) was born in Moscow, graduated from its university and fought in the wars against Napoleon. A skilled linguist, he was a diplomat by profession, serving from 1819 in Georgia and Persia, where he was later murdered during an attack on the Russian embassy to Tehran.[51] Griboyedov associated with the St Petersburg *littérateurs* of his day, and was arrested in the wake of the Decembrist uprising, only to be released after three months of questioning. He wrote a little during his spare time, and produced one work of significance, his masterpiece of Russian theatre, *Woe from Wit*.

Completed in the spring of 1823, *Woe from Wit* is a verse comedy in four acts. The action takes place during the early 1820s in the Moscow house of Famusov, a government official. The plot is straightforward. Chatsky, a young serf owner, returns to Moscow after three years abroad and immediately calls on Famusov's daughter, Sophia, with whom he fell in love before setting off on his travels. In the meantime, Sophia has fallen in love with Molchalin, Famusov's secretary. Molchalin professes his love for Sophia, but his real passion is for her maid, Liza, and his insincerity is soon revealed to the audience. Meanwhile, during a ball at Famusov's house, a rumour is spread that Chatsky has gone mad, because he cannot refrain from insulting people and talking to them in incomprehensible terms. Chatsky delivers a tirade about the Russian infatuation with France, but no one listens. In the final act, the mysterious Repetilov appears on the scene. He is a member of the English Club in Moscow and informs Chatsky that he has become involved with a secret society that discusses things like 'Parliaments and Juries'. Sophia then discovers Molchalin's deception, and Famusov sends him away, along with Chatsky, who has been dismissed as a Jacobin and a madman.

These ostensibly simple scenes serve as a platform for Chatsky's attacks on Moscow society, particularly its slavish imitation of French culture, and its servility. The main theme is that Chatsky's learning has made him disrespectful of convention and authority. He makes people around him feel uncomfortable by his constant jibes, and, as Sophia remarks to him, appears to have nothing good to say about anyone. Like Famusov, he denounces Muscovite gallomania, but unlike Famusov he equally despises Moscow. At the end of Act 3 in a long monologue, Chatsky expresses his hostility towards both France and Russia, claiming that there is a 'sick craving for abroad' and asking, 'When shall we rise against this alien tyrant, Fashion?'[52] Like Starodum in *The Minor*, he rails against a system that awards sycophancy rather than merit. When asked why he refuses to join the service, Chatsky replies, 'I'd like the Service. It's the servility that makes me sick.'[53] Famusov exclaims that Chatsky must have joined the Carbonari: 'He's on the verge of preaching liberty!', 'He doesn't recognize Authority!'[54]

Chatsky is also portrayed as an educated man surrounded by people who sneer at learning. Famusov denounces reading and eventually calls for all books to be burned.[55] Griboyedov himself claimed that 'In my comedy there are twenty-five fools to one reasonable man, and this man, of course, stands in conflict with the society surrounding him.'[56] Ultimately Chatsky's 'wit' – here meaning his education – leads to his 'woe', his isolation from society. He is unable to live abroad, but is surrounded by fellow countrymen who blindly imitate French customs. He is an early incarnation of the superfluous man, the progressive individual driven to despair by the unyielding conservatism of his society.

Banned by the censor from either publication or performance, *Woe from Wit* quickly established itself as the most notorious forbidden play of Nicolaevan Russia. It was rapidly distributed in manuscript copy, and its circulation soon belied its banned status. It has been claimed that by 1830 as many as forty thousand manuscript copies were in circulation across Russia.[57] In January 1825, Pushkin's friend from the lycée Ivan Pushchin visited him at Mikhailovskoe and brought with him a copy of *Woe from Wit*. As T. J. Binyon relates, 'Pushkin had begun to read this aloud, commenting as he went, when someone else drove up to the house. He looked out of the window, seemed embarrassed, and hurriedly opened a miscellany of religious texts which lay on the table. A moment later, a short, red-haired monk with a flowing beard came in.'[58] Herzen retrospectively compared the play's impact to that of Pyotr Chaadayev's first *Philosophical Letter*, published in 1836, in which he claimed that Russia had contributed nothing to world culture:

> such is the power of the spoken word in a land of silence, unaccustomed to free speech, that Chaadayev's *Letter* shook all thinking Russia. And well it might. There had not been one literary work since *Woe from Wit* which made so powerful an impression. Between that play and the *Letter* there had been ten years of silence, the Fourteenth of December, the gallows, penal servitude, Nicholas.[59]

Belinsky, writing in 1841, argued that the play had 'great significance both for our literature and for our society', calling it an 'outpouring of bilious, thunderous indignation at a rotten society of worthless people' who live according to the 'dilapidated traditions of olden times', concerned only with petty things like 'rank, money, gossip, the abasement of human dignity'.[60]

Scenes from *Woe from Wit* were regularly given illegal, impromptu performances in radical circles, and then from 1829 individual acts were occasionally staged at the Imperial Theatres.[61] Its first full public performance took place on 30 January 1831 in St Petersburg, although with many cuts. It remained completely banned in the regions until 1863,[62] and was not performed anywhere in its full original version until 1895. Its reputation, however, was already well established. A review by Bulgarin claimed that anyone who could read Russian was already familiar with the play. Its success as a literary text was explained, claimed Bulgarin, by the fact that it was a '*narodnyi*, Russian thing' and that all Russians could believe in its characters. The language was 'truly colloquial, natural'. But the main reason for its success was 'the sense of ardent love for the fatherland on which the comedy is based'.[63] Another review noted that the theatre was always full for *Woe from Wit*, something that did not always happen with Russian plays.[64]

Why was the play initially banned? Here it is interesting to contrast its later reputation with contemporaneous views. The arch-conservative Vigel claimed not to know why permission was refused for publication or performance, implying that he saw nothing particularly subversive about it.[65] Bulgarin, a friend of Griboyedov, was full of admiration for the work, perhaps because he shared many of its sentiments about Russian gallomania. He offered to publish extracts in his short-lived journal the *Russian Thalia* in 1825, although the censor objected to the scenes where 'a girl of good family spends a whole night in her bedroom with an unmarried man and emerges with him shamelessly'.[66]

In time, however, Griboyedov's masterpiece came to be regarded as an implicit attack on serfdom and autocracy – in other words, on the existing social and political structures of imperial Russia. Herzen regarded Chatsky as the most obvious, if still a tendentious, literary representative of the Decembrist movement:

> In his exasperated, jaundiced thoughts, his youthful indignation, one can detect a healthy impulse to action; he feels what it is he is dissatisfied with, he beats his head against the stone wall of social prejudices and tests whether the prison bars are strong. . . . Chatsky could not have lived with his arms folded, neither in capricious peevishness nor in haughty self-deification; he was not old enough to find satisfaction in grumbling sulkiness, nor young enough to enjoy the self-sufficiency of adolescence. The whole essence of the man lies in this restless ferment, this working yeast.[67]

For the Hungarian writer René Fülöp-Miller, *Woe from Wit* constituted a 'fiery protest against the prevailing order of things . . . a terrible indictment of the

Government and society in general'.[68] For the Soviet historian S. S. Landa, the play depicted the triumph of 'the romantic idea of the heroic individual rejecting the stagnant reality of serf Russia'.[69]

It is perhaps a measure of Griboyedov's talent that *Woe from Wit* appealed to such a broad range of constituencies. By directly addressing the issue of society's apparent alienation from its own native customs while simultaneously transforming spoken Russian into a literary gem – many lines from *Woe from Wit* remain popular aphorisms in Russia today – he demonstrated the possibilities for a national repertoire. At the same time, however, his play also indicated how the pursuit of a national repertoire could expose, magnify and denounce uncomfortable realities about the country. Hence the powerful appeal of the play to radicals.

Similar conclusions can be made about Nikolai Gogol's theatrical masterpiece, *The Government Inspector*, a five-act comedy set in a district town in an unidentified part of Russia during the 1830s. It begins with an announcement from the local prefect that a government inspector, travelling incognito, is expected in the town imminently. The prefect is clearly concerned that endemic bribe-taking and poor standards, such as in the local hospital and school, will be exposed. News then arrives of a stranger who has rented a room at the local inn. The stranger is Khlestakov, a low-ranking official from St Petersburg with a habit of absconding without paying his bills. Assuming that Khlestakov must be the inspector, the prefect hastens to the inn to ingratiate himself. Khlestakov assumes that the prefect has come to reprimand him, believing that the innkeeper has submitted an official complaint on account of unpaid meal bills. The prefect's misunderstanding prevails, and Khlestakov becomes his guest. At the prefect's house, Khlestakov is bribed by a succession of local officials, including the district judge, the postmaster, the superintendent of schools and the warden of charitable institutions, all anxious that their maladministration is about to be exposed and reported back to St Petersburg. At this point, Khlestakov realizes they have mistaken him for an inspector, and he is advised by his servant, Osip, to flee. Prior to his departure, Khlestakov, for personal amusement, declares his love for the prefect's daughter, Mary, and they quickly become engaged. While Khlestakov then makes his escape on the false pretext of urgent business, the prefect and his wife boast about the great life that awaits them in St Petersburg. All the characters gather to congratulate them. Then the postmaster, having perlustrated Khlestakov's mail and discovered his true identity, announces that he was not the inspector. As all the characters express disbelief and anger, a gendarme appears to announce the arrival of the real inspector.

The Government Inspector was completed late in 1835 and was initially banned by the censor. Influential friends of Gogol persuaded Nicholas I to read the play, however, and the tsar personally approved it for performance. It premiered at the Alexandrinsky on 19 April 1836 to a packed house, with Nicholas I himself watching appreciatively from the royal box.[70] Although later interpreted as a satirical attack on tsarist maladministration of the regions and a fundamental indictment of the imperial regime, *The Government Inspector* was intended by Gogol primarily to show Russian types on stage and to break away from the neoclassical rigidity that continued to dominate the repertoire. Gogol was effectively an advocate of a national repertoire that reflected the realities of Russian life. 'For heaven's sake,' he exclaimed in 1836, 'give us Russian characters, give us ourselves, our own scoundrels and cranks! On stage with them, subject them to general laughter! . . . We are grown so indifferent from watching insipid French plays that now we are afraid to look at ourselves.'[71]

Gogol's motives in advocating a national repertoire should not be misinterpreted, however. He was fundamentally apolitical and once insisted that 'I have always avoided politics. . . . It is not the poet's job to worm his way into the worldly market place.'[72] In a letter to the poet V. A. Zhukovsky, he confided that he 'had not at all wished to make fun of the established order of government, but only of those who deviated from this order. I was angered both by the spectators who didn't understand me and by myself for being the cause of the misunderstanding.'[73] The playwright, of course, had little influence over the way his work was interpreted.

The response to the premiere of *The Government Inspector* suggested that the public objected to the depiction of Russian types as irredeemably corrupt. The critic Pavel Annenkov recalled that the audience was unsure as to how to react and laughed in all the 'wrong' places, 'but the common verdict to be heard from all parts of the elite public was: "This is something inadmissible, a slander and a farce".'[74] Gogol was bitter about the reaction, complaining soon after his play opened,

I am not angry at what people say. . . . I am not angry, because the people who are annoyed and turn away from me find their own features in my characters and rail accordingly . . . but I am saddened by the ignorance which reigns in the capital. . . . You put rogues on the stage, and everyone is

furious. Let the rogues get angry, but people I did not at all regard as rogues
are livid. . . . The capital is most squeamishly insulted, because the morals
and manners of half-a-dozen provincial officials have been put on the stage.
What would the capital say if its own manners had been touched upon,
however lightly?[75]

Bulgarin's initial response was lukewarm. In his review of the premiere, he
suggested that a comedy cannot be based on 'administrative abuses' and that
it would be a pity if audiences who lacked knowledge of the Russian provinces
were to gain the impression that towns like the one depicted by Gogol, where
no one possesses any redeeming moral features, actually existed. Bulgarin
concluded that Gogol had written a farce peopled with caricatures, and the
audience had enjoyed the performance in so far as it smiled and laughed. The
play was unlike contemporary life, although it was clearly based on recognizable aspects of it – such as the way people dressed – and endeavoured to discuss
it. Ultimately Bulgarin evaded the uncomfortable fact that Gogol's discussion
of Russian reality focused on 'administrative abuses' by claiming that this was
a representation not of Russian but of Ukrainian or Belorussian life (Gogol
himself was Ukrainian).[76]

The response of the Moscow public was equally cool. One critic, discussing
the audience that witnessed a Moscow performance, explained that this was
the elite public,

rich, official, nurtured in boudoirs, for whom visits to the theatre are one
of life's duties, not a joy, nor a pleasure. This public is on that happy
eminence of public life, where the trivial concept of national character
disappears – where there are neither passion and feeling nor original
thoughts, where everything merges and is engulfed in the immutable
concept, so terrifying to the ordinary man, of propriety. This public shows
neither grief nor joy, neither need nor satisfaction, not because it has never
experienced them, but because it is improper, vulgar. Brilliant dress and a
cold, dead face, these are the distinguishing features of the society that
stooped to see that all-Russian play, arising not from imitation, but from
the author's own, possibly bitter, feeling. Looking at the public while
making my way to a seat between the acting and state councillors,
apologising to the gentlemen owning several thousand souls, I
involuntarily began to think – it's hardly likely that *Revizor* [*The
Government Inspector*] will please them. . . . And thus it was; *Revizor* did not

grasp or move the public in the theatre, only made it laugh a little without delighting it. Even in the interval a half-French whisper of indignation and complaint could be heard. 'Mauvais genre!' The terrible sentence with which high society brands talent which has the good fortune not to please it. . . . We need two theatres, because the public is divided into two huge categories. But until we have them, we shall go to enjoy ourselves where the others go to rest and sleep after dinner; happily they sleep so sweetly that they do not twitch even at the noisiest transports of the public that truly loves art.[77]

Like *Woe from Wit*, then, *The Government Inspector* generated considerable interest because of its skilful depiction of indigenous types. But at the same time it held up a mirror to uncomfortable realities, or at least demonstrated how the search for *narodnost'* could unsettle audiences instead of reaffirming their self-perceptions.

If the theatrical masterpieces of Griboyedov and Gogol pointed to the possibilities for a national repertoire, they were nevertheless exceptional. There remained a glaring disparity between the intelligentsia's ambition for theatre and the mainstream repertoire. Vaudevilles and melodramas fashioned from foreign models continued to predominate. One oft-noted change during the second quarter of the nineteenth century was the appearance of plays dealing with merchants. Merchants had featured in a small number of plays written during the second half of the eighteenth century, but had then largely disappeared until the 1830s, when they reappeared in popular works such as Shakhovskoi's romantic drama *The Bigamist* and P. G. Grigorev's vaudeville *The Merchants*.

It is not necessary to agree with the view that explorations of the 'merchant theme' reflected the 'growth of antifeudal forces' or the 'democratic strivings of Russian literature and theatre' to acknowledge their existence.[78] Furthermore, lest we assume that mention of 'bourgeois' themes on stage is an exaggeration of Soviet historiography, it is worth quoting Vigel on the late 1820s:

tragedy and high comedy were completely abandoned; they were replaced by so-called petty bourgeois [*meshchanskie*] dramas and comedies (comédies bourgeoises); particularly abundant were melodramas and vaudevilles; in a word, the moving or intelligently funny [*umno-zabavnoe*] had to give way to the ghastly and repulsive or obscenely buffoon.[79]

Such developments are often alleged to have been a reflection of the steady embourgeoisement of audiences, especially in Moscow. Maikov, who ran the Moscow Imperial Theatres before taking up the post of director in St Petersburg in 1822, wrote that merchants constituted 'the greatest share of the spectators'.[80] Occasionally, however, the significance of the merchant theme is exaggerated. One historian sees plays about Kuzma Minin, the Nizhny Novgorod merchant who played a crucial role in organizing the national militia that expelled the Polish garrison from Moscow in 1612 – such as N. A. Polevoy's *Kuzma Minin the One-Armed* and N. V. Kukolnik's *The Hand of the Almighty Saved the Fatherland* – as indicative of this genre.[81] Yet while Minin was definitely a merchant (*kupets*), these plays were arguably more representative of the *national* theme in Russian drama than anything else.

For the vast majority of actors in the Russian empire, day-to-day existence involved a struggle against exploitation at the hands of the theatrical administration – or, in the regions, impresarios – and against widespread public condescension towards their vocation. They were deprived of many rights and were subject to the moral censure even of audiences who regarded theatre-going as a mark of respectability. At the Imperial Theatres, where working conditions were assumed to be more tolerable, the arbitrariness of officialdom often made an actor's life miserable and unpredictable. In 1822, the governor of St Petersburg, Miloradovich, imprisoned the well-known tragic actor Vasily Karatygin in the Peter and Paul Fortress for forty-two hours for allegedly insulting director Maikov by failing to stand up in his presence.[82] In 1836, the governor of Moscow took offence at the humorous portrayal of an officer on the Imperial stage and ordered the theatre pupil involved to undergo three days of house arrest, with only 'bread and water' for sustenance.[83] Such was the low esteem in which most thespians were held that a decree of 1827 stipulated that government officials could become actors (as distinct from tyrannizing actors) only if they relinquished their rank.[84] The decree both reflected and reinforced the widely held view that acting was a vocation of low social status.[85] It was to be some years before a concerted effort was made to reverse this situation and to take a stand against the widespread abuse of Russia's actors.

For a few, however, a career in acting turned out to be socially rewarding. During the second quarter of the nineteenth century, a number of leading actors at the Imperial Theatres acquired great reputations and became notable celebrities who were respected by officialdom and feted by the intelligentsia.

The most prominent among them were Shchepkin, Karatygin and Mochalov, but others such as Yakov Bryansky (1790–1853), Ivan Sosnitsky (1794–1871), Alexander Martynov (1816–60), Ekaterina Semenova (1786–1849) and Varvara Asenkova (1817–41) should not be overlooked. When the status of honorary citizenship (*pochetnoe grazhdanstvo*) was extended to actors in 1839, in practice it was accorded only to a few of such leading actors of the Imperial Theatres.[86]

One contemporaneous observer suggested that the growing number of talented artists demonstrated that 'the foundation of Russian life is not unfavourable for stage art, and that love for theatre [is] gradually spreading and taking root in the Russian public'.[87] The emergence of high-profile celebrity actors was significant for another reason. It confirmed and enhanced theatre's growing status among educated Russians as an institution that performed an important public role. Anatoly Altschuller has even suggested that 'The influence of the theatre upon the social and spiritual life of the country owed at least as much to the appearance of a constellation of brilliant actors as it did to the writings of any of the authors who are perhaps better known to history.'[88] This view is eminently justified. Talented actors made theatre real and demonstrated its capacity to portray the complexities of individual lives, as well as to exert a powerful influence over a wider audience. As certain leading actors began to attract the regular attention of critics and to inspire discussion about their fictional roles and their interpretations of characters, they contributed to theatre's emerging reputation as a public forum for the exploration of various issues. Moreover, the fact that several of these actors were acquainted with members of the intelligentsia reinforced the impression that theatre was perceived as a real or potential ally of Russian society's educated critics.

Shchepkin emerged during this period as the premier actor of his generation, in terms of both his talent and his celebrity. He was a close friend of many leading writers, radicals and conservatives, westernizers and Slavophiles, including Pushkin, Gogol, Sergei Aksakov, Herzen, Belinsky, Turgenev, Nekrasov, Granovsky, Shevchenko and others. He mingled with Moscow's intellectuals at Bazhanov's coffee house near Theatre Square in the centre of the city.[89] Their association with him and with other actors indicates just how much they expected from the theatre – it was not only the text of the play that was important, but also the performance. Such associations led to the Malyi being dubbed Moscow's 'second university' and the 'house of Shchepkin'. Shchepkin's steady rise from serfdom to metropolitan stardom also illustrated what was possible in terms of social mobility, even though his transformed circumstances were hardly typical for actors. But he was, as Laurence Senelick astutely observes, 'the emblem of change and progress in nineteenth-century Russia, change effected not through political evolution but through art'.[90]

Shchepkin strove for realism in acting, an ambition that corresponded powerfully with the aims of contemporaneous realist playwrights. He created his best roles in national satires, including Famusov in *Woe from Wit* and the prefect in *The Government Inspector*. But he also excelled at the common man, notably in *The Sailor*, in which he played a seaman who returns home after many years at sea only to discover that his wife has since remarried and his daughter, now grown up, no longer recognizes him. Belinsky summed up Shchepkin as follows: 'The triumph of his art consists not only in knowing how to evoke laughter and tears at the same time, but also in knowing how to interest the spectator in the fate of a common man and make him sob and tremble at the suffering of some sailor.'[91]

Shchepkin's position as the leading actor at the Moscow Imperial Theatre and his association with members of the intelligentsia created an uneasy tension. It made him suspect in the eyes of the authorities, who were still coming to terms with the steady expansion of interest in theatre and the rise of the celebrity. In 1857 the governor-general of Moscow, A. A. Zakrevsky, described the genial actor in a secret letter to the chief of the gendarmes, V. A. Dolgorukov, as someone who 'wants revolutions and is ready for anything'.[92] While there is no doubt that this was an exaggeration, it reflected official concern about the sociability of Moscow's leading cultural figure. Shchepkin was a loyal subject, but he did not regard himself by any means as a member of the establishment, despite his position at the Imperial Theatres. Commenting on his performance of Famusov in *Woe from Wit*, he noted that the character is a nobleman, 'and there's nothing lordly about me, I haven't a lordly manner, I'm a man of the people, and this puts me in complete discord with Famusov'.[93]

The growing importance of actors as symbols of wider social and political tensions was most evident in the debate between critics and others over the two great tragedians of the time, Vasily Karatygin and Pavel Mochalov, a debate that reflected a series of dichotomies, including St Petersburg versus Moscow, and order versus freedom, as suggested by contrasting acting styles. Karatygin (1802–53) encapsulated the order and discipline of St Petersburg, as well as its Frenchified customs. Tall and handsome, he was a master of declamation and pose, qualities suited to the imported melodramas of the period. His confident stage presence bespoke authority and discipline, and he used make-up to great effect. In these senses, Karatygin also represented the artificiality of St Petersburg, its deliberate theatricality. Mochalov (1800–48) was the most prominent member of a distinguished acting dynasty. His father, Stepan Mochalov (1775–1823), was a serf of the landowner N. N. Demidov and performed in his domestic theatre, as did his wife, Avdotya. In 1803 Stepan joined the troupe of Maddox's Petrovsky Theatre in Moscow, and in 1806, when the troupe was taken over by the directorate of Imperial Theatres, he and his family received their freedom. The Mochalovs raised two prominent Russian dramatic artists, Pavel and Maria (married name Frantsieva, 1799–1862). Maria initially performed in Moscow, then in the provinces, and finally ran her own venture in Voronezh. Pavel also had two actor brothers, Vasily and Platon, and a daughter, Ekaterina, who became an actress.

Mochalov was the greatest romantic actor of his generation. In contrast to Karatygin's punctilious attention to attire, he possessed an apparent disregard for outward appearance, preferring to concentrate on inner mood. His short and dishevelled appearance also contrasted with Karatygin's imposing stature. Mochalov's strengths as an actor lay in his reputed ability to project passion through his voice and to touch the hearts of audiences. He eschewed make-up, preferring to portray his characters by feeling his way into them and capturing their moods. He attained his greatest heights in the works of Shakespeare and Schiller, but also excelled in the plays of Kotzebue, Kukolnik and Polevoy. His greatest role was Hamlet, in Polevoy's translation, as the enraptured Belinsky testified:

> For the first time we were shown how an actor can completely renounce his own personality, forget himself and live another's life, or, better still, let us say make his own life that of another, and thus for a few hours deceive himself and two thousand spectators. . . . My God! we thought, here is a man walking on the stage without any instrument connecting him with us, there is no electrical conductor between us, yet we feel his impact on us; like a magician he oppresses us, tortures us, or rouses us to enthusiasm at his will, and our souls are powerless to withstand his magnetic charm.[94]

Indeed, Belinsky was passionate about Mochalov to the point where he practically dismissed Karatygin altogether:

Karatygin boldly plays every kind of part and is the same in all of them, or better still is never intolerable, something that fairly frequently happens to Mochalov. This is the result not of a many-sided talent, but of lack of real talent. . . . I consider acting to be a creative art and the actor an independent creator, not the slave of the author. That is why our incomparable Shchepkin is so often superb in the poorest parts.[95]

Karatygin and Mochalov performed many of the same parts, and critics soon began to compare them. After Sergei Aksakov saw Karatygin perform in St Petersburg, he insisted that 'Karatygin is made for the leading parts of heroes and emperors; Mochalov for the leading roles of lovers and young princes. If they go from one *emploi* to another they are both unsatisfactory.'[96] A kind of civic patriotism was evident in the way Petersburgers defended Karatygin and Muscovites Mochalov, and this was intensified in 1833, when each visited the other's theatre for a guest performance. Karatygin, nevertheless, won over many Muscovites, while Mochalov found it difficult to make a good impression in St Petersburg. The critics, on the other hand, were almost unanimous in declaring Mochalov to be ultimately the better actor. Mochalov was never to return to St Petersburg, but Karatygin ventured once more to Moscow, in 1835, when he took part in a performance of Schiller's *Mary Stuart* with his great rival. (Karatygin played the part of Leicester, Mochalov that of Mortimer.)

Mochalov himself was full of praise for Karatygin. Others, however, remained sharply divided over the two actors. It was not a question of talent, since few disputed the fact that both were accomplished artists. It was rather a matter of style, and what each style was understood to represent. An anonymous reviewer of the joint performance in *Mary Stuart* wrote that 'The most aristocratic section of the public . . . was for Karatygin; the middle part half and half; the lower for Mochalov.'[97] Shchepkin summed up the difference as follows: 'Mochalov has warmth, fire, the spark, the divine spark . . . your Karatygin is uniformed St Petersburg; drawn up and buttoned to the chin, appearing on stage as on parade.'[98] As Bertha Malnick aptly puts it, 'Both were part of their troubled time, Mochalov the romantic embodiment of its impulse towards self-expression, Karatygin the very epitome of its outward grandeur.'[99]

During the first half of the nineteenth century, and especially from the 1820s, theatre and theatre-going consolidated their positions as the epitome of refinement, the mark of social status and respectability. This was both a cause and a consequence of growing state control over theatrical life, particularly in the capitals, where the Imperial Theatre monopoly was beginning to crystallize.

Yet the period from the 1820s to the 1850s also demonstrated that theatre was no longer the exclusive province of the loyalist stratum of the establishment. Radical members of the emergent intelligentsia identified the stage as a potential means of influencing society and challenging prevailing norms of identity, while theatrical reportage increasingly acted as a conduit for the discussion of issues of broader social and political significance. Differing views about audiences reflected latent disputes about elitism and populism, and growing demands for the Russification of the repertoire, in the face of the elite's dogged attachment to French culture, exposed the potential of theatre to unsettle society. And as theatre established itself as a prominent feature of metropolitan culture, leading actors acquired something akin to celebrity status.

The theatrical mirror reflected a growing diversity of social groups and interests, from the privileged and Frenchified circles which congregated at the Mikhailovsky, to the more variegated or democratic audiences which were appearing elsewhere. Moreover, a small number of brilliant new plays reminded observers that the dramatic stage possessed the capacity to reflect aspects of Russian social reality. For all the oppression and censorship of Nicholas I's reign, the stage had emerged as a significant factor in public life. And it was on the verge of making an important breakthrough for civil society in Russia.

Chapter 3

FREEDOM OF THE THEATRES

The quarter century from the mid 1850s to the late 1870s was a period of rapid and often turbulent change in Russia. Following the country's defeat in the Crimean War, Alexander II embarked on a series of reforms designed to modernize Russia's economic and social infrastructure and reassert its status as a great power. The emancipation of the serfs, the creation of new institutions of local government (the *zemstva*), the expansion of education and a moderate relaxation of censorship laws all contributed to the unprecedented animation of Russian society and the development of public life. The professional classes – such as physicians, teachers and lawyers – developed rapidly and soon began to organize their own associations, while the growth of commerce and industry fostered a new business elite and contributed to the expansion of the urban population. The first professional revolutionary organizations, advocating the overthrow of the tsarist regime, also emerged during this period.

It was within this broad context that Russian theatre began to play an increasingly confident and assertive role in public life. In the prolific and popular playwright Alexander Ostrovsky the stage at last found its ideal chronicler of ordinary Russian life, or more accurately of the lives of the inhabitants of Moscow and the Volga basin. His great dramas acted as powerful lightning rods for a new generation of critics, among whom Nikolai Dobrolyubov, Apollon Grigorev and Nikolai Chernyshevsky stood out, and between them the dramatist and his critics gave Russians new ways of seeing and talking about themselves. Ostrovsky was pre-eminent, but he was far from being the only playwright to produce original works on authentic Russian themes. The period from the 1850s to the 1870s also witnessed important contributions from Ivan Turgenev, Alexander Sukhovo-Kobylin, Mikhail

Saltykov-Shchedrin, Alexei Pisemsky and Alexei Potekhin, to name but a few. The conclusion of one journalist, writing of the Moscow stage in 1864, that 'translations and adaptations have almost entirely disappeared from the theatrical repertoire' was something of an exaggeration, but it nevertheless reflected the steady emergence of original works on Russian themes by native playwrights.[1]

The growing importance of the stage and of theatrical criticism was assisted to some extent by the expansion of the press. By the 1850s, the *Northern Bee* was no longer the only newspaper officially permitted to review and comment on performances at the Imperial Theatres, and from 1862 preliminary censorship on theatrical articles was abolished.[2] After the closure of *Pantheon* in 1856, the main periodical publication devoted to theatre was the *Theatrical and Musical Herald* (1856–60), alongside two serial collections of plays, *The Dramatic Anthology* (1858–62) and *The Anthology of Theatrical Plays* (1858–9). The 1860s and 1870s saw the publication of several short-lived specialist newspapers, including: *Playbills and the Interval* (1864–5), the *Russian Stage* (1864–5), the *Interval* (1866–8), *Music and Theatre* (1867–8), *A Map of the Capital's Shows* (1873) and *Petersburg Dramaturgy* (1878). But the majority of theatrical reportage and criticism continued to appear in 'thick' journals, such as the *Contemporary* and the *Herald of Europe*, and in mainstream newspapers such as the *Petersburg Gazette*.

The most important issue for theatre as a public institution capable of contributing to the development of civil society in St Petersburg and Moscow was the Imperial Theatre monopoly. From the 1850s onwards, as theatrical life flourished in the regions – where there were few official restrictions on the organization of entertainments – the monopoly was reasserted and defended in governmental circles for political reasons, although the economic motives which originally gave rise to it continued to be cited in official pronouncements. Under the influence of the 'great reforms' and the invigoration of public life, however, calls for the monopoly's abolition were soon heard, especially during the 1870s and early 1880s. For complex reasons that will be explored below, it was finally abolished by Alexander III in 1882, clearing the way for a new era in the theatrical history of the capitals.

The immense south-facing walls of the Moscow Kremlin rise imperiously above the Moscow River, the vital stretch of water that linked the old capital to Russia's main river routes and that for centuries had served as a lucrative conduit of trade and commerce. On the southern side of the river lies the district of Zamoskvoreche, which in the nineteenth century was a rich and bustling community of artisans and merchants. It was here in 1823 that Alexander Ostrovsky was born. Within a few decades he established himself as Russia's greatest playwright, renowned in particular for his carefully observed portrayals of the Zamoskvoreche community and its colourful inhabitants.

Ostrovsky initially pursued a legal career. In 1840 he was admitted to Moscow University to read law but failed to complete his studies. Through his father, a lawyer, he obtained work as a court clerk, an experience he was to use to great effect in his dramatic characterizations. His real passion, however, was the theatre, and he soon began to devote all his time to writing for the stage. His first play, *The Bankrupt*, was completed in 1849 and was soon published in the literary journal the *Muscovite*. But it was immediately banned from public performance on account of its portrayal of merchants as dishonest, and the playwright was put under police surveillance. His first play to be performed to a public audience was *Don't Get Into Someone Else's Sleigh*, in 1853.

Ostrovsky's output was prodigious and he single-handedly transformed the repertoire of Russian theatre. In all he wrote forty-seven original plays, including comedies, dramas, tragedies and historical chronicles. During his lifetime, forty-six of his original single-authored plays were staged. Seven plays which he co-authored, one that he translated from Italian, and six which he adapted were also performed. This amounted to a grand total of sixty performed works by the time of his death in 1886. Together they accounted for 2,914 performances at the Malyi and Alexandrinsky theatres, more than one thousand performances in private theatres of the capitals, and approximately twenty thousand performances in regional theatres. It has also been calculated that 'no fewer than ten million spectators' saw a play by Ostrovsky during his lifetime.[3] His best works included *Poverty Is No Vice* (1853), *The Storm* (1859), *Enough Stupidity in Every Wise Man* (1868), *The Forest* (1870), *Wolves and Sheep* (1875), *The Heart Is Not a Stone* (1879), *Talents and Admirers* (1881) and *Guilty Without Guilt* (1883). Such works were particularly prominent in the repertoire of the Moscow Malyi, and soon the 'second university' and 'house of Shchepkin' acquired a third alias: 'house of Ostrovsky'.[4]

Most of Ostrovsky's plays are notable for their careful attention to the details of everyday life, portrayals of traditional customs, use of the vernacular and snippets from old folk songs. His characters are drawn from real people, and his plots, which can be dark and painful, are often based on the tribula-tions and machinations of real people. As such, Ostrovsky is commonly regarded as the founder of realism in Russian drama. The critic Nikolai Dobrolyubov (1836–61) called his works 'plays of life'.[5] For many, the true-to-Russian-life nature of Ostrovsky's works, especially the use of a vernacular that is often difficult to translate, explains why he remains relatively unknown outside Russia. It should be noted, however, that although Ostrovsky's works are regarded as quintessentially Russian, the everyday life depicted in his *oeuvre* is based more specifically on his observations of life in Moscow and the Volga region, the areas of his personal experience and the locations of most of his plays.[6] Nevertheless, his plays often deal with situations that are essentially universal, even if the context can be impenetrably Russian.[7] A regular and oft-noted motif, for example, is the phenomenon of *samodurstvo* (petty tyranny) and the *samodur* (the petty tyrant), a word formed from *samoderzhets* (autocrat) and *durak* (fool). Examples include Bolshov in *It's a Family Affair* (a new title given to *The Bankrupt*) and Dikoi in *The Storm*.

It is testimony to Ostrovsky's impact and influence that his plays exposed several underlying fissures in Russian society. Dobrolyubov observed that they divided people into two camps, 'the old and the young, the rich and the poor, the self-willed and the meek'.[8] For a time, Ostrovsky simultaneously appealed to Slavophiles and westernizers, but for different reasons. The former hailed his richly detailed portrayals of ordinary life, while the latter regarded him as a major critic of the social order and its alleged back-wardness. The extent to which the meaning of Ostrovsky's work could be contested was particularly evident in the critical responses to what is perhaps his greatest play, *The Storm*. This five-act drama was premiered at the Moscow Malyi in November 1859. Set in the town of Kalinovo on the Volga during a summer in the late 1850s, it tells the story of a married woman, Katerina Kabanova (Janáček's opera *Katya Kabanova* is based on the play), who is clearly oppressed by her family and social environment and seems to welcome the idea of death. She reacts to her circumstances by having an affair, but, unable to live with herself or those around her, she confesses to her family before throwing herself into the Volga. The clear message of the play is that Katerina's suicide is prompted not simply by shame, but by the whole oppressive environment in which she lives.

For Dobrolyubov, the significance of *The Storm* lay in its exposure of the petty tyranny, the *samodurstvo*, of family life, which he considered a microcosm of the social and political order, the 'dark kingdom' that he referred to in two critiques of Ostrovsky, 'The Kingdom of Darkness' (1859) and 'A Ray of Light in the Kingdom of Darkness' (1860). Katerina, in this interpretation, was cast as a heroic representative of the struggle against tyranny, although her suicide suggests resignation rather than fighting resolve. The conservative critic Apollon Grigorev (1822–64) rejected this interpretation and argued that the significance of Ostrovsky's work lay in its national character, its *narodnost'*.[9] During the 1860s, however, the notion of *narodnost'* became increasingly associated with radicalism, notably through the efforts of Chernyshevsky, but also partly as a result of Ostrovsky's plays and Dobrolyubov's influential interpretation of them.[10]

According to the theatre historian Anatoly Altschuller, 'Whereas in 1820 it could be said that many characters were created as much by the actors as by the playwright, by about 1850, when Ostrovsky's plays began to appear, the persona of the author had become central in the creation of theatre.'[11] This view has much to commend it in the light of Ostrovsky's impact, but the significance of actors for the realization of his work on stage should not be underestimated. It is noteworthy that Shchepkin, the greatest Russian actor of his age, struggled when it came to performing Ostrovsky's roles, apparently because, while Shchepkin was concerned with the universal characteristics of man, irrespective of class or nationality, Ostrovsky's interest was in depicting the lives and habits of a specific milieu. Shchepkin's inability to comprehend Ostrovsky's purpose was particularly manifest when he performed the part of the merchant Bolshov in *It's a Family Affair* at the Malyi in January 1861. The critics concurred that it was one of his least impressive performances: Bolshov is an unsympathetic *samodur*, yet Shchepkin endeavoured to show him in a sympathetic light. As one critic observed, 'This was no petty tyrant, who makes his whole family tremble at a glance. . . . We saw a good-natured, rascally old man – and that's all.'[12] The actor who most effectively incarnated Ostrovsky's characters was Prov Sadovsky (1818–72).

Ostrovsky and others created a dramatic literature that reflected the lives of ordinary urban Russians, and this in turn fostered a growing awareness of a broader stratum of society. As one observer put it in 1864, 'Drama is the consciousness of the life of the people [*narod*].'[13] This was a potentially dangerous development for the tsarist regime, in that growing artistic recognition of the *narod*, especially in the context of emergent revolutionary populism, was not necessarily compatible with autocracy in the longer term. Although the government had embarked on a reform programme under Alexander II, there was no intention to revise the fundamental premises of the political system. As theatre asserted its position as a forum in which the lives, values and concerns of the *narod* were publicly examined, the government was to respond by temporarily reasserting its control of theatrical life in the capitals.

By the mid nineteenth century, the monopoly of the directorate of Imperial Theatres on public entertainments in St Petersburg and Moscow had reached its apogee as a result of accumulated legislation targeted mainly at masquerades and concerts. Until its abolition, the original economic rationale for it was emphasized in all formal statements. In the late 1850s, however, in response to tentative suggestions from a special committee that private theatres might once more be permitted, government officials began to invoke political reasons (in private correspondence and classified memoranda) for retaining the monopoly. In March 1856, as the Crimean War ended and its bleak consequences for the state's finances became evident, a special committee was set up to examine ways of reducing deficits in the Imperial Theatre budget. The economically motivated monopoly evidently ensured that audiences could attend only state theatres, yet it was still unable to guarantee sufficient income. The committee was formally chaired by the Minister of the Imperial Court, V. F. Adlerberg, who appointed the writer and government official V. A. Sollogub (1813–82) to take general charge of its affairs.[14] In September 1857 Sollogub travelled to France, Prussia and Austria to study the administrative and financial arrangements of theatres there.[15] In March 1858 the committee finally began its work (using Sollogub's data about foreign theatres as the basis of its deliberations) and submitted its report to the tsar two months later.[16]

The report began by observing that most European theatres were private commercial enterprises and that, with the exception of the 'highest patriotic stages' supported by courts and governments, most received little or no state support. The tsarist government was therefore committing far more money to theatre than its European counterparts – six times as much as the Prussian government, for example. According to the report, this was because *every* theatre in St Petersburg and Moscow was run by the government.[17] The Russian state theatres also employed more people: the St Petersburg drama troupe had 190 more actors than the Comédie-Française, and the St Petersburg ballet troupe had 261 more members than the Paris Opéra.[18] An additional problem was that the Imperial Theatres were rarely allowed to open during Lent and were closed during the summer, as a result of which their overall box-office takings were lower than those of European theatres that were not subject to the same performance restrictions.[19] The report also argued that the government provided 'excessive' financial support to its Italian and French troupes.[20] According to Sollogub's data, in 1857–8 the following amounts (in rubles) were spent on the St Petersburg troupes:

Russian drama	44,232
Russian opera	85,153
German	85,925
Italian	123,701
French	179,150
Ballet	193,448[21]

This imbalance between expenditure on Russian-language theatre and foreign troupes or foreign-language theatre was compounded by two facts. Firstly, the ballet troupe was staffed by large numbers of non-Russians; and secondly, the troupe that received the least resources, the Russian drama troupe, performed most often. In 1857 in St Petersburg there was a total of 603 theatrical performances by the various troupes:

Russian drama	201
Russian opera	83
German	75
Italian	80
French	107
Ballet	57[22]

Moreover, although the Russian drama troupe performed in Russian, much of its repertoire consisted of translations or adaptations from western European, notably French, plays. The implication of these statistics, therefore, was that the directorate, and by association the government, was neglecting Russian in favour of foreign theatre. It is possible that defeat in the Crimean War made this idea less palatable to committee members.

The committee concluded that the fundamental cause of Imperial Theatre deficits was the monopoly and the reluctance of the directorate to allow impresarios to run some of the capitals' theatres. Referring to Catherine II's decree of 1783 (which, it argued, already allowed for a European style of theatrical administration, thereby hinting that the monopoly might be illegal),[23] the report advocated that private theatres be permitted, but only for foreign troupes, leaving open the question of whether there should be private *Russian* theatres in St Petersburg and Moscow:

> The restoration of such regulations could soon bring about significant savings in current theatre expenditure. Permitting private theatres will give the directorate the chance to free itself from the burden of its superfluous personnel. The transfer of foreign troupes to impresarios, with guarantees from the latter and the granting of benefits to them, in accordance with the procedure established in Paris for the three Imperial Theatres (Odéon, Opéra-Comique and Théâtre-Italien), will provide for a reduction of at least one-third of government expenditure on foreign troupes. But to what extent one or several private Russian theatres could be useful, and whether foreign performances would gain in merit with the intervention of private interests – on this the Committee does not make bold to express its conclusion, not knowing in advance the will of Your Imperial Majesty.[24]

The wording of the report, however, concealed disagreement between committee members. Sollogub, having observed the wider European theatrical scene at first hand, was probably the chief advocate of private theatres, and certainly the broadly favourable impression of private theatres that pervades the committee's report appears to reflect his experience. Moreover, in his memoirs he blamed the poverty of the Russian repertoire in the mid nineteenth century on the lack of private theatres, although he did not elaborate on how they would have remedied the situation.[25] But there was considerable opposition to the idea of private theatres from other committee members. Gedeonov, director of Imperial Theatres, argued that theatre possessed an ideological significance that made such freedom undesirable, claiming that, 'Moral education should conform with the form of government, and theatre, as a public institution, should be directed towards the aims of the government.' He attempted to establish a connection between the proliferation of private theatres and political change, arguing that during the French Revolution, when 'freedom of the theatres' was decreed in 1791, the number of theatres grew rapidly, many proving to be 'political'. He also alluded to the spread of popular theatres in Berlin during 1848–9. Although these theatres were the *result* of revolution, not its cause, in Gedeonov's mind the link was sufficient warning against 'freedom of the theatres'.[26]

Adlerberg was also hostile to the proposal. Although he signed the committee's report, he then expressed strong opposition to liberalization in a secret memorandum to Alexander II, arguing that Russian literature, which would find a popular outlet in private theatres, had a 'political tendency' often inclining towards the 'overthrow of the existing order'. Private theatres would be politically dangerous, in that they would become platforms for people 'desiring a revolution' and would 'have an effect upon all estates, powerfully and quickly, and the more so on ordinary people'. Nor was censorship an effective guarantee against oppositional sentiment in theatres. 'It should not be forgotten,' wrote the minister, echoing Gedeonov, 'that in all revolutions private theatres have served as a means for the excitement of the passions, and that their propagation in France and Germany is the fruit of revolutions.'[27] Adlerberg's wariness about 'revolutionary' literature extended beyond Russian works. Later in 1858 he prevented the director of Imperial Theatres A. I. Saburov (to whom Gedeonov had relinquished the post) from staging Goethe's *Egmont*, which celebrates Dutch resistance to Spanish rule in the sixteenth century, declaring, 'There is no possibility whatsoever of improperly and carelessly pulling out of the archive a work that has been there for about half a century and is in essence revolutionary, although it is based on historical facts. Veto.'[28]

Such arguments persuaded the tsar, who annotated Adlerberg's secret memorandum with the statement that 'private Russian theatres will not be introduced in the capital', a statement that was reiterated word for word in Alexander's formal response to the committee's report on 16 May 1858.[29] In 1862, Alexander also withdrew the directorate's authority to allow *ad hoc* private performances with entry fees and playbill announcements, although this regulation appears to have lapsed within a couple of years.[30] Exceptions were made for some performances with philanthropic aims. In St Petersburg, for example, Sunday schools, the Samsonievsky People's Reading Room, the Literary Foundation and the free daily schools on the Petersburg Side area of the city were permitted one amateur performance each in the run-up to Holy Week.[31] The merchant Nikolai Kalgin was also granted permission by the tsar to organize amateur performances in the St Petersburg shopping arcade, Passazh, in aid of the Tauride School.[32]

The newly articulated political rationale for the monopoly was re-emphasized in 1868 in response to a plan by the St Petersburg police chief, F. F. Trepov, to create a people's theatre. Proposals for private people's theatres had started to appear during the 1860s. The earliest petitions were from V. Mordvinov (1862), R. Zotov (1862) and P. F. Sekretarev (1863). In 1865, requests were made by P. A. Litvinov-Iurkevich for the right to set up a people's theatre in Kronstadt, and by the inhabitants of transfluvial (*zarechnyi*) St Petersburg to organize a similar venture. These were all rejected on the basis of the tsar's resolution of 16 May 1858.[33]

Trepov, however, believed that a people's theatre would improve the morals and intellects of ordinary people. It would distract 'the ordinary person in leisure hours from crude enjoyments, drunkenness, and the idleness and depravity that are inseparable from them', while providing him with 'instructive examples, an inconspicuous way of inculcating in him an aversion to vice and notions of virtue, civic duty, honest labour, thrift and so forth'.[34] The tsar, despite his earlier resolutions, instructed Adlerberg to establish a commission to discuss the proposal in detail,[35] but it came to nothing: Adlerberg remained strongly opposed to a people's theatre and to what he regarded as its inevitable form, a private theatre.

Setting out his position in a lengthy letter to the Minister of Internal Affairs, Adlerberg pointed out that the issue had been discussed ten years previously, reiterated his main objections, and insisted on their enduring validity. There was no dramatic literature that ordinary people could understand, and the vaudevilles and farces that dominated the Imperial Theatre repertoire would not improve the educational level of the people. The *narod* remained insufficiently educated for theatre, possessing no concept of 'civic duty' (such as the duty to obey police orders), and any surplus from meagre wages was spent on wine. Inexpensive theatre tickets would never be cheaper than the minimum amount of wine required to bring someone to a 'revelling state of spirit'. And when, asked the minister, could the working classes actually go to the theatre, since they laboured 'from 5 a.m. to 8 or 9 p.m.'? Theatre in itself would not reduce drunkenness because people could drink at work, and could drink 'before, during and after' a performance. The *narod* would not understand plays; it only understood 'vulgar farces and pantomimes', freely available in *balagany* on Admiralty Square during Holy Week and Easter.[36] Moreover, a people's theatre would cultivate among ordinary people 'ideas hostile to the existing order'. Censorship would not be able to control this; it could not even control the press, 'with the difference that the press only influences the educated class'. A people's theatre would be a 'powerful and harmful instrument of revolutionary propaganda'. Finally, although the proposed theatre would be private, it would not make any money, even with government support, as the entry fee would have to be low to admit the *narod*.[37] Trepov's plan was also opposed by the chief of the gendarmes, P. A. Shuvalov, who argued that the commercial imperatives of a private people's theatre would cancel out any social use it might have. As an example, he pointed to the 'immoral' repertoires of provincial theatres.[38]

The last official statement of the Imperial Theatre monopoly before its abolition was contained in the revised 'Statute on the Prevention and Suppression of Crimes', a series of regulations concerning public order published in the 1876 *Digest of Laws*. The section entitled 'Special Rules Regarding Public Amusements and Entertainments in the Capitals' included various clauses which affected the directorate (clauses 159–79).[39] Clause 159 confirmed, on the basis of Adlerberg's 1854 regulation, that 'The right to give public masquerades and concerts in the capitals belongs exclusively to the directorate of Imperial Theatres.' The use of the term 'masquerade' was an archaic echo of the language used in early nineteenth-century sources. Although masquerades were still organized by clubs and societies, in practice the term signified the directorate's monopoly on all theatricals. One unpublished compilation of the relevant statutes rephrased the key sentence to make it accord with actual practice: 'The exclusive right to give public stage performances in both capitals belongs to the directorate of Imperial Theatres.'[40]

The other clauses emphasized the economic motives for the monopoly, placing careful restrictions on the right to organize different kinds of entertainment. In most cases where the directorate was allowed to grant permission to private individuals or institutions to organize masquerades or concerts, it could levy a tax. The most favoured institutions were the St Petersburg and Moscow Noble Assemblies, which could provide up to six masquerades a year for their members. Clubs and similar venues were allowed to organize masquerades for members and guests, but only with the approval of the government and the payment of 25 per cent of the takings to the directorate. Philanthropic societies were prohibited outright from organizing masquerades but, with the agreement of the directorate, could organize public concerts. Readings of dramatic works at such concerts, 'even if not in costumes', were not permitted. Public balls with lotteries and so forth could be organized by philanthropic societies, but only once a year and at the directorate's discretion. This was also the case for other popular amusements such as acrobatics and conjuring. The decree that abolished the monopoly in 1882 simply nullified articles 159–79 of these 'Special Rules' without reference to earlier pronouncements on the directorate's authority.

During the mid nineteenth century, the theatre industry in regional Russia continued to expand and soon became, in the words of one historian, 'the centre of the cultural life of the provinces'.[41] It has been calculated that in the late 1850s there were approximately forty-three provincial theatres, and that by the beginning of the 1870s there were 102 troupes, sixty-one of them permanent.[42] The main precondition for this expansion was the absence of formal restrictions on the organization of theatrical enterprises by impresarios. The police remained officially responsible for monitoring the activities of regional theatres, and in 1842 the Third Section requested from the Ministry of Internal Affairs a list of all regional troupes and their repertoires in order to ensure that impresarios were not staging prohibited plays.[43] Otherwise the only major constraints on the development of regional theatricals were practical ones: limited resources for the construction of dedicated buildings, and a lack of audiences to support permanent or even itinerant troupes.

Constraints of this kind gradually began to disappear during the second half of the nineteenth century. The abolition of serfdom and the development of trade and commerce resulted in a steady increase in the size of the urban population. It has been estimated that between 1860 and 1897 the total population of the empire grew from 74.1 million to 126.4 million. Between 1863 and 1897, the population of St Petersburg increased from 539,500 to 1,264,900 and that of Moscow from 462,500 to 1,038,600.[44] This in turn helped to stimulate the growth of the theatre industry, as new audiences appeared and more people sought work as actors. Growing demand for entertainments during the 1850s and 1860s was evidenced by the construction of new theatre buildings, such as those at Nizhny Novgorod (1855), Archangel, Kiev, Nikolaev, Tambov (all 1856), Uralsk (1858), Ufa (1861), Orel, Ryazan (both 1862), Kostroma, Rostov-on-Don (both 1863), Smolensk (1864), Saratov (1865), Kaluga, Novocherkassk and Taganrog (all 1866).[45] New buildings were often designed as replacements for older ones, but they nevertheless testified to growing interest in the theatre.

The organization of regional theatricals was highly dependent on impresarios. The most prominent example was Pyotr Medvedev (1837–1906). After graduating from the Moscow theatre school, he acted in various towns, including Kostroma, Tver and Saratov, and then from 1862 concentrated on management, organizing ventures in Saratov, Kazan and elsewhere. The experience of Shchepkin had demonstrated that the provincial circuit could be significant for the cultivation of major talents, and this became increasingly evident during the second half of the nineteenth century. Several future stars of the Imperial Theatres, such as Maria Savina, Vladimir Davydov,

Konstantin Varlamov and Alexander Lensky, developed their skills in one of Medvedev's troupes. Yet the successful careers of such stars should not obscure the fact that, for the majority of thespians, conditions on the provincial circuit were often harsh. Ostrovsky alluded to this in his portrayals of provincial actors, such as Schastlivtsev and Neschastlivtsev in *The Forest*, or Shmaga in *Guilty Without Guilt*. It was an issue that later led to the formation of a professional actors' association (see chapter 6). The fortunes both of actors and of impresarios were closely dependent on the vagaries of the entertainment market, and indeed by 1889 Medvedev's material position as an impresario had become unsustainable. He nevertheless found employment first in St Petersburg as a régisseur and then as an actor at the Alexandrinsky.[46]

In marked contrast to the mid-century expansion of regional theatre, the Imperial Theatre monopoly was effective in restricting the number of theatres in St Petersburg and Moscow. Only one major theatre building was constructed at this time, namely the Imperial Mariinsky in St Petersburg, completed in 1860 to house the state opera and ballet troupes. Yet the efficacy of the monopoly did not mean that other entertainments were unavailable in the capitals. As official pronouncements on the monopoly confirmed, a range of clubs and societies could organize masquerades, concerts and other theatricals during the regular theatre season (normally late August to April or May), although usually only for members. Club theatricals normally consisted of a series of short stage acts, including singers, magicians, and often readings of scenes from plays. Club venues in St Petersburg alone included the Artists' Club, the Russian Merchant Mutual Aid Society, the Russian Merchant Assembly, the Noble Assembly, the German Club and the Petersburg Society of Lovers of Stage Art.[47]

Most private entertainments approved by the directorate occurred outside the regular theatre season and during holidays when the Imperial Theatres were closed and would not have to compete for audiences. They included fairgrounds, pleasure gardens, cabarets, concerts and popular festivals such as the *narodnye gulian'ia*. The latter took place in parks and squares during holidays and included a variety of games, rides, *balagany* and other fairground attractions such as ice hills, roller coasters and merry-go-rounds. During Shrovetide and Easter, the impresario Vasily Malafeyev organized popular *balagany* in St Petersburg. Summertime pleasure gardens, organized by other impresarios such as Alexei Alekseyev-Yakovlev, were increasingly popular, and by 1870 there were seven in St Petersburg. During the 1870s and early

1880s, Mikhail Lentovsky organized a variety of summer amusements, including an operetta theatre in the Hermitage summer garden in Moscow. Temporary theatricals also accompanied the St Petersburg Manufacturing Exposition in 1870, where Malafeyev received special permission to organize a people's theatre, and the Moscow Polytechnical Exposition in 1872, where the Malyi Theatre actor Alexander Fedotov ran a similar venture.[48]

Other private ventures were permitted at the directorate's discretion if they provided the sort of entertainment that the Imperial Theatres tended to eschew. An early example was the Children's Puppet Theatre in St Petersburg (1841–7). During the 1860s and 1870s, in response to the interest in *variété* and operetta, the directorate granted permission for the Theatre of V. K. Berg (1866–76) and the Théâtre Bouffe (1870–8, latterly known as the Opéra Bouffe) in St Petersburg, and for similar entertainments at the Solodovnikovsky Passazh and the Povarskaya Street Theatre in Moscow. These were essentially music halls and were not considered serious alternatives to the Imperial Theatres.[49]

Performances of legitimate drama outside the Imperial Theatres were confined initially to a few household theatricals. Known as 'family evenings', these were usually organized by circles of artists and literary figures and were not open to the public. During the 1850s in Moscow, for example, family evenings were organized by the amateur actor N. I. Davydov at his house where banned plays such as Ostrovsky's *It's a Family Affair* were performed with the participation of the author himself. Similar gatherings were organized by the Morkov Circle in Moscow, which counted the writers Alexei Pisemsky and Modest Pisarev among its members. The most important circle was the Artistic Circle in Moscow. Founded in 1865 by, among others, Ostrovsky, Nikolai Rubinstein and Vladimir Odoevsky, as a forum where writers, actors, musicians and painters could exchange ideas about the arts, it also organized lectures, exhibitions, musical evenings, and readings of plays for members. In 1867 it was granted permission to give private performances of full costume dramas for members, and in 1868 these performances were opened to the public. The directorate's willingness to countenance the new theatre is possibly explained by the fact that it was organized by the Imperial Theatre actor N. E. Vilde.[50]

Another figure who received permission to organize private theatricals, although not full costume dramas like the Artistic Circle, was the Imperial Theatre actress Anna Brenko (1849–1934). Brenko joined the troupe of the Malyi in February 1878 and remained there until October 1882, when she was dismissed as part of a general reduction in Imperial Theatre staff.[51] Soon after joining the Malyi, Brenko was prompted by dissatisfaction with its routines to organize her own ventures, despite remaining officially employed by the Malyi. During an interview in 1905 she explained her decision to set up a new theatre:

> While working at the Malyi Theatre, I was suffocated by the awful customs and the bondage. Freedom of art was my ideal. I saw so much unfairness that my soul was troubled by these awful customs, and I resolved to fight this evil. I decided to create a theatre on different principles, free from routine and bureaucracy, a theatre where fraternity and association on honourable terms would reign.[52]

In 1879, having received permission to organize public readings of 'scenes from plays',[53] Brenko put together an amateur troupe from among students of the Petrovskaya Academy called 'Free Performances of Artists' that gave performances during the summer, many of the proceeds from which (no doubt contrary to official expectation) went to arrested students and their families.[54] Emboldened by that success, Brenko organized amateur performances in Moscow from September 1879. From January to April 1880 these were given at the Solodovnikovsky Passazh Theatre.[55] Then in September 1880, Brenko's troupe moved to the so-called Pushkin Theatre. The formal title of the theatre was 'The Drama Theatre of A. A. Brenko in the House of Malkiel', after the millionaire merchant S. M. Malkiel who turned one of his houses on Tverskaya Street into a theatre. It was also known as the 'Theatre Near Pushkin's Statue', 'The Pushkin Theatre' or just 'Brenko's Theatre'. Malkiel let Brenko have the theatre for twenty-one thousand rubles per annum, to be paid in advance in two six-monthly instalments.[56] The venture was initially financed by Brenko's husband, the lawyer and music critic Osip Levenson, whose considerable financial resources she was able to draw upon. Writing of the Pushkin's first season in her memoirs, Brenko acknowledged that 'Without my husband my pockets were empty.'[57]

As with her other ventures outside the Malyi, Brenko received permission to stage only 'scenes from plays'.[58] Yet the Pushkin opened on 9 September 1880 with a full-length costume performance of Gogol's *The Government Inspector*. In this sense, the new theatre initially had a 'semi-legal' existence.[59] Despite artistic success, Brenko's enterprise encountered financial difficulties towards the end of its first season. A tax of forty or fifty rubles per performance had to be paid to the directorate,[60] and after the assassination of Alexander II all theatres were required to close for six months, damaging box-office revenues.[61] Brenko made an effort to save her theatre from collapse shortly before the abolition of the directorate's monopoly, and we will return to her story below. Her theatre was significant because, by staging full-length costume dramas without permission, it was the first private venture to breach the letter of the regulations with impunity.

It is worth noting here that the directorate's willingness to grant permission for some private ventures has resulted in historiographical confusion as to what should be considered the first private theatre to appear in the capitals after the consolidation of the monopoly. Many sources make the claim for Brenko's enterprise,[62] while others give the accolade to the theatre at the 1872 Moscow Polytechnical Exposition.[63] More than one reference guide to Russian theatre states that the theatre of the Artistic Circle was the first but then goes on to make similar claims for the Pushkin Theatre.[64] In the early Soviet period it became customary to refer to Brenko's as the first private theatre, a reputation apparently based on comments made by Brenko herself during an interview with the writer Vladimir Giliarovsky in 1905.[65] Yet when it was established Brenko's venture did not attract special attention and was not considered the first private theatre. 'The winter season has presented us with a new private theatre,' observed one under-whelmed correspondent.[66] Another simply included the new theatre among a list of Moscow's other entertainment venues, including the two Imperial Theatres, the Artistic Circle, the Solodovnikovsky and the theatre at the German Club.[67] It is clear that ascertaining what was the first private theatre ultimately depends on definitions. If private theatres are defined simply as non-state enterprises, all of the enterprises mentioned above were private theatres, and the first one to appear during the period of the monopoly was the Theatre of V. K. Berg in 1866. If private theatres are defined as non-state theatres staging serious drama in full costume, the theatre of the Artistic Circle was first. If they are defined as theatres that circumvented the monopoly and were completely independent, none was a private theatre because they all existed with the permission of the directorate and paid taxes to it. Brenko's theatre was distinct because it staged full costume dramas for ticket-buying audiences without permission, yet with impunity.

Thus, before the end of the monopoly the directorate periodically granted permission for private ventures if they were unlikely to challenge the Imperial Theatres' domination of the market for legitimate theatre.[68] In other words, although by the late 1850s the monopoly was defended for political reasons, its original economic motives remained evident in the way it was applied by the directorate.

From the late 1860s the monopoly was attacked by a number of writers who argued that it was responsible for declining standards in the Russian theatre. In 1867, the prominent publisher and theatre enthusiast Alexei Suvorin described the capital theatres as 'mediocre' and suggested that, in the absence of competition, they were likely to remain so. 'Russian theatre,' he insisted, 'can flourish only with freedom of the theatres.'[69] A few years later, Suvorin claimed that, despite increased demand for theatre occasioned by population growth, standards of performance and of playwriting were declining. The capitals' theatres were run by bureaucrats with no artistic training, while censorship and paltry royalties inhibited talented writers from working for the theatre. The Alexandrinsky's box-office revenues were buoyant only because it was the sole Russian drama theatre in St Petersburg. Suvorin observed that 'in the capital of the Russian kingdom there are only two Russian theatres [the Alexandrinsky and the Mariinsky] and five foreign ones: the Mikhailovsky, the German, the Bouffe, the Berg, and the Italian opera' and wondered if this was to enable Russians to learn foreign languages. Competition was his proposed solution: 'If required to summarize all that I have said about the shortcomings of our theatre, I would say that the most rational way of eliminating them consists in the freedom of the theatres.'[70]

Another critic was the journalist Mikhail Katkov, who asked, 'Why do we have full freedom of private enterprise in theatrical affairs everywhere except the capitals, where it would be particularly fruitful?' If such freedom was harmful, reasoned Katkov, it could not be allowed in the provinces. Seeking to allay the fears of conservatives, he claimed that freedom of the theatres would not remove government surveillance; unreliable people would not be allowed to establish theatres, and the repertoire would still be monitored. For Katkov, the fear that competition would harm the Imperial Theatres was unfounded: 'The absence of competition, as the condition of these theatres demonstrates, has not saved them from decline.' Foreign experience showed that 'free competition' did not disadvantage privileged theatres, but rather prevented them from sinking into 'routine'. Katkov alluded to a possible alternative to liberalization, whereby state theatres could be leased to private individuals, but he dismissed this option, arguing that the 'monopolist-speculator' would be no better than the state. Such a measure would only work if free competition were permitted at the same time.[71] Elsewhere Katkov argued that 'full freedom of competition in the field of theatrical enterprises' would solve the problem of deficits in the state theatres because it would ensure profitability.[72]

There were other detractors of the monopoly. The critic Alexander Volf argued that the unsatisfactory condition of the St Petersburg theatres could not be rectified under the monopoly because as long as the theatrical administration enjoyed unchallenged domination of the market, with a guaranteed income, it need not revise its ways, its adherence to outmoded traditions.[73] The lawyer and critic Alexander Urusov claimed that, unless private theatres were permitted, Russian theatre would become 'weak and degenerate'.[74]

The argument that the monopoly impeded the development of the Russian theatre was central to the three most extended and influential critiques of the situation, written by Ostrovsky during 1880 and 1881. In the first, 'Club Stages, Private Theatres and Amateur Performances', he insisted that 'The theatrical monopoly has brought significant harm to the development of stage and dramatic art in Russia, in that it has assisted the rise of club and other similar stages . . . The main, if not the only, cause of the decline of the Russian stage and public taste is the theatrical monopoly.' Ostrovsky argued that the development of a public culture (*obshchestvennost'*) in the capitals had increased the 'thirst for elegant spectacles', but because private theatres were prohibited this demand could only be satisfied 'furtively', by clubs and assemblies that organized 'family musical and dancing evenings'. Moreover, financial limitations (club members were admitted free of charge and paying guests were few in number) meant that such 'light entertainments' could not become serious theatrical ventures.[75]

Ostrovsky accused the directorate of neglecting Russian drama and fearing competition. The lack of competition would not matter if the administration valued Russian theatre, but since the unification of the Imperial Theatres in 1842 the directorate's priority had been 'trifling economies, petty reductions in expenditure'. This was especially so under the management of Baron Kiester, an official in the Ministry of the Imperial Court who was granted responsibility for the Imperial Theatres from 1875 to 1881, taking over from S. A. Gedeonov (director since 1867, not to be confused with his father A. M. Gedeonov, director from 1834–58), although he did not formally assume the post of director. Kiester, who was widely disliked in St Petersburg, focused on making economies in Imperial Theatre expenditure and was accused of neglecting Russian art.[76] The consequent decline of theatre, according to Ostrovsky, hindered the Russian capacity for self-expression, despite a demand for 'native [*rodnoe*] art' in Moscow, the main geographical focus of his concerns. For the 'patriot' the confinement of theatricals to clubs was hopefully 'only a sad episode, a temporary calamity'.[77] Furthermore, none of the private theatres that had been allowed were significant, partly as a result of restrictions imposed by the monopoly: for example, the Théâtre Bouffe in St Petersburg had failed because the directorate's tax had ruined its manager.[78]

In his second critique, 'A Note on the Condition of Dramatic Art in Russia at the Present Time', which he started working on in February 1881,[79] Ostrovsky argued that Moscow required a national theatre to cultivate patriotism among its inhabitants. Since the state-run Imperial Theatres were incapable of fulfilling that task, the new theatre should be financed privately by Moscow merchants. The city needed a theatre that would exert the 'civilizing influence of dramatic art' on its changing population and also express its historical and national identity. The population of Moscow had doubled since the 1850s, but the growing industrial and merchant class was deprived of theatricals because only the Malyi was allowed to stage drama (by this time the Bolshoi was largely reserved for opera and ballet), and even this was reserved mainly for the 'official public', including the richer merchants, many of whom were too European in dress, habits and customs.[80] Fortunately, reflected Ostrovsky, Muscovites who emulated Europe were a minority, but the playwright was alarmed that many regarded European culture as a benchmark. These people were harming Russian art and had 'spoiled the Russian repertoire; writers have begun to adapt to its taste'.

Ostrovsky warned that the demand for 'aesthetic satisfaction' was urgent and that its absence 'could have a harmful influence on social morality'. 'The population of Moscow is mainly mercantile and industrial; Moscow is the trade centre of Russia, the meeting place of six railways that convey on a daily basis a huge quantity of people belonging to the trading *soslovie*.' Moscow was also the 'patriotic centre of the state':

> Taking into consideration all the above, it is impossible not to conclude that Moscow needs, first and foremost, a Russian theatre, national, all-Russian. This is an urgent business – the issue of a Russian theatre in Moscow comes before the issue of freedom of the theatres and is independent from it. A Russian theatre in Moscow is an important, patriotic business.

For Ostrovsky, a proper Russian theatre, capable of reaching a wider audience, would aid the spread of patriotic sentiment among ordinary people. 'A national theatre is a sign of the coming of age of a nation, like academies, universities, museums.' 'Patriots' had to build this theatre, 'worthy representatives of the rich Moscow merchants' for whom the theatre is mainly intended. Ostrovsky concluded by stating that if his ideas reached government circles and were approved, he would happily take on the task himself. He claimed to know Moscow merchants who desired a new theatre and were prepared to finance it.[81] His third critique of the monopoly, contained in 'On the Causes of the Decline of Dramatic Theatre in Moscow', largely reiterated the arguments developed in his previous writings.[82]

Ostrovsky's three papers indicated that he preferred a two-stage introduction of private theatres. Firstly, he wanted the right to establish a model national theatre using merchant capital, and only then should there be general freedom of the theatres. He was convinced that 'speculation' would not lead to a national theatre, and that, without one, freedom of the theatres might actually make matters worse, in that it would simply mean more operetta and melodrama. For Ostrovsky then, cultural (notably Muscovite) patriotism was the driving issue for the theatre, and neither the government (in the shape of the directorate) nor free competition could be trusted to promote it. And, crucially, Ostrovsky was one of the few people concerned about the effects of the monopoly who, as we will see, had the ear of the government when the issue of theatre reform was placed on the agenda following the assassination of Alexander II in March 1881.

The Imperial Theatre monopoly was finally overturned on 24 March 1882, when the new tsar, Alexander III, instructed the senate to abolish the 'exclusive right of the directorate of Imperial Theatres to organize public masquerades and concerts' in St Petersburg and Moscow.[83] Private theatres could now be organized without prior approval from the directorate. In order to understand this change in policy, it is necessary to examine the series of events that took place between the accession of the new tsar and the spring of 1882, in particular the personnel changes within the upper echelons of government, the financial crisis at Brenko's theatre and her energetic efforts to resolve it, and Ostrovsky's project for a privately funded national theatre in Moscow.

On 17 August 1881, A. V. Adlerberg (who had succeeded V. F. Adlerberg in 1870) was replaced as Minister of the Imperial Court by Illarion Vorontsov-

Dashkov.[84] A soldier by training, Vorontsov-Dashkov had participated in the Russo-Turkish War of 1877–8, had commanded the emperor's bodyguard at Gatchina, and was the principal organizer of the Holy Brotherhood (1881–3), a secret society which was really a royal bodyguard designed to protect Alexander III and root out sedition. Its 729 members had to support Great Russian interests and tended to be aristocrats, although other groups such as merchants were also represented.[85] The potential significance of the change was noted by Ostrovsky: 'With the removal of Adlerberg one ought to expect great changes in the theatre administration.'[86] There is no evidence that Vorontsov-Dashkov had any interest in theatrical affairs, and Ostrovsky's initial optimism about reform was based simply on the fact that Adlerberg – who had upheld the views of his predecessor on private theatres – had gone, as had Kiester.

The first step towards the realization of Ostrovsky's hopes was taken on 3 September, when the new minister appointed Ivan Vsevolozhsky as the new director of Imperial Theatres. The playwright I. V. Shpazhinsky suggested to Ostrovsky that the time was 'very opportune to renew the petition of our society regarding permission for it to open theatres in both capitals or, at least, in Moscow. They say that, at the present time, the government is inclined to favour the freedom of the theatres.'[87] Shpazhinsky was referring to the Society of Russian Dramatists and Composers, established in Moscow in 1874 to represent the interests of dramatists (composers were admitted to its ranks in 1877). Ostrovsky was the society's chairman from its foundation until his death in 1886. It is not clear what 'petition' Shpazhinsky was referring to, but the society appears to have lobbied the government on behalf of certain individuals – for example, Alexander Fedotov, organizer of the theatre at the 1872 Moscow Polytechnical Exposition – for the right to set up theatres.

Shpazhinsky met with Vsevolozhsky soon after his appointment and informed Ostrovsky that the new director wanted to increase state funding for Russian theatre.[88] Hopes for reform were raised further when, on 12 October, Vorontsov-Dashkov established a commission to review the administration of the Imperial Theatres on the grounds that the statute of 1827 was outdated (see p. 48).[89] It was chaired by Vsevolozhsky and included the following members: A. F. Yurgens, manager of the St Petersburg Office of the Imperial Theatres; I. L. Dzyubin, secretary of the chancellery of the Ministry of the Imperial Court; A. P. Frolov, manager of the Theatre School; and two officials attached to the Ministry of the Imperial Court named Emelyanov and Lange. The commission was entitled to invite Imperial Theatre artists and other specialists if deemed necessary, and it invited Ostrovsky, Alexei Potekhin, and Dmitry Averkiev.

The commission held its first session on 20 October,[90] and five days later Vorontsov-Dashkov presented it with an agenda consisting of sixteen questions. In addition to considering the general question whether the Imperial Theatres were fulfilling their task of supplying 'aesthetic pleasure', the commission was asked to review several administrative matters, the role of the theatre school, and dramatists' royalties. Only the fourth question alluded to the monopoly: 'If it is inconvenient to keep all theatres under the direct administration of the directorate, which of them could be passed on to private enterprise and on what conditions?'[91] The commission, however, was not asked to question the monopoly as such, and it is clear from its protocols and correspondence that it envisaged 'private enterprise' as a franchise system whereby the directorate would retain control of all theatres in the capitals but permit impresarios to run some of them as leases. Vsevolozhsky argued that any private enterprise should be granted 'only under the supreme control of the director of Imperial Theatres'.[92] During February and March 1882, for instance, discussions were held as to whether to transfer the German troupe to 'private enterprise', but what was intended was that an impresario would run the troupe and pay rent to the directorate for the use of the new Malyi theatre building in St Petersburg (also known as the Apraksin Theatre after its owner, Count Apraksin), constructed between 1876 and 1878.[93] The motive for proposing to lease theatres to impresarios was mainly financial but also aesthetic. An anonymous report in the directorate's archive about limiting expenditure argued that the use of an impresario would enrich both the revenues and the artistic work of a theatre, since the directorate employed too many people of doubtful use who interfered in artistic matters.[94]

The commission met thirty-four times between 20 October 1881 and 14 April 1882. During that time the monopoly was abolished, but it was never considered by the commission, which focused on reforms within the Imperial Theatre system and raised the issue of private theatres only in another context. The sources suggest that the commission was ambivalent about the monopoly. On the one hand there was a clear desire for the directorate to retain control of all theatres, yet one report (on dramatists' royalties) referred to the 'harmful theatrical monopoly'.[95] Thus, although the monopoly was abolished during the period in which the commission met, there does not appear to have been a direct link between the two developments.

Let us now consider the claim that Anna Brenko was responsible for the end of the monopoly. During the summer of 1881 Brenko began to petition the authorities for the full right to run her theatre – in other words, to stage, legally, full-length costume dramas, without having to give a portion of box-office revenues to the directorate. Initially she approached the governor-general of Moscow, V. A. Dolgorukov,[96] who forwarded her petition to Vorontsov-Dashkov when the latter was appointed Minister of the Imperial Court. The matter was finally settled by the tsar who agreed that Brenko could run her theatre for ten years without paying tribute to the directorate. Brenko was then informed by Baron Kiester that she could run her theatre for two years under the 'previous conditions'.[97] Dolgorukov supported Brenko with another letter, which she presented to the new Minister of Internal Affairs, N. P. Ignatev, whereupon the tsar, realizing that his initial instruction had been ignored, dismissed Kiester on 19 August.[98]

Vitenzon suggests that Brenko's petitions compelled Alexander III to instruct Vorontsov-Dashkov to establish the theatre reform commission.[99] This would appear, however, to be conjecture founded on chronological circumstance rather than on corroborative evidence. In fact, almost two months elapsed between Kiester's dismissal and the commission's establishment (12 October), during which time other interventions were made that more plausibly explain the decision to consider reform. Notable in this respect was a paper submitted by the Imperial Theatre actor F. A. Burdin to Vsevolozhsky on 6 September. Burdin claimed that the 'present decline' of Russian theatre was a result of 'indifference, not to say contempt, on the part of the theatrical administration'. Productions were carelessly and shabbily staged, and there was a desperate need for effective régisseurs. He also implied neglect of national art: 'Russian plays are given with old greasy scenery, poor furniture, pitiful costumes, often without wigs, not taking into consideration that the wig constitutes the main element in the actor's make-up, imparting a certain originality of physiognomy.' Ballet, opera and French theatre, he argued, were treated differently. Burdin also drew Vsevolozhsky's attention to the harmful effects of ubiquitous benefit nights and poor remuneration for dramatists, pointing out that the 1827 statute was still being used as the basis upon which playwrights received royalties, even though the statute was officially regarded as 'obsolete'.[100] Given that these were all issues that the commission was asked to consider, it seems likely that it was Burdin rather than Brenko who influenced the decision to review theatrical practice. Besides, there is no reference to Brenko in any of the commission's papers or in the letter from Vorontsov-Dashkov to Vsevolozhsky by which the commission was established.

Brenko's theatre continued to stage performances during late 1881 and January 1882.[101] In November 1881 it was confirmed that the Pushkin would be granted full independent status.[102] 'I have secured freedom of private theatres in the capital,' claimed Brenko. 'My cherished dream of the freedom of Russian theatre from the monopoly of the Imperial [Theatres] has been realized.'[103] In January 1882 Dolgorukov reminded Brenko that she still had to wait for the formal decree on private theatres before 'opening' her theatre, implying that a decision to abolish the monopoly had been taken.[104] The decree came too late for Brenko, however, whose theatre did not survive, closing on 7 February 1882, seventeen months after it opened.[105] As for her claim that she had overturned the monopoly, this was probably an exaggeration, unwittingly perpetuated by historians. Brenko's efforts to secure 'full freedom' for her theatre are likely to have played some role in the monopoly's demise, but the precise nature of that role is not clear from the sources. A stronger case can be made for the influence of Ostrovsky.

Ostrovsky was already working on 'A Note on the Condition of Dramatic Art in Russia at the Present Time' when Alexander II died. Hopeful of reform under the new administration, he initially asked his brother, a government official, to speak with the new Minister of Internal Affairs, N. P. Ignatev, about his proposals for a new theatre.[106] As Russia's leading dramatist, Ostrovsky was appointed to the theatre reform commission on 1 October,[107] setting out for St Petersburg at the end of the month and remaining there until 20 March 1882. On 5 November he presented a paper on the 1827 statute to the commission and, according to the actor, writer and acquaintance of Ostrovsky, I. F. Gorbunov, it made a 'powerful impression'.[108] It appears, however, that because the commission was not concerned with the issue of the monopoly, Ostrovsky used much of his spare time in St Petersburg to lobby officials about his ideas on private theatres. In a letter to his wife, dated 11 November 1881, he wrote that Ignatev had visited him and that he (Ostrovsky) and his brother had returned the visit, during which the dramatist had read his paper 'on private theatres' and presented the minister with a copy. This was the above-mentioned 'Note on the Condition of Dramatic Art', in which Ostrovsky called for a national theatre to be established in Moscow. According to Ostrovsky, Ignatev agreed with everything he said.[109] On 24 November Ostrovsky (on the recommendation of Shpazhinsky) presented Ignatev with a petition from the Society of Russian Dramatists and Composers regarding Alexander Fedotov's desire to set up a 'Russian Theatre in Moscow'.[110] Three months later, on 19 February 1882 (and the reasons for the delay are unclear),

Ignatev passed Ostrovsky's paper and the society's petition to Alexander III. On the same day, Ostrovsky was granted permission, as chairman of the society, to organize a national theatre in Moscow. Formal notification of the tsar's approval was sent to Ostrovsky by Dolgorukov, who would have the right to veto its repertoire.[111] A truncated version of Ostrovsky's paper was published in the *Government Herald* on 9 March 1882, according to which the tsar had inscribed on the paper the important statement 'It would be highly desirable to realize this idea, which I completely share.'[112]

In the midst of these developments, the monopoly was dismantled. An initial step was taken on 21 October 1881, when Vorontsov-Dashkov informed Vsevolozhsky that the directorate was no longer to levy money from private individuals who organized theatrical entertainments.[113] In March 1882 Vorontsov-Dashkov submitted a short report to Alexander III recommending the abrogation of the monopoly. The monopoly, observed the minister, 'had the main purpose of protecting the economic interests of the directorate'. However, it also allowed the directorate 'to decline all the initiatives of private impresarios in organizing theatres and concerts. The capitals were thus deprived of private theatres and the mass of the public, in its pursuit of aesthetic pleasure, was compelled by the shortage of seats in the theatres to seek more accessible if not always suitable forms of entertainment.' Vorontsov-Dashkov sought to allay any concern that competition would result in greater expenditure for the directorate by stating that it 'can attract the best stage talents, prepared to go on the imperial stage for a smaller fee'. The minister argued that the monopoly was 'harmful' because 'this tax kills private theatrical enterprise and deprives artist-toilers . . . of the opportunity to earn a crust'. He concluded that 'it is hardly in keeping with the dignity of the Imperial Theatres to base their prosperity on compulsory dues from private individuals and societies'.[114] Vorontsov-Dashkov's essential rationale for asking the tsar to abolish the monopoly was thus that there was a paucity of suitable theatrical entertainments in the capitals, a situation that was detrimental both to members of the public seeking 'aesthetic pleasure' and to thespians seeking work. On 24 March Alexander III duly brought the monopoly to an end.

While the decision to abolish the monopoly was made during the period in which the theatre reform commission was deliberating on matters pertaining to the Imperial Theatres and Brenko and Ostrovsky were seeking official permission for their own projects, the precise relationship between these developments is unclear. What is certain is that the commission did not examine the monopoly, and that Brenko was granted permission for her theatre four months before the formal end of the monopoly. The crucial link was probably Ostrovsky, and indeed Vorontsov-Dashkov's report reflected issues that the dramatist had explored in his various papers. Yet the minister's report contained little by way of an historical explanation for the decision. It simply suggested that a greater number of suitable theatrical entertainments were needed in the capitals and that the monopoly prevented their development (confirming, incidentally, that the monopoly had been effective). That much was already clear. Why then had the government decided to grant freedom of the theatres?

The end of the monopoly was part of a trend in nineteenth-century Europe that saw the gradual removal of legislation protecting the exclusive rights of a small number of theatres to stage serious drama in major cities. Notable examples were the Theatre Regulation Act (1843) that ended the monopoly of Drury Lane and Covent Garden in London,[115] and the Declaration of the Freedom of the Theatres (1864) that abolished the patent, or licensing, system in France.[116] The Russian reform differs from these examples in two fundamental respects, however, prompting questions about its purpose.

First, in England and France the theatre monopolies were largely ineffective. In London, the monopoly applied only to legitimate theatre, and new entertainment venues circumvented the regulation by using pianists to provide musical accompaniment to the action, thereby ensuring that performances were not classified, at least officially, as legitimate.[117] In this manner, theatres proliferated across early nineteenth-century London to meet increasing demand, leading to what one historian has termed the 'growing obsolescence' of the patent system.[118] According to another commentator, 'Sooth-sayers prophesied a further out-break of theatre-building [after the Theatre Regulation Act], but in fact the demand was already satiated. Between 1843 and 1860 not a single important new theatre was opened in London.'[119] Likewise in France, 'the concept of restrictive patents had become obsolete' by 1864.[120] The system limited the number of theatres, but was not intended to prohibit private theatres.[121] Instead, it was designed to determine what kinds of production (tragedy, vaudeville, opera, etc.) could be staged by individual ventures. Genre control proved difficult to enforce, however, and a growing campaign for freedom of the theatres persuaded the provisional government of 1848 to review the licensing system, although it was finally abolished only in 1864.[122] By contrast, the Russian Imperial Theatre monopoly proved effective in restricting the growth of legitimate theatre and controlling the theatrical affairs of St Petersburg and Moscow in general, and private theatres were established in significant numbers only after its abolition. Amateur and club theatricals appear to have grown in popularity during the mid nineteenth century, but, as will be argued below, they did not constitute implicit challenges to the monopoly and exercised a negligible influence on the decision to abolish it.

Secondly, in England and France the repeal of the theatre monopolies accompanied broad programmes of liberalization. In England, electoral reform and free trade occupied the centre of contemporary debates, and in France Napoleon III was embarking upon the liberal phase of his rule, which included the removal of state restrictions on a range of private enterprises. By contrast, the Russian reform occurred during the political reaction that followed the assassination of Alexander II in March 1881. Dealing a famous blow to the liberals, Alexander III issued a manifesto declaring his strict adherence to autocracy.[123] This was followed by a series of counter-reforms designed to rein in much of the autonomous public activity created by the 'great reforms' of the 1860s and 1870s. Why then should a decision have been taken to allow private theatres to exist in the capitals subject only to police approval, a decision that appears to contradict Alexander III's agenda? The fact that the tsar is often portrayed as a keen patron of the Russian arts does not provide a straightforward answer, since it fails to explain why, in the context of reaction and repression, such support entailed the liberalization of entertainment legislation. We should also remember that 'freedom of the theatres' had been rejected on political grounds under the tsar's predecessor.

Four possible explanations for the reform suggest themselves. Two of them can be dismissed quite easily, while the others require further examination. The first explanation, advanced by Danilov, is that the government liberalized the rules on theatrical entertainments in order to divert the populace from political issues following the recent regicide.[124] This view, echoed in much of the Soviet-era literature on Russian theatre,[125] is not supported by any of the documentary evidence relating to the decision.[126] Even if the measure was designed to facilitate the spread of theatricals, as Vorontsov-Dashkov's report implies, there is no evidence that the government believed they would have a pacifying effect on potentially seditious or rebellious types. Vorontsov-Dashkov's remark that the monopoly forced the public to seek out entertainments that were 'not always suitable' was likely an echo of Ostrovsky's complaint that the monopoly had encouraged the growth of club theatricals, but that complaint reflected a concern about artistic standards, not a belief that such entertainments were politically unsafe. Moreover, although the Adlerbergs no longer had any influence, it is highly unlikely that their long-standing opposition to private theatres on the grounds that they appeared to accompany revolutions was suddenly replaced by the diametrically opposite view.

If the political explanation is unpersuasive, was there a financial reason for the decision? We have already seen that proposals to lease some of the directorate's theatres to impresarios were not related to the issue of the monopoly, and it is equally clear that its abolition was not designed to rid the administration of expensive theatres. (After all, it could simply have closed them down, a solution that was not considered.) The directorate would of course lose income after the monopoly's abolition, because it would no longer be able to levy a portion of box-office revenues from private theatres. The amount it would lose was in fact relatively small. For example, in 1880 the directorate's total income from all Imperial Theatre performances was 1,453,095 r. 33 k., while its total income from private entertainments was a mere 20,327 r. 8 k.[127] Yet the tax made it difficult to run private theatres, when permitted. The government, therefore, as Vorontsov-Dashkov's report indicated, acknowledged the financial limitations imposed on theatrical enterprise by the monopoly. But the removal of the tax does not in itself explain the decision to allow private theatres to exist in the capitals without the directorate's sanction; it merely shows that one of the stumbling blocks to the viability of private theatres had been addressed.

Some historians have alluded to a third reason for the monopoly's abolition, namely the growing demand for entertainments (such as the holiday enter-tainments, family evenings and club theatricals noted above), together with pressure from some writers and impresarios for freedom of the theatres.[128] Ostrovsky regarded family evenings and club theatricals as evidence of a latent demand for legitimate theatre that could not be satisfied under the monopoly. The dramatist and critic Pyotr Gnedich claimed that amateur performances flourished in St Petersburg during 1878–9 because private theatres were forbidden,[129] and Danilov described family evenings as the 'concealed organizing of a private drama stage'.[130] By removing the monopoly, such activities could be channelled into serious legitimate theatre, as Ostrovsky suggested. On the face of it, this interpretation has much to commend it. Ostrovsky had lambasted club theatricals in 'Club Stages, Private Theatres, and Amateur Performances' and appears to have influenced officials with his ideas about reform. There are, however, significant caveats. Club theatricals and amateur performances did not abate after 1882 but maintained their popularity. In 1888, for example, one commentator noted that club stages with talented performers continued to exist but were simply not reported in the press,[131] and Savva Mamontov's family evenings continued long after his Private Opera opened in Moscow in 1885.[132] It is also worth observing that the absence of the monopoly outside the capitals did not prevent the appearance of vibrant club theatricals.[133]

The persistence of club and amateur theatricals in St Petersburg and Moscow might have been a consequence of the commercial uncertainties entailed in running permanent theatres after 1882 (clubs, for instance, were smaller and enjoyed other sources of income). Yet it also suggests that such theatricals were popular in their own right and were not simply substitutes for legitimate theatre. Moreover, before 1882 some of the organizers of club performances, and many of their participants, were Imperial Theatre artists.[134] In 1901 the Russian Theatre Society (which had emerged in the 1890s as a national regulatory association for theatre people) received a letter signed by twenty-four actors who complained of being unable to find work in St Petersburg's clubs on account of the number of Imperial Theatre artists employed by them.[135] Clearly, then, this was not merely an underground entertainment scene organized by people who were excluded from legitimate theatre, as Ostrovsky had implied. This does not mean that he failed to persuade the new administration that the monopoly had encouraged such entertainments, which in turn had impeded the development of Russian art. Indeed, although there is no corroborative evidence, Vorontsov-Dashkov's comments about unsuitable entertainments were probably prompted by Ostrovsky's critique. But it was the mistaken *critique* that was influential, not demand for legitimate theatre *per se*.

Interpreting the decision as a response to pressure from writers is also problematic. Of all the monopoly's critics whose views had been published during the 1870s, only Ostrovsky was involved with theatrical reform during 1881 and 1882. As noted above, however, he had advocated that a new national theatre should be established *before* the abrogation of the monopoly. He initially sought permission for his own private venture, not full freedom of the theatres. Moreover, pressure from impresarios like Brenko does not provide a fully convincing explanation. Quite apart from the fact that the link between her petitions of 1881 and Vorontsov-Dashkov's report of March 1882 is unclear, it is important to emphasize that Brenko already had her theatre (albeit under difficult conditions) and that the directorate had likewise granted permission to several impresarios to run ventures during the 1860s and 1870s. The directorate, in other words, had effectively regulated the theatrical life of the capitals while accommodating a number of requests for private theatres and could have continued to do so.

While there is little evidence of a sudden rise in demand for theatricals on the eve of the monopoly's abolition, in November 1881 Vsevolozhsky noted in a report submitted to Vorontsov-Dashkov that 'very often many charitable societies and individuals' approached him with requests for permission to organize 'concerts and performances'. He went on to explain that, since the 'issue of the freedom of the theatres' had arisen, and in order to avoid troubling Vorontsov-Dashkov each time a request was received, he wanted the right to grant permission for 'charitable performances and concerts', to which the minister agreed.[136] Yet this was a reference to ad hoc theatricals organized for charitable purposes, which the directorate had long permitted on a case-by-case basis. Vsevolozhsky was presumably seeking to lighten the bureaucratic load in view of the demand for such events. But this does not in itself indicate a demand for full-time private theatres; nor does it explain why such theatres were soon able to exist without the permission of the directorate (which Vsevolozhsky ran) and in competition with the Imperial Theatres. The evidence, therefore, does not lend strong support to the view that it was demand that persuaded the government to abolish the monopoly. Vorontsov-Dashkov may have been right to claim that the 'mass of the public' wanted 'aesthetic pleasure', but his comments were founded on broad assumptions rather than growing clamour for the end of the monopoly.

This brings us to a fourth possible explanation, one that focuses on the new administration. Although Alexander III's reign is normally described by historians in terms of economic growth and political reaction, earlier chroniclers of his reign concentrated on portraying the tsar as a nationalist and generous patron of native culture who resisted the notion of Russia as a westernized or westernizing country and instead emphasized its own deep-rooted customs and beliefs, as symbolized by seventeenth-century Muscovy.[137] The new emphasis was prompted by several events and developments, including Russia's diplomatic humiliation at the Congress of Berlin in 1878, the 'rediscovery' of Asia and the assassination of Alexander II, and it was supported by Konstantin Pobedonostsev, the reactionary Procurator of the Holy Synod who became one of the most influential figures in Alexander III's administration, Vorontsov-Dashkov, Ignatev and others. Alexander III's

Muscovite revival defined itself in opposition to the westernist ambitions of Peter the Great (which had dominated political, cultural and economic thinking from the early eighteenth century) and was evident in, for example, the policy of Russification, efforts to strengthen the position of the Orthodox Church, and the construction of churches that imitated the Muscovite style, most prominently the Cathedral of the Resurrection of Christ (or the Saviour on the Blood), built on the spot where Alexander II was assassinated.

On a more personal level, the tsar's ardent Slavophilism was expressed in his anti-Germanism. His antagonism towards the prominent 'German element' at his father's court, which included the Adlerbergs and Kiester, was strengthened by his marriage to a Danish princess, Dagmar. Spending time in Denmark while tsarevich, he was influenced by Danish hostility to Bismarck, who had seized Schleswig-Holstein from Dagmar's father.[138] This influence was further reinforced by Alexander's difficult relationship with his Germanophile father. During the Franco-Prussian War, for example, Alexander II supported Bismarck, while the tsarevich placed his sympathies with France.[139]

As heir to the throne, Alexander shunned court life, preferring music and painting to balls and parades. He also resented the domination of foreign languages at court, and insisted on speaking Russian when he became tsar.[140] His inclinations were further evident in his patronage, as first honorary chairman, of the Imperial Russian Historical Society.[141] His dislike of court life was accompanied by an apparently genuine affection for the customs of ordinary Russians, and he appeared to identify with the *narod* rather than with the westernized circles of St Petersburg. For Kovalevsky, 'This was in truth a Russian *narodnyi* tsar, a tsar-nationalist.'[142] Alexander III demonstrated his Russianness by patronizing indigenous arts. He supported the Russian Musical Society, granting it the building of the St Petersburg Bolshoi Theatre and funds for the construction of the Conservatory.[143] He was a diligent collector of Russian art, notably by the Itinerants, or Wanderers, and founded the Russian Museum in St Petersburg to house his collection. As for theatre, his diary as tsarevich indicates that Alexander attended performances two or three times a week.[144]

Alexander III's administration thus contained elements that were disdainful of the court and dismissive of western culture. In that context, the abolition of the Imperial Theatre monopoly is more readily explicable. The new tsar was well disposed towards Ostrovsky's project for a national theatre in Moscow, and his dislike of the westernized court perhaps explains his willingness to entrust the new venture to private enterprise rather than to the directorate, which was, after all, part of the court administration. The idea of a theatre not run by the state appeared to complement the notion of a national theatre. Ostrovsky had hoped to establish his proposed venture before full freedom of the theatres was granted. Perhaps this was not understood by Vorontsov-Dashkov and Alexander III, or not clearly articulated by the playwright. At any rate, Ostrovsky failed to attract sufficient funding for his national theatre and the project lapsed. Ostrovsky subsequently attributed that failure to the abolition of the monopoly, writing that 'after I was granted permission for a private theatre the monopoly of the Imperial Theatres was rescinded, and profiteering, which had long awaited this moment, was unbridled and greedily threw itself on the spoils . . . To start a solid business at such a time was unwise: it was not possible to compete with people who had nothing to lose.'[145] Ostrovsky was, however, granted an opportunity to influence the direction of the Imperial Theatres when he was appointed artistic director of the Moscow Malyi. Unfortunately, this occurred only six months before his death in 1886. But his fundamental claim that the directorate had to be deprived of its exclusive right to organize legitimate theatre in the capitals had been accepted by the new administration, and the stage was set for the eventual emergence of new theatres.

The abolition of the monopoly, then, should be understood as a reaction to the perceived inability of the directorate to promote Russian theatre. From the 1850s onwards concerns had been expressed that the directorate favoured foreign troupes over Russian ones, and that native theatrical art was suffering as a consequence. During 1881 and 1882 Burdin's paper to Vsevolozhsky, the lobbying of Brenko and more particularly Ostrovsky brought these concerns to the attention of the new administration, which was clearly predisposed in favour of measures that might be construed as promoting indigenous Russian culture. Viewed in that context, the reform does not seem at odds with the new administration's agenda. Although it was understandably regarded outside the government as an act of liberalization, it was certainly not intended as a concession to progressive circles. In fact, paradoxical as it may seem, it is more accurate to see the abolition as part of Alexander III's conservative-nationalist programme.

The monopoly's abolition was immediately welcomed by cultural activists, and soon came to be regarded as a significant turning point in the development of late imperial Russian culture. For contemporaries, it constituted the 'freedom of the theatres' that some writers had demanded during the mid nineteenth century. One commentator claimed that the monopoly had impeded 'the development of free art' and that with its abrogation private theatres had 'received the right of citizenship'.[146] This view was even shared by certain officials within the directorate, notably Vladimir Pogozhev, who described it as the 'emancipation of artistic labour', seeing the consequences for the Imperial Theatres as no less serious than the consequences of the emancipation of the serfs for the nobility.[147] For Nikolai Drizen, a theatre historian and editor of the Imperial Theatre yearbook, Alexander III had 'liberated' the Russian theatre.[148] Contemporaries also associated the end of the monopoly with an anticipated invigoration of theatrical life. One observer immediately welcomed the reform as 'very gratifying', claiming that it would undoubtedly yield 'wholesome fruits' for Russian art in general and that private theatres, 'the benefits of which have, in recent years, been much talked about in the press', would soon appear.[149] At the end of 1882, one journal depicted the monopoly as a rotten oak tree whose collapse had enabled the mushrooming of new, if so far undistinguished, theatres (see figure 14).[150] In 1900, Pogozhev described the 'huge consequences' of the reform, including 'the appearance of a whole series of theatres in St Petersburg and Moscow', while 'the best artistic talents of the provinces began to be drawn to the capital' and 'for the first time the Imperial Theatres had to reckon with private competition'.[151] Later historians have generally concurred with these early assessments of the reform's significance, claiming that the monopoly placed severe restrictions on the development of Russian theatre, and that its abolition helped to facilitate its 'golden age'.[152]

The removal of the monopoly, of course, did not in itself lead to the proliferation of theatres or generate the innovation that characterized much of their late imperial activity, but it established the formal conditions that enabled impresarios to organize private theatres without hindrance from the state. In that sense, even though the theatrical worlds of St Petersburg and Moscow were not to be transformed overnight, the demise of the monopoly was of major symbolic significance, marking a vital stage in the campaign for greater control over the production of late imperial Russia's theatrical culture by its fledgling civil society.

Chapter 4

METROPOLITAN IMPRESARIOS

The abolition of the Imperial Theatre monopoly meant that, for the first time since the late eighteenth century, private commercial theatres could be established in the capitals without the prior approval of the state. Although there was no sudden proliferation of theatres, within two decades the theatrical landscapes of St Petersburg and Moscow had been transformed almost beyond recognition. The two cities possessed six Imperial Theatres between them in 1882. By 1901, the five remaining imperial stages had been joined by fourteen private commercial theatres in St Petersburg and twelve in Moscow. (The Bolshoi Kamenny had closed in 1886 – the building was acquired by the Russian Musical Society and, after extensive reconstruction, became the permanent home of the St Petersburg Conservatory.) In addition, there were seventeen 'pleasure garden enterprises' in St Petersburg and four 'summer enterprises' in Moscow which included theatrical entertainments.[1] During 1902, no fewer than forty-two summer theatres were counted in the environs of St Petersburg, and the number was expected to rise during the following summer.[2] As private, non-governmental ventures, these theatres demonstrated the capacity of civil society to create new artistic institutions, even though many had a short duration. They also demonstrated the capacity of theatre to contribute to the further development of late imperial Russia's civil society.

Who were the pioneers of private commercial theatres in the capitals? Why did they establish theatres? What obstacles did they face? What contributions did their enterprises make? In addressing these questions, attention will be paid to four individuals who were especially instrumental in the development of the capitals' vibrant commercial theatre culture after 1882: Fyodor Korsh, Savva Mamontov, Alexei Suvorin and Mikhail Lentovsky. Together they represented the growing confidence of impresarios that freedom of the theatres provided them with a much-needed opportunity to make a significant impact on the entertainment worlds of St Petersburg and Moscow. Their stories illustrate both the institutional emergence of a theatrical civil society in the capitals – that is to say, theatres that were independent of the state – and the growing cultural pluralism of urban Russia, a key characteristic of a genuine civil society.

The most famous of the theatrical enterprises to appear after 1882 was the Moscow Art Theatre (1898–present) of Konstantin Stanislavsky and Vladimir Nemirovich-Danchenko, which has been the subject of many studies and will be covered in chapter 7. While its reputation for technical innovation and cultural prominence is deserved, the historiographical attention accorded the Moscow Art Theatre and its co-founders has tended to obscure the contributions of other prominent impresarios who established important theatrical ventures before 1898, some of which prefigured the reforms that were subsequently attributed to Stanislavsky and Nemirovich-Danchenko. Other notable examples of the successful private theatre included the Korsh Theatre (Moscow, 1882–1917), the Mamontov Private Opera (Moscow, 1885–1904) and the Suvorin Theatre (St Petersburg, 1895–1917). Mamontov's operatic enterprise is included here as an example of what could be achieved under freedom of the theatres. In each of these three cases, private wealth helped to guarantee survival. Lentovsky, by contrast, lacked private resources, and hence his ventures proved more transient.

The Korsh, Mamontov and Suvorin theatres, as independent enterprises supported by private wealth, contributed to the wider social trend that was gradually challenging the state as the curator of artistic culture and the arbiter of identity. The leading figures behind these theatres were all representatives of Russian modernization: Korsh was a lawyer who had benefited from the 1864 judicial reform; Mamontov was a railroad magnate who had benefited from the state's economic policies; and Suvorin was a publisher who had benefited from the contemporaneous rise of the newspaper industry and the spread of literacy. But why did they establish theatres?

Fyodor Adamovich Korsh (1852–1923) was born in the Caucasus, the son of a doctor in the Georgian Grenadiers. After studying Oriental languages at the Lazarevsky Institute, he read law at Moscow University, where he acquired his passion for theatre. He indulged his interest by organizing amateur dramatics, and according to one account always ensured that the proceeds from such performances went to 'poor and indigent people'.[3] Lest it should be assumed, however, that Korsh was motivated by sympathy for impoverished Muscovites, we should remember that the only way to gain permission to stage amateur theatricals for ticket-buying audiences in Moscow before 1882 was to donate the proceeds to charity. After graduating in 1872, Korsh worked as a barrister, gaining a prominent position among the Moscow *advokatura*. The extent of his involvement in the theatre between 1872 and 1882 is unclear, but the rapidity with which he established his enterprise after the abolition of the Imperial Theatre monopoly suggests that he was relatively well connected and involved at some level.

Within a few months of the announcement on the freedom of the theatres, Korsh had organized a troupe of actors and actresses for what became the first permanent private theatre in Moscow. It opened on 30 August 1882 under the official name of the Russian Drama Theatre, although it was popularly known as the Korsh Theatre. The date of the inaugural performance was significant because it was also the traditional opening night of the Imperial Theatre season, signalling that Korsh's venture was to compete directly with the state-sponsored drama theatre in Moscow, the Malyi. Indeed, it was initially located only a few streets away from the Malyi, in the Lianozov House on Gazetnyi Lane. It subsequently moved to purpose-built premises on Petrovsky Lane designed by the architect Chichagov. The new theatre building was constructed on land owned by the Bakhrushin family, one of whose scions was soon to establish the first Russian theatre museum (see chapter 5). Korsh paid the Bakhrushins an annual fee for use of the land, initially 8,000 rubles, rising to 12,600 by the end of the 1880s, and to 13,000 by the end of the 1890s, although this was still less than the 20,520 rubles he had been paying for use of the Lianozov House.[4]

Korsh formed his troupe from the remnants of Anna Brenko's venture at the Pushkin Theatre, and among the notable talents that he inherited were Modest Pisarev, Vasily Dalmatov, and Vasily Andreyev-Burlak. His initial suggestion that the new theatre be organized as a share-holding venture met with a negative response from the troupe, and he also failed to secure financial support from the Moscow duma or from business interests.[5] As a result, the new venture was initially funded from Korsh's private resources. The financial records of the theatre show that each year he personally made up the difference between income and expenditure, the level of his contributions serving as a general indication of the wider commercial fortunes of his theatre:

Season	Korsh's contribution
1883–4	40,294 r. 36 k.
1884–5	21,219 r. 70 k.
1885–6	21,677 r. 85 k.
1886–7	10,456 r. 55 k.
1887–8	5,215 r. 45 k.
1888–9	2,162 r. 25 k.
1889–90	7,480 r. 30 k.[6]

The fact that Korsh was gradually able to reduce his personal subsidies suggests that his theatre managed to establish itself as a commercially viable enterprise. Consequently, in 1885 Korsh again attempted to organize his theatre on a stock-holding basis. In a brochure designed to attract investors, he emphasized that his venture had survived for three years and now had the right to exist. Moreover, the recipe for success had been discovered and would be adhered to: 'In the course of time, the character of the theatre has been definitively formed; the comparative failure of big plays, with expensive sets, has shown that security for the success of the enterprise lies exclusively in the careful performance of pure comedy, with an impeccable ensemble.'[7] The theatre, wrote Korsh, had followed this aim energetically during the previous season, and he provided statistics indicating that performance returns were favourable. It is not entirely clear whether a joint-stock company was created, but it is probable that the sharp reduction in Korsh's personal contributions to the theatre's finances from the 1886–7 season was made possible by contributions from other investors. Either way, the evidence indicates that the new theatre was a commercial success in the 1880s. During the second half of the 1890s, Korsh's personal contribution temporarily climbed again. During the 1896–7 season, it amounted to over eighteen thousand rubles, but dropped the following season to just over three thousand. By 1905 Korsh was receiving money from the theatre's accounts, ranging from a few hundred to a few thousand rubles per annum.[8]

In her memoirs, Anna Brenko implied that Korsh was motivated by hopes of pecuniary gain: 'Korsh knew that large revenues can come from theatre and continuously shouted that it is a golden business.'[9] The comment perhaps betrays a certain bitterness on Brenko's part over the financial collapse of the Pushkin, and is somewhat belied by Korsh's own investment in the enterprise. Korsh himself later claimed that he was motivated by four main aims:

1) to give the Moscow public a stage that would satisfy its growing theatrical-aesthetic needs, 2) to give the most talented provincial artists the opportunity to work and perfect themselves in conditions more favourable and regular than in the provinces, 3) as far as possible to promote the well-being of dramatic literature by staging the works of new dramatists, 4) to make the best dramatic works of native and foreign authors as accessible as possible to the greatest number of the public and to the growing young generation by staging these works at generally accessible performances with prices reduced to a minimum.[10]

The repertoire of the Korsh Theatre included some notable firsts. Chekhov's first major play, *Ivanov*, was premiered there in November 1887, as were one of the earliest Russian productions of Ibsen's *A Doll's House* (November 1891, with the title *Nora*) and the first Moscow production of his *An Enemy of the People* (1892–3 season). Plays with historical themes figured prominently, but with varying degrees of success. They included Bukharin's *Izmail*, centred on the capture of the fortress of Izmail during the Russo-Turkish wars of the second half of the eighteenth century, and featuring national heroes like Rumiantsev, Suvorov and Potemkin; François Coppée's *The Jacobites*; and Pierre Berton's *A Marseille Beauty*. But the repertoire, at least until 1907, was dominated by the Russian classics, especially the works of Ostrovsky, Gogol, Griboyedov and Fonvizin, most of them brimming with comical and satirical characters. In general, Korsh did not interfere in the artistic side of the theatre, being content to provide the entrepreneurial energy for it. As one actress recalled, 'It seemed that he was always on the move, aspiration personified.'[11] Yet Korsh took a keen interest in literary work, successfully adapting and translating several foreign plays for the Russian stage, notably Victorien Sardou's popular comedy *Madame Sans-Gêne*, as well as writing a few plays himself, such as *The Matchmaker*.

The claim that the Korsh Theatre exercised 'a colossal influence on many other Russian stages' is probably an exaggeration.[12] But it was innovative in several important respects. Its very durability confirmed that, by the 1880s, there was sufficient demand for a new theatre in Moscow. Korsh pioneered the inexpensive matinée performance in order to attract young people and students to his theatre. At the imperial Malyi, only approximately 130 seats out of 1,100 cost less than one ruble (thirty to sixty kopeks). The Korsh Theatre had a capacity of 1,300, and during its matinée performances at least half the seats cost less than one ruble, with 256 seats costing as little as ten to thirty-five kopeks.[13] Even if the intention was to ensure regular full houses, Korsh certainly succeeded in his professed aim of making performances 'generally accessible'. Moreover, the Korsh Theatre was the first in Russia to be completely illuminated by electric lighting (although not, as claimed, the first in the world: London's Savoy Theatre beat it by several months).[14] In addition, the first production of a historical drama to strive for detailed authenticity (N. A. Chaev's *Vasily Shuisky*) was staged at Korsh's theatre. Finally, the Korsh Theatre had important symbolic significance, in that it demonstrated that a durable private theatre, free of the routines of the Imperial Theatres, was possible in the capitals. During the twenty-fifth anniversary celebrations in August 1907, in one of the many telegrams sent to Korsh, the writer and dramatist Evgeny Chirikov offered his congratulations and expressed the hope that 'we are all still working in a free theatre without the surveillance of depressed noncommissioned officers'.[15]

Savva Mamontov (1841–1918), like Korsh, was not a native of Moscow. He was born into a Siberian family which had relocated to Moscow by the early 1850s. Mamontov studied law at Moscow University, again like Korsh, but instead of pursuing a legal career joined the family business, predominantly railway construction, largely at his father's prompting. Savva's real interests, however, lay in the arts. He had learned to sing as a child, and during the 1860s became involved, much to his father's chagrin, with a Moscow student circle dedicated to theatre reform.[16] During the winter of 1872, while holidaying in Rome, the Mamontov family surrounded themselves with young artists and students, and on his return to Moscow the inspired Savva participated in the Artistic Circle. In addition to singing, Mamontov dabbled competently in acting, sculpture, writing and directing.

Mamontov's cultural tastes were a complex blend of traditionalism and modernism. He was reputedly fond of the Latin phrase 'Ars longa, vita brevis' (life is short, art endures),[17] and he displayed a keen interest in a variety of artistic styles without seeming to privilege one over the other. He established an 'artists' colony' at his country estate of Abramtsevo during 1872–3, where representatives of the Itinerants, among them Ilya Repin, Valentin Serov and the Vasnetsov brothers, Apollinary and Victor, went on to develop the Russian style in art.[18] He and his wife also displayed an interest in old Russian folk crafts, and fearing their demise as the country modernized, promoted peasant crafts at Abramtsevo.[19] They also constructed an old-style church on the estate in 1882, after a design by Victor Vasnetsov. But Mamontov's encouragement of traditional Russian styles in art and architecture was not dogmatic or exclusivist. His support for modernism, for example, was expressed in his sponsorship of Sergei Diaghilev's *Mir iskusstva* (World of Art) in 1898 to the tune of twelve thousand rubles, almost half of the journal's costs.[20] Mamontov's generous sponsorship of the arts soon earned him the sobriquet of Moscow's Lorenzo de' Medici,[21] and his reputation is reflected in the fact that his portrait was painted by at least two of the great artists of the time, Mikhail Vrubel and Repin.

Mamontov's passions for music and the visual arts found their natural expression in opera, which he was fond of producing on an amateur basis at his home. In 1884, however, he conceived the idea of establishing his own commercial opera theatre in Moscow. His motives are unlikely to have been financial. Mamontov was already very wealthy, and he anyway continued to pursue his other business interests. According to Rossikhina, who has produced the most scholarly history of the Private Opera to date, the immediate impetus came from two musical events of 1884 which together persuaded Mamontov that he could offer the Moscow public something valuable. The first was a performance of N. S. Krotkov's opera *The Scarlet Rose* before a specially invited audience at Abramtsevo, the success of which convinced Mamontov that the work he sponsored was starting to receive the 'serious, sincere approval of connoisseurs'.[22] Shortly afterwards Mamontov was invited to organize a performance of Robert Schumann's *Manfred* music as part of a concert held in celebration of Nikolai Rubinstein, and again his efforts were warmly received.[23] This lends credence to the view that Mamontov's primary intention was to demonstrate the possibilities for opera, particularly through the application of modern art to its staging. Contemporaries commented that the Private Opera signalled a self-conscious break from traditional routines, meaning the production practices of the Bolshoi.[24] More broadly, Mamontov appears to have believed in the wider social responsibilities of art, and is reputed to have claimed that artists and poets are the 'property of the people [*narod*]' and that 'the country will be strong if the people are imbued with an understanding of them'.[25] He also maintained that it was the task of civil society to organize the arts. According to music historian Abram Gozenpud, 'Mamontov was convinced that industry and art could be developed in Russia only with the aid of private initiative.'[26]

The Private Opera Theatre duly opened on 9 January 1885. It was initially located in the premises of the Korsh Theatre on Gazetnyi Lane for its twice-weekly performances; when the Korsh moved in the autumn of 1885, the Private Opera remained there, although it subsequently relocated to the

Solodovnikovsky theatre building.[27] Like Korsh, Mamontov devoted considerable energy and resources to his theatre but delegated artistic matters to others. The first director of the Private Opera was Krotkov, and although Mamontov's son later claimed that the enterprise was his father's 'favourite child',[28] there was some reluctance to publicize his involvement too openly: the playbill for the opening night made no mention of the theatre's owner, but described it as the 'Private opera troupe in Moscow of N. S. Krotkov'.[29] The inaugural production was Dargomyzhsky's *Rusalka*, the critical response to which foreshadowed the general reaction to the Private Opera for the next two decades: the scenery, especially for the underwater kingdom, produced from sketches by Victor Vasnetsov, was well received, but there was less enthusiasm for the singers and the musicians, who were no more than adequate.[30] Nevertheless, the Private Opera soon gained a reputation for staging challenging productions, especially of works by native composers, which the Imperial Theatres had generally neglected, even though the several Russian operas staged by Mamontov during the first season were the least well attended.[31] The financial fortunes of Mamontov's venture were mixed. It initially operated for two seasons, was temporarily liquidated in 1887, and was then resurrected in 1896. It almost closed again in 1899 after Mamontov was implicated in a financial scandal involving his other businesses, but was kept going by some of the performers as the Association of the Russian Private Opera until 1904.[32]

Alexei Sergeyevich Suvorin (1834–1912) was born into a peasant family in the village of Korshevo in Voronezh province. In 1851, he graduated from the Voronezh military school, but soon abandoned an army career for primary school teaching and journalism. In the early 1860s, he became a full-time journalist, moving to Moscow and then St Petersburg. Suvorin gradually established a reputation for himself as a journalist and writer, but suffered a personal tragedy in 1873 when his wife was shot dead by her lover. Although he remarried two years later, he devoted most of his energy to his work. In 1876, he raised the money to buy the failing newspaper the *New Times*, which he proceeded to revitalize into 'the nation's most powerful newspaper'[33] and which, together with his major publishing house, secured his fortune.[34] Suvorin also gained a reputation for his political views, initially flirting with liberalism in the 1860s, but subsequently transforming himself into a prominent – and notoriously antisemitic – conservative who advocated strong central authority of the Hobbesian type.[35]

Like many public figures of the time, Suvorin indulged his predilection for the arts, especially the theatre. He was a keen amateur dramatist – his best-known plays included *Tatyana Repina*[36] – and was well connected in cultural spheres, counting Chekhov among his regular correspondents.[37] Suvorin was also an active member of the St Petersburg Literary-Artistic Circle, and it was the success of the circle's production of Gerhart Hauptmann's previously banned *Hannele* that persuaded its members, notably Alexander Kugel, Pyotr Gnedich and Pavel Lensky, to establish a permanent theatre.[38] Suvorin emerged as the principal investor and chief organizer. This augured well for the fortunes of the new theatre, in that Suvorin's considerable financial resources would be able to shield it from commercial unpredictability. Indeed, in June 1897 Suvorin confided to his diary that he expected the theatre to suffer losses once again in the forthcoming season, but that he was not inclined to abandon the project.[39]

Like Korsh and Mamontov, Suvorin delegated everyday artistic matters to others, inviting the provincial actor Fadeyev to form a troupe and to direct performances. He also invited Evtikhy Karpov to work as a régisseur in the new theatre. By his own account, Karpov was surprised at the invitation because he was not personally acquainted with the publishing baron and, more importantly, 'Our social views were very different.'[40] Karpov was, however, reassured by Gnedich, who had approached him on Suvorin's behalf, that the aims of the new theatre were purely artistic and that it would eschew any political tendency.[41]

The Suvorin Theatre opened on 17 September 1895 and quickly became the most important private theatre in St Petersburg.[42] Suvorin appears to have permitted his régisseurs a fair degree of independence. He himself was disinclined towards Ostrovsky and reputedly found Ibsen's plays cold,[43] yet the theatre's inaugural production was Ostrovsky's *The Storm* and its second was Ibsen's *A Doll's House*. There were times when the repertoire reflected his own rather controversial views, such as in 1900, when the theatre gained notoriety for its production of the blatantly antisemitic drama by V. Krylov and S. Litvin *Contrabandists (The Sons of Israel)*. But it also staged relatively progressive drama, often producing works that were neglected by the Imperial Theatres and even by other private theatres in Russia. Among the notable premieres were Lev Tolstoy's *The Power of Darkness* (1895), A. K. Tolstoy's *Tsar Fyodor Ioannovich* (1898), Alexander Sukhovo-Kobylin's *The Death of Tarelkin* (1900) and S. A. Naidenov's *Vaniushin's Children* (1901). *The Power of Darkness* had in fact been banned, but Suvorin used his connections to persuade the censor to permit its production. The play was premiered on 16 October 1895, two days before it was staged at the Alexandrinsky Theatre and three days before it appeared at the Korsh Theatre. The censor had expunged only Mitrich's scathing comments about the banking system in Act 3, but after five performances they were reinstated with the censor's permission.[44] With such influence wielded by its impresario, the Suvorin Theatre soon became something of a cultural authority in the imperial capital.

This brief introduction to three of the major theatrical impresarios of late imperial Russia suggests that, in establishing private theatres, Korsh, Mamontov and Suvorin were motivated not by politics or pecuniary interests but by an affection for the theatre. Their agendas were emphatically cultural, with very few apparent exceptions. It is often suggested that members of Russia's new professional and especially business elites were drawn to the arts by something other than mere enthusiasm, namely by the need for 'social approval' within a culture that was fundamentally hostile to entre-preneurialism and 'vulgar profiteering'.[45] Although many Russians embraced and excelled at entrepreneurialism, social prestige did not necessarily result from money-making of this sort, as it often did, for example, in nineteenth-century Britain. By contrast, the pursuit of intellectual and artistic activities was regarded as an honourable endeavour because such activities were supposedly concerned with truth-seeking rather than personal gain. Hence, it is argued, the number of businessmen who patronized the arts.[46] While there might be some validity in this view, it should be emphasized that the body of evidence relating to the impresarios discussed above contains no real indication that their theatrical patronage was in any sense a self-conscious bid for social status. In fact, Mamontov's reluctance to have his name printed on the playbills of his Private Opera suggests a degree of diffidence in declaring his patronage of the arts, despite the esteem it would have brought him in some circles. Whatever their motives, the activity of the impresarios undoubtedly possessed wider significance as a relatively high-profile dimension of civil society. Moreover, although largely devoid of political ambition, these vibrant, independent cultural institutions further undermined the tsarist regime's monopoly on identity by promoting (most likely unwittingly) a sense of cultural pluralism – that is to say, a situation in which a rich multiplicity of cultural interests, producers and identities appear able to coexist. This was particularly evident in their explorations of the Russian past and its folklore, to which we now turn.

As commercial enterprises, the theatres of Korsh, Mamontov and Suvorin were obliged to adopt repertoires that appealed to popular taste. Although all three received financial backing from their wealthy patrons, none could afford to function as a fully subsidized organization in the manner of the Imperial Theatres. Their audiences generally consisted of members of the intelligentsia, including writers and artists, as well as professionals, merchants and students,[47] and in order to maintain the support of this relatively diverse range of people, preference was normally given to works with a proven ability to attract a broad audience. This meant that the repertoires of the Korsh and Suvorin theatres tended to be dominated by light comedies and the Russian classics; and when Mamontov needed to bolster his box-office takings he invited popular Italian singers to join his troupe. Occasionally, however, these three theatres experimented with genres and themes that were not guaranteed to win popular approbation, even though they might draw critical acclaim. Notable in this respect were the Korsh Theatre's production of N. A. Chaev's *Tsar and Grand Duke of All Rus, Vasily Ivanovich Shuisky*, the Private Opera's production of Rimsky-Korsakov's operatic adaptation of Ostrovsky's *The Snow Maiden*, and the Suvorin Theatre's production of A. K. Tolstoy's *Tsar Fyodor Ioannovich*. Although the numbers of performances of the first two were not especially high, and although they were not commercial successes, they were arguably the most important productions staged by Korsh and Mamontov in that they established critical reputations for their ventures. *Tsar Fyodor Ioannovich* likewise strengthened the reputation of the Suvorin Theatre, but unlike the other two productions it enjoyed considerable commercial success. These three productions were important not simply because they coincided with an intellectual interest in history and folklore, but because they did so with a lavishness and extravagant attention to detail hitherto unseen in the Russian theatre. They stood out in bold relief from the mainstream repertoire as ambitious and studious explorations of Russia's heritage, not merely improvised spectacles intended to hypnotize audiences.

The new theatres' excursions into the Russian past are particularly intriguing for occurring at a time when the state was promoting Muscovite Russia as a model of stable autocratic government. Perhaps the most famous example of the late imperial court's fascination with Muscovy was the St Petersburg winter ball of February 1903, at which Nicholas II appeared as Tsar Alexei Mikhailovich.[48] Official interest in Muscovy can be traced at least to the reign of Nicholas I,[49] but it achieved especial prominence under Alexander III, who believed that the gradual westernization of Russia, particularly during and after the reign of Peter the Great, was responsible for the revolutionary agitation that had resulted in the assassination of his father. According to

Richard Wortman, Muscovy 'provided a model of an ethnically and religiously united people, ruled by an Orthodox tsar.'[50] But this model was derived from a carefully selected period of Muscovite history, namely the era following the Time of Troubles (1598–1613), during which Muscovy had been torn apart by dynastic disputes, social unrest and foreign invasion, and prior to the accession of Peter the Great (1689). As Wortman explains,

> The historical narrative of seventeenth-century Muscovy associated the origins of the Russian nation with the affirmation of monarchical authority after the breakdown period of 'Troubles' at the beginning of the seventeenth century. The seventeenth century was the paradigm for a recrudescence of state power that could reunite an administration divided in the previous reign by considerations of legality and institutional autonomy.[51]

In striking contrast to the regime's preoccupation with a supposedly unified seventeenth-century Muscovy in which tsar and people lived in harmony, the new private theatres of the late nineteenth century revisited the Muscovy of the late sixteenth century and the Time of Troubles. The Korsh Theatre's production of *Tsar and Grand Duke of All Rus, Vasily Ivanovich Shuisky* dealt with an era of monarchical usurpation, while the Suvorin Theatre's *Tsar Fyodor Ioannovich* depicted a period of weak rule and dastardly machinations behind the throne after the death of Ivan the Terrible – hardly positive portrayals of Muscovy and its political attributes. Whether this view of the Russian past was pursued in deliberate opposition to that of the state is unclear, and in fact unlikely. After all, most of the plays that had been written about Muscovy were understandably set amidst events that were conducive to gripping drama. It nevertheless confirms that the theatrical representations of Muscovy were not conceived as a means of bolstering state propaganda. Moreover, while the state's 'resurrection' of Muscovy was evidently inspired by political insecurity, the theatrical impresarios appear to have been motivated chiefly by an interest in Muscovite culture. This is certainly the impression given by the performance reviews, which tended to draw attention to the producers' efforts to ensure historical authenticity in terms of costumes, scenery and atmosphere.

The Korsh Theatre's production of Chaev's *Tsar and Grand Duke of All Rus, Vasily Ivanovich Shuisky*, or *Vasily Shuisky*, was the biggest event of its second season, 1883–4. It was directed by A. A. Yablochkin, and the expenditure on sets and costumes was so enormous (thirty-five thousand rubles) that the production almost bankrupted Korsh. Furthermore, despite critical approval, *Vasily Shuisky* failed to attract consistently large audiences and there was no box-office return on the investment. The production was nevertheless one of the most significant theatrical events of the 1880s and 1890s, notably because it was the first to aspire to historical authenticity, sixteen years before the Moscow Art Theatre became famous for similar endeavours. The costumes were designed from historical drawings, the furniture and weapons were copied from period originals held in the Kremlin armoury (where Chaev was a curator), and the make-up of the actor who played Shuisky was based on a rare portrait that the theatre had managed to track down abroad.[52] While such efforts might appear unsurprising by today's standards, they were innovative for 1883, particularly when compared to the lacklustre productions at the Imperial Theatres, which paid little heed to temporal or geographical accuracy.

The text of Chaev's play does not appear to have survived, at least in published form, and the reviews of performances at the Korsh Theatre reveal little about its structure, except that it was a simple chronicle and that its interest for audiences lay in its production style, its 'historical kaleidoscope'.[53] Vasily Shuisky was a leading boyar who reigned as tsar between 1606 and 1610. He had been Boris Godunov's great rival until Godunov's death in 1605, and had plotted to remove his successor, the False Dmitry, before the latter was beaten to death by a mob in 1606. Most of Shuisky's reign involved struggles between Moscow and a variety of rebellious movements, some supported by Sweden and Poland. When King Sigismund III invaded Muscovy and captured Smolensk, Shuisky was deposed and for the next three years Muscovy was governed by a boyar council.

The opening night of *Vasily Shuisky* was described by one critic as 'an unquestionable and fully deserved success'. The parterre was 'completely full' and only a few of the boxes were empty. Moreover, 'In terms of production and performance, nothing more could be wished for.' The performers were talented, and great expense had been lavished on the production. Both Chaev and Korsh, continued the reviewer, had made a 'prominent contribution' to society with *Vasily Shuisky*, immediately establishing the artistic importance of the new theatre. Statistics cited by the same critic indicate the scale of the production: there were thirteen different scenes (each with its own backdrop), 275 costumes and 950 props. 'The audience ardently applauded after each scene.'[54] Another reviewer confirmed the positive reception of the production, observing that 'The scenery is all new and very effective.'[55] Particular praise was reserved for the carefully choreographed crowd scenes, as another observer remembered:

> The best scene of the play was 'At the Novgorod market'. This is the scene between the people and Mikhail Skopin-Shuisky, who is persuading the Novgorodians to stand up for Rus. Ivanov-Kozelsky skilfully recited Skopin's monologue, but the first place undoubtedly belonged to 'the people'. The talented régisseur Yablochkin staged this scene wonderfully. His crowd 'lived', and when the action reached the execution of the traitor Tatishchev, the reality of the performance made the audience quiver.[56]

In contrast to *Vasily Shuisky*, Rimsky-Korsakov's opera *The Snow Maiden* was based on a traditional Russian folk tale, which Ostrovsky had popularized as a play, rather than on historical events. Mamontov's production nevertheless drew upon authentic Russian costumes and architecture for several scenes, notably the depiction of Tsar Berendey's palace. Premiered at the Private Opera on 8 October 1885, *The Snow Maiden* is a blend of mythology, paganism and folk customs. The opera's eponymous character is the child of Grandfather Frost and the Spring Fairy. Yarilo (the Sun) disapproves and withdraws his rays from her village, leaving it in a state of perpetual winter. To protect her from Yarilo, the Snow Maiden is kept hidden in a forest, guarded by a wood spirit. She is eventually tempted out of the forest by the sound of humans at play. Mizgir falls in love with her, but the Snow Maiden does not reciprocate. Tsar Berendey offers a reward to anyone who can win her heart. The Spring Fairy proceeds to use pagan magic to enable the Snow Maiden to fall in love. She gives her heart to Mizgir, but just before their wedding Yarilo touches her with a ray of sun, and the heroine melts. The inconsolable Mizgir drowns himself.

The critical response to *The Snow Maiden* was almost unanimous: the singers and the orchestra were substandard, but the scenery and props signalled a major turning point in the application of the decorative arts in the Russian theatre. S. Kruglikov, for example, attacked the orchestra but wrote, 'The costumes and the scenery are fresh, distinctive and beautiful. Even the magical transformations are not lacking in effect, despite the fact that they do not take place in time to the music. The direction is also meticulous, and all the folk [*narodnyi*] scenes are characterized by animation, intelligence and veracity.'[57] Another critic concluded that 'The costumes and the sets are very good; evidently a lot of money has been spent on them.'[58] One reviewer, praising its originality, referred to the production as 'a new era in the chronicle of our musical life',[59] while another remarked upon its 'wealth of imagination, style and splendour' and observed that 'Since the time when the Meiningen troupe was resident with us, we have not had occasion to see anything of similar artistic merit on any Russian stage.'[60]

The production of *The Snow Maiden* also allowed reviewers to wax lyrical about Russian art and music, even if they were relatively unimpressed by the technical aspects of the performance at the Private Opera. One critic pointed out that new operas with a 'Russian character' are a rarity and that 'it is impossible not to be ardently sympathetic towards the idea of serving Russian art'. He continued, 'to the lovers of patriotic art, one may recommend becoming acquainted with this work'.[61] Another asserted that 'Of the most recent composers, only Mussorgsky can compete with Rimsky-Korsakov in the portrayal of everyday (particularly historical-everyday) scenes, but in the portrayal of magical elements perhaps no one nowadays is in a position to contend with him.'[62] The explanation for the success of *The Snow Maiden* lay in Mamontov's long-standing support for modern Russian artists and their work on folk culture, much of it carried out at Abramtsevo. The sets, for example, were based on sketches by Victor Vasnetsov, and were worked on by, among others, Konstantin Korovin and Isaac Levitan. Research for the production had been conducted in Tula province (although the playbills claimed that it was based on costumes from Ryazan and Smolensk).[63] Like the Korsh Theatre before it, and the Suvorin Theatre and Moscow Art Theatre after it, the Private Opera had succeeded, albeit through a fairy tale, in conveying to audiences a sense of cultural veracity and of the possibilities of native Russian art.

The Suvorin Theatre's production of A. K. Tolstoy's *Tsar Fyodor Ioannovich* was both an artistic and a commercial success. It was premiered on 12 October 1898, two days before the more famous Moscow Art Theatre production. By the spring of 1900 it had already reached its hundredth performance, a considerable number by the standards of the Russian repertoire, which tended to stage large numbers of plays and perform them infrequently.[64] Tolstoy's play centres on the rivalries between the Shuisky family and Boris Godunov for influence over Tsar Fyodor (reigned 1584–98), the frail successor to Ivan the Terrible and the last of the Riurikid dynasty. When Godunov has the supporters of the Shuiskys arrested, they incite a rebellion and seek to have Fyodor divorced from his wife (Godunov's sister) so that they can proclaim Dmitry (another son of Ivan the Terrible) as tsar. Fyodor is willing to relinquish the throne, but the idea of divorcing his wife sends him into a rage and he allows Godunov to deal with the Shuiskys. The Suvorin Theatre was permitted to stage a largely uncensored version of the play. The excisions related to religious figures such as the Metropolitan, who did not have significant parts within the story.[65]

The production was highly praised by the critics for its effective staging and the quality of the acting. One reviewer claimed that during several scenes the audience was able to forget that it was watching a theatrical event, and that the play 'transported them to the remote epoch of the reign of the "meekest" son of the Terrible tsar'.[66] In a more extensive review, the same writer recorded that the actor in the main role, Orlenev, had succeeded in portraying the various facets of Fyodor's personality – his weak character and limited intelligence, as well as his 'elevated soulful qualities', the 'pure soul of the ideal Christian'. The actor Tinsky was a 'genuine Godunov' who depicted the 'most important feature' of his character, namely 'his striving for a noble aim, for the good of the Russian land'. Moreover, in even the smallest details it was 'historically faithful'.[67] According to another critic, the performance was a 'great success' and was a 'genuine triumph' for Orlenev: 'It can justifiably be said that Orlenev created the role of Tsar Fyodor.' The critic also remarked favourably on the historical details and external effects, notably 'the horseman moving at full speed across the stage, the departure from the church with the ringing of the bells, the breaking of the fence and so on'.[68]

As theatrical impresarios, Korsh, Mamontov and Suvorin thus made an important contribution to the development of late imperial Russia's civil society, but not merely because their enterprises augmented the growing number of private, non-state institutions that enjoyed reasonably high public profiles. Equally if not more important were the cultural pluralism and flexibility of identity that the impresarios and their theatres appeared to reveal. As individuals, Korsh, Mamontov and Suvorin exemplified the new professional and entrepreneurial elites that the 'great reforms' of the 1860s and 1870s had created. They were the astute, university-educated businessmen of urban Russia who had benefited from, as well as contributing to, the ongoing process of modernization in Russia.

Yet their fundamental modernity did not constrain their cultural interests, but rather expanded them. Between them the impresarios identified with a variety of styles and tastes, and constantly seemed to resist uniformity, to defy neat classification according to cultural or even at times occupational identity. Simultaneously inhabiting the contemporaneous worlds of progressive ideas, conservatism, commerce and the professions, as well as dabbling in the curiosities of Muscovy and native Russian crafts, the patrons of private theatre appeared to possess composite identities, none of whose components predominated for any length of time. In other words, Korsh, Mamontov and Suvorin arguably typified the 'modularity' that Ernest Gellner suggested is the essential precondition for an effective civil society. They did not allow their modernity to monopolize their identity, nor was the state able to manipulate their approach to imperial Russia's Muscovite legacy. It might be suggested, therefore, that the activity of the theatrical impresarios of late imperial Russia simultaneously cultivated and exposed both the 'institutional and [the] ideological pluralism' considered essential to civil society. Of course, the identification of a perhaps superficial cultural pluralism does not in itself demonstrate the existence of a robust civil society. The examples highlighted here, however, collectively suggest that the state's capacity to influence theatrical life was weakening as civil society advanced.

Korsh, Mamontov and Suvorin all established a particular type of theatre, namely the artistically serious and financially sustainable (if only because shored up at key moments by wealthy patrons). Yet the theatrical landscapes of St Petersburg and Moscow after 1882 also witnessed many ephemeral ventures which were unable to withstand commercial pressure, despite fashioning their repertoires for mass audiences. Notwithstanding their lack of durability, such enterprises bore further testimony to the tentative emergence of a commercial theatre culture in the capitals. They included the St Petersburg ventures of A. F. Kartavov, who staged Russian drama at the Malyi (Apraksin) Theatre between 1882 and 1885, and G. A. Arbenin (pseudonym of Sergei Palm, son of the dramatist A. I. Palm), who staged operettas and vaudevilles at the same venue from 1885 to 1895. Examples from Moscow included the theatres of K. O. Shcherbinsky (1885), Maria Abramova (1889–90) and Elizaveta Goreva (1889–91). Although Abramova had inherited a fortune and Goreva's companion was able to bankroll her venture, a combination of financial mismanagement and lukewarm critical responses to productions led to the failure of both theatres.[69] The most prominent impresario who represented this type of enterprise was Mikhail Lentovsky. His circumstances differed from those of Korsh, Mamontov and Suvorin in two significant and related respects. First of all, Lentovsky initially pursued a career in acting and devoted himself entirely to the theatre. Secondly, he had no financial resources from other interests or businesses which he could draw upon to bolster his ventures. This partly explains why Lentovsky found it difficult to establish his theatres as commercial successes: during the 1880s and 1890s, the market remained too weak to maintain private theatres without some level of subsidy.

Lentovsky was born in Saratov in 1843.[70] His father had once performed as a violinist in a serf orchestra, but later trained as a feldsher, a career that he expected the young Mikhail to pursue. In 1861, however, following an inspirational performance by the popular provincial actor Nikolai Rybakov in Saratov, Lentovsky decided to abandon his education for an acting career. In October 1862 he wrote to Shchepkin, declaring his passion for theatre and appealing for financial assistance to bring him to Moscow.[71] The veteran actor was so moved by the letter that he agreed to help, and Lentovsky duly arrived in the city in January 1863 to live and learn the theatrical arts in the actor's house. Although Shchepkin passed away a few months later, there was still time to instil a few basic principles in the young enthusiast and to introduce him to the Malyi Theatre, where he performed for a short time.

Between 1865 and 1869, Lentovsky developed his craft in various provincial theatres. In 1869, he joined Pyotr Medvedev's troupe, intending to work winter seasons in Kazan and summer seasons in Saratov, but within a few months he transferred to Kharkov, where he gained his first experience as a régisseur in Nikolai Dyukov's company. During the 1871–2 season Lentovsky was based in Odessa, where he worked with the circus impresario Wilhelm Sur in the capacities of artist, régisseur and manager. Then in 1873 he was invited to return to the Malyi Theatre in Moscow, where he remained until 1882, performing mainly in operettas.

While employed as an Imperial Theatre artist, Lentovsky also pursued other ventures. He performed as a *kupletist* – a reciter of couplets, or singer of satirical songs – in places like the Slavyansky Bazaar restaurant in central Moscow. In 1876 he became involved with the Artistic Circle, and in 1877 organized the circle's summer entertainments, mainly operettas, at the Moscow zoological gardens. In the winter of 1878, he received permission from the directorate of Imperial Theatres to rent the Solodovnikovsky Passazh Theatre, which he renamed the Bouffe, for performances of *variété* and operetta.

Lentovsky's most durable enterprise was the Hermitage summer garden in Moscow, which he rented from 1878 to 1893. A pleasure garden with a theatre, a restaurant and an outdoor stage, the Hermitage catered to a wide cross-section of the Moscow population, including merchants, artisans, members of the intelligentsia and nobility.[72] Lentovsky expended great effort in renovating the gardens, in 1880 building a new wooden theatre, and in 1882 installing gas lighting around the gardens and constructing a new outdoor stage called the Fantastical Theatre.[73] His aim, he later wrote, was to 'enhance the convenience and pleasure of the visiting public'.[74] In addition to running the Bouffe in the winter and the Hermitage in the summer, Lentovsky pursued several ventures outside Moscow. For example, in 1881 he organized a drama theatre in Nizhny Novgorod, as well as entertainments at the Arcadia gardens in St Petersburg.[75]

The abolition of the Imperial Theatre monopoly meant that Lentovsky no longer had to limit his theatrical entrepreneurialism to summer entertainments or *variété* and operetta. In November 1882 he left the government stage as part of a general reduction in the number of state-employed actors (although he retained the right to refer to himself as an 'artist of the Imperial Theatre'), and in the same month opened the Skomorokh in Moscow, his most important venture yet, intended as a people's (*narodnyi*) drama theatre. The inaugural production was Dmitry Averkiev's *The Comedy of the Russian Nobleman Frol Skobeyev*, with Lentovsky in the title role, one of his favourites. The theatre closed in 1883 for financial reasons, but later reopened at a different location.[76]

By this time, Lentovsky had established a solid reputation as an impresario, and he was invited to organize the official entertainments at Khodynka Field in Moscow to mark the coronation of Alexander III in May 1883. The programme reflected the blend of music and spectacle that Lentovsky liked to produce. The entertainments began at midday with fairground peep-shows, puppet booths, swings, seesaws and an army chorus. At two o'clock there was a burst of cannon fire, followed by orchestral marches and the ringing of bells. After a procession entitled 'The Beautiful Spring', performances commenced in four theatres which had been constructed around the field: extracts from *Ruslan and Liudmilla*, *The Hump-Backed Horse* and *Ermak Timofeeich*, and a harlequinade and *divertissement*. The celebrations concluded at nine o'clock with a spectacular firework display.[77]

Lentovsky's influence and ambition were further demonstrated in the spring of 1885, when he succeeded in bringing the celebrated dancer Virginia Zucchi to Russia, as part of a troupe of Italian artists. She was engaged to perform at one of his shorter-lived ventures – the Kein-Grust at Livadia, St Petersburg – as the *première danseuse en chef* for two thousand francs per month.[78] Zucchi then went on to dance at the imperial ballet for several years.

What motivated Lentovsky as an impresario? In so far as he possessed an ideological perspective beyond genuine enthusiasm for the stage, it was that entertainment should take precedence over education in theatre, that visual spectacle was more appealing than serious psychological drama. Lentovsky had a reputation for producing stunning special effects on stage, the most notable example being his popular production of *Voyage to the Moon*, based on Offenbach's operetta, which was staged more than sixty times between 1883 and 1885, and in which audiences were dazzled by elaborate effects, including a giant electric moon and an erupting volcano.[79] It was this kind of emphasis on the fantastical and fairytale worlds of the stage that earned Lentovsky the popular sobriquet 'magician and wizard'. Closely connected with his views on spectacle was his conviction that theatre should endeavour to attract the widest possible audience, not just a narrow section of educated society.[80] It was no coincidence that the full title of the Skomorokh, in its first incarnation, was 'Skomorokh: a Theatre of Popular and Generally Accessible Productions'.

Yet Lentovsky's restless enthusiasm for organizing popular entertainments belied a constant struggle to find support for his enterprises and to make them commercially viable. In 1882, saddled with debts, he contemplated abandoning the theatre business altogether, and only the timely assistance of Suvorin persuaded him to continue.[81] As he prepared to relaunch the Skomorokh in 1886, a sense of weariness pervaded Lentovsky's correspondence. In August of that year, in a letter to Lev Tolstoy that is reputed to have inspired thoughts of writing a play for a *narodnyi* audience, *The Power of Darkness*, he appealed for the author's support:

> Without outside help, and with great exertion on my part, I have begun the construction of a theatre for *narodnyi* and generally accessible performances. Turning to you, not for the sake of ingratiation, not for the sake of any mercenary aims, but from some feeling incomprehensible to myself, I hasten to inform you first of the forthcoming business. Trusting in your most loving spirit, I request your moral support for my worn-out heart.[82]

At the same time, he wrote to a certain Konstantin Mikhailovich:

> I consider it necessary to inform you that on 1 October 1886 I am opening a theatre for *narodnyi* and generally accessible performances, which I am building with my own feeble resources and with great exertion on my part. I am not requesting the help that you promised (albeit a small amount) – I

am only reminding you. I don't need money personally – it's necessary for the business, which you consider to be not insignificant. Help me only if you can, or rather want to.[83]

The new incarnation of the Skomorokh, which opened with a performance of Ostrovsky's *Poverty Is No Vice* (Lentovsky claimed that Ostrovsky's works were to be at the centre of the repertoire), lasted until 1897, but it was never able to shake off financial problems and was funded largely on credit. Although the troupe was relatively small – twenty-four actors and sixteen actresses, plus a chorus of twenty-three during the 1886–7 season[84] – Lentovsky had always provided his employees with generous salaries, and this constituted his biggest expenditure by far.[85] During the 1887–8 season, his total monthly expenditure at the Skomorokh amounted to 15,618 rubles, of which 7,200 were spent on the troupe, excluding the chorus. The next largest expense was the rental of the theatre (1,000 rubles), followed by the orchestra (975 rubles) and fees for the gas company for heating and lighting (900 rubles).[86] Moreover, because Lentovsky intended his theatre to be generally accessible, tickets were relatively cheap, ranging from ten kopeks to one ruble, and consequently box-office receipts never constituted a significant source of income.[87] This state of affairs was often compounded by poor attendance figures. During the 1886–7 season, the highest attendance was an impressive 3,615 people, but the lowest was a mere 340. Most performances drew in approximately 2,000 people. Total attendance for the season was 131,892.[88]

Despite financial difficulties, Lentovsky managed to keep open his main ventures, the Hermitage and the Skomorokh, during the 1880s. But the margin of commercial success was small. For the 1888–9 season, the total revenue from all his theatres amounted to just over eighty-eight thousand rubles, while his expenditures were just over eighty-two thousand.[89] By the early 1890s, Lentovsky's financial problems were mounting and he was compelled to abandon his main enterprises. The Skomorokh was taken over by A. A. Cherepanov, one of Lentovsky's former actors, in 1891 and the Hermitage closed in 1893. Lentovsky went into semi-retirement, surviving on his Imperial Theatre pension. He worked for a few years (1898–1901) as a régisseur at Mamontov's Private Opera, and died in 1906.

Lentovsky was arguably the most energetic theatrical impresario in Russian history. According to one of his obituaries, he constructed or substantially renovated a total of eleven theatres, mostly in Moscow and St Petersburg.[90] In addition to his main enterprises, he organized several short-lived ventures, including theatres in the Malkiel House (1883) and Lianozov House (1887) and the 'Theatre of the Nineteenth Century' (opened 1891). A tremendous enthusiast and effective organizer, Lentovsky was clearly also very determined. Contemporaneous accounts portray a bold and defiant individual. One acquaintance from 1875 recalled that Lentovsky 'had one thin overcoat, which he proudly wore unbuttoned in twenty degrees below zero as a sign of absolute contempt'.[91] Yury Bakhrushin left this description:

> One day, going downstairs to the museum [Alexei Bakhrushin's theatre museum], I found father showing the museum to someone who looked like a coachman. The guest was in lacquered bottle-shaped boots and a long, dark blue coat, girdled by a Caucasian waistband, and he held in his hands an expensive fur hat with a sable band, which he didn't part with for a minute. When walking about he jingled, like spurs, with a multitude of trinkets, dangling from him on a silver chain on the side of his long coat. A curly gipsy beard with keen streaks of grey, thick black eyebrows and a penetrating gaze made his face unfriendly and sullen. The celebrated Moscow 'magician and wizard' M. V. Lentovsky left me with a sense of some inexplicable fear.[92]

But despite his energy and his eventual fame, Lentovsky was consistently unable to make his ventures a commercial success. Given the wide range of genres he worked with, as well as his popularity as a producer, it seems unlikely that the explanation lies with what he staged. Rather, his insistence on cheap ticket prices and expensive stage effects, as well as his huge wage bill, were partly to blame. The large number of ventures he pursued may also have overstretched his resources. But what really set him apart from the likes of Korsh, Mamontov and Suvorin was the absence of any large fortune made in the legal profession, the railway industry or the publishing industry which could be used to shore up his theatres. While the number of theatrical venues proliferated during the late nineteenth century, financial viability clearly remained elusive for many entrepreneurs. The institutional emergence of a theatrical civil society in the capitals, for all its achievements, demonstrated that the longer-term survival of an enterprise was still largely dependent on private wealth.

Chapter 5

DISCOURSES OF DECLINE

By the 1890s, Russian theatre appeared to be experiencing one of the most prosperous and felicitous periods in its history. The sheer number of theatres across the empire was unprecedented. The economic development of Russia during the 1880s and 1890s ensured that industrialization and urbanization continued to advance at a steady pace, and the expansion of the urban population facilitated the further spread and consolidation of commercial culture, as the massed ranks of new town and city dwellers fostered demand for a wide variety of leisure pursuits.[1] One result of these developments was the rapid proliferation of theatrical venues. Whereas by the beginning of the 1870s there were sixty-one permanent theatrical troupes in regional Russia, by the early 1890s there were 127 theatres in provincial urban centres alone, including six opera and twenty-four operetta theatres.[2] Moreover, it has been estimated that by 1899 there were 2,134 entertainment venues in the provinces, including 216 theatres, thirty-two concert halls, forty-two circuses, and hundreds of clubs and amateur societies.[3] As noted at the beginning of the previous chapter, by 1901 the Imperial Theatres had been joined by fourteen private commercial theatres in St Petersburg and twelve in Moscow. The theatres of Korsh, Mamontov, Suvorin and Lentovsky were only the most prominent and accomplished examples of cultural enterprises produced by the burgeoning commercial entertainment market. One actor from Moscow, astounded by the abundance of entertainment venues that he discovered while living in St Petersburg, described the situation as a 'theatrical bacchanalia'.[4]

The numerical expansion of theatrical venues during the 1880s and 1890s was accompanied by renewed efforts to establish specialist theatrical journals devoted to critical and theoretical issues. They included the *Theatrical World* (1884–93), *Theatre and Life* (1884–93), the *Artist* (1889–95), *Theatrical News*

(1894–1903), *Theatre and Art* (1897–1918) and several other, shorter-lived publications. In addition, widely read commercial daily newspapers devoted considerable space to theatrical news and regularly provided performance reviews. They included the *Daily News*, the *New Times* and the *Stock-Exchange Gazette*. In the midst of what seemed like an endless stream of theatrical journalism, one commentator concluded that the extent of Russia's interest in the stage was unique, insisting that even in France the theatre did not attract as much attention.[5] Lev Tolstoy drew attention to this phenomenon in 1898 in the opening lines of his essay *What Is Art?* 'Pick up any newspaper of our time,' he wrote, 'and in every one of them you will find a section on theatre and music.'[6]

The history and achievements of the stage in Russia began to receive greater publicity, both at home and abroad, and in a manner which suggested that the country's theatrical tradition was viewed with a sense of civic pride. The Vienna International Theatre Exhibition of 1892 included a Russian section, and although only the Imperial Theatres were represented it nevertheless provided an opportunity to showcase some of the work of the St Petersburg and Moscow stages to the rest of Europe. The manager of the St Petersburg Imperial Theatres, Vladimir Pogozhev, organized the section, which measured five hundred square metres and emphasized the history and structure of theatrical affairs, largely ignoring contemporaneous stage art. It included photographs of theatre people, publications from the archive of the directorate, such as the recently inaugurated *Yearbook of the Imperial Theatres*, illustrations of costumes, examples of stage props, plans of Imperial Theatre buildings, including information on heating and ventilation, playbills, performance programmes, information about the theatre schools, and mannequins with costumes, mainly from operas.[7] While it was the Austro-Hungarian and German sections of the exhibition that attracted the most attention, the writer and critic Alexander Pleshcheyev was able to report of the Russian area, 'foreigners admire our section'.[8]

The growing civic pride in Russia's theatrical achievements also manifested itself in the foundation of the world's first theatre museum, opened in Moscow in 1894 by the industrialist and stage enthusiast Alexei Bakhrushin (1865–1929) on the basis of his vast collection of theatrical memorabilia. The museum constituted a further example of the way in which civil society was beginning to contribute to Russia's theatrical culture, demonstrating once again the significant role played by private resources in the development of theatre's public profile after 1882. Curiously, Bakhrushin's 'autobiography' – a typed summary of his career extending to just over one page – makes no mention of his business interests, but rather emphasizes his life-long interest in the arts, his collection of books on theatre, and his work for the Russian Theatre Society (see chapter 6) and other organizations.[9] The museum was gifted to the city in 1913, becoming part of the Academy of Sciences, and was named for its founder after the Bolshevik revolution.[10]

If the numerical expansion of venues, the appearance of new specialist journals and the exhibition of achievement suggested that Russian theatre was flourishing by the 1890s, contemporaneous theatrical reportage was, in an apparent paradox, permeated with a discourse of decline. The following comment, from 1890, was not untypical: 'In Moscow the number of theatres increases every year, the number of enterprising impresarios is increasing – but the theatrical business is not improving at all. It is declining . . . This is unquestionable.'[11] In 1895, one observer declared that the theme of 'decline' had now become a 'platitude'.[12] Writers for the new specialist journals regularly bemoaned a range of deficiencies which allegedly debased the standard of dramatic art or rendered it inaccessible to ordinary people. Their complaints, taken together, amounted to a fundamental rejection of commercial entertainment as incompatible with the higher ideal of theatre as an elevated school for the people.

Some critics complained about the standard of the repertoire. Although the classics – Shakespeare, Schiller, Molière and so forth – continued to be performed on a regular basis, and the works of Ostrovsky were now firmly established, the repertoires of most theatres continued to be dominated by unexceptional plays written by a handful of contemporary dramatists. They included Shpazhinsky, Potekhin and Averkiev, but the most prolific was Victor Krylov (pseudonym of Victor Alexandrov, 1838–1906), who authored or adapted no fewer than 115 plays, mostly in the style of melodrama or drawing room farce. Krylov regarded himself primarily as an entertainer, not an educator, and the prevalence of his works in the late nineteenth-century repertoire was referred to pejoratively as the *krylovshchina* (roughly meaning 'the reign of Krylov').[13] Ostrovsky's prediction that 'speculation' would not on its own improve artistic standards seemed vindicated; the promulgation of full freedom of the theatres prior to the creation of a national theatre had simply led to more melodrama and operetta. The Imperial Theatres were no exception. The point was that the advent of new private theatres in the capitals had been expected to provide a solution.

The cultural intelligentsia did not regard the genres favoured by Krylov and others as intrinsically serious. Yet the benefits system encouraged the relatively rapid composition of a large number of such plays. Benefit nights – whereby a particular artist was celebrated and received a substantial share of the box-office takings – were in theory abolished in 1882, but they continued to take place in practice. Artists who were awarded benefits were entitled to select the plays in which they would perform, and the custom was to choose one that had never been staged. Hence the demand for new plays, many of which were never heard of again after the benefit night. In such conditions, plays of literary worth were seldom performed. At the beginning of 1885, one reviewer lamented that the whole season had produced nothing of value. Several plays staged at the Imperial Theatres had proved successful in terms of revenues, including P. D. Boborykin's *Doctor Moshkov*, Shpazhinsky's *The Sorcerer*, Nemirovich-Danchenko's *The Dark Coniferous Forest* and Krylov's *The Ghosts of Fortune*, but none of these, claimed the critic, possessed any literary merit.[14] A decade later, another critic complained that Russian dramatists were not producing any plays with a 'serious social motive'.[15] There were exceptions, notably the realist didactic dramas of Lev Tolstoy – *The Power of Darkness* (1886), *The Fruits of Enlightenment* (1889) and *The Living Corpse* (1900) – but they were by no means typical of the repertoire of the 1880s and 1890s. In the provinces, according to one observer, the problem was compounded by the fact that, after the declaration on freedom of the theatres, the best artists sought work in the capitals and regional stages were left with the less talented thespians.[16]

Others complained that economic conditions rendered theatre either too expensive for ordinary people, or too inexpensive to make it commercially viable for impresarios, especially in the provinces. In 1885, the theatre journalist Alexander Sokolov observed that new theatres were appearing in the capitals, especially Moscow, but that in the provinces things were in 'decline', even though the large number of amateur theatricals indicated that there was considerable demand for stage entertainments. As Sokolov put it, 'The theatre perishes, but love for the theatre increases.' His explanation was that theatres were 'materially inaccessible' and that domestic amateur theatricals therefore constituted a means of satisfying the widespread interest in the stage.[17] In 1886 the theatrical newspaper edited by Sokolov, the *Prompter*, even reproduced the above-mentioned article of 1842 showing how to construct a little temporary stage at home (see p. 46 above).[18] The vogue for amateur theatricals was also served by published collections of plays suitable for domestic performance, such as *For Domestic and Amateur Performances*, which appeared during the late 1890s. Each issue of Fyodor Kumanin's periodical *Theatromane* (1895–8) contained a play and his *Theatrical Library* (1891–4, 1896–8) was entirely devoted to the publication of plays.

The issue of accessibility occasionally took unexpected forms. In a letter to the *Prompter* in July 1885, a 'simple spectator' noted that while the governor of St Petersburg, P. A. Gresser, a keen advocate of theatricals, had the interests of audiences at heart, he ought to bear in mind the needs of the 'average theatrical public'. The writer claimed that audiences were being 'fleeced', even though art was meant to be accessible to all. The problem was that the buffet and restaurant prices at the Arcadia and Livadia summer gardens were 'not accessible to all'. The reader continued, 'We will not, of course, appeal to the authorities regarding a legislative inducement to lower the price of a sandwich, but we think that it is the direct business of the authorities to provide a legal counterbalance to such prices which are established in so-called luxurious restaurants.'[19] While the cost of refreshments was hardly central to the theme of decline, the letter nevertheless illustrated a perception that a visit to the theatre was not readily affordable for all inhabitants of the city.

This kind of complaint reflected the fact that theatre audiences were increasingly diverse, an inevitable result of the spread of theatrical venues. One observer, M. V. Karneyev, claimed in 1887 that most theatres now possessed a 'mass audience' with 'no individual opinion, no fixed ideals'.[20] Lower-class audiences could be seen even at the Korsh Theatre, especially during matinée performances, for which the tickets were relatively inexpensive. As in the first half of the nineteenth century, the growing variety of spectators generated a certain condescension on the part of some observers, including theatrical journalists, in particular towards provincial audiences. This was indicated, for instance, by a satirical sketch depicting two gentlemen conversing in the foyer of a provincial theatre during an interval in a performance of *Hamlet*. One of the gentlemen is accompanied by an English friend who does not understand Russian, but because he has seen *Hamlet* many times in England and has read it, he understands what is happening. The other gentleman expresses surprise – he did not know that *Hamlet* had been translated into English.[21]

A third theme in the discourse of decline focused on artists' salaries. In an 1885 examination of the decline of the theatrical business, one observer wrote that impresarios were unable to make sufficient profits. He rejected the idea that the problem was caused by the 'absence of a new repertoire' or 'the miserliness of the public'. Instead, the root of the dilemma lay in rising prices which had resulted in greater expenditure on artists' wages, especially in operetta theatres, which were popular in the provinces. This meant that impresarios could not make money from their enterprises, the conclusion being that theatrical affairs could be improved only if salaries were reduced.[22]

A related complaint concerned the apparent overextension of the theatre industry. In an article entitled 'The Economic Basis of the Theatrical Question in the Provinces', the actor Dmitry Karamazov noted that the 'sorrowful situation' of theatrical affairs outside the capitals was constantly lamented, and wrote of 'the decline of the artistic level of the provincial stage'. The number of provincial stages and actors kept increasing, observed Karamazov, but so did the number of failed ventures. This resulted in large numbers of actors falling into hardship. For Karamazov, the only thing that appeared *not* to be increasing was the amount of artistic talent. This was in marked contrast to the condition of provincial theatre during the 1850s and 1860s, when there were fewer ventures but 'their artistic level was higher'. Karamazov acknowledged that reducing the number of theatres would result in a considerable amount of thespian unemployment, but he concluded that it would be preferable to sacrifice some than to let all suffer.[23]

When Sokolov's trade newspaper the *Prompter* closed down in 1886, the editor explained the decision as follows: 'The contemporary decline of theatrical affairs, both in the provinces and in the capitals, means that organs dedicated exclusively to theatres are deprived of material.'[24] In the same issue, the difficult material circumstances of commercial theatre were underlined by the report that, on 5 February 1886, Vasily Berg, popular showman and impresario of the first private St Petersburg theatre (1866–76), had been laid to rest in the city's Smolensk cemetery, having passed away 'in extreme poverty'.[25]

In 1893, the ballet critic Valerian Svetlov noted that, despite all the talk of decline, the two capitals possessed decent theatres, namely imperial and private.[26] Yet the Imperial Theatres and the decent private theatres of St Petersburg and Moscow survived because they had access either to state subsidies or, through their wealthy patrons, to substantial private resources. For the majority of theatres, seeking to entertain or even enlighten mass audiences, resources remained scarce. It is no coincidence that most of the complaints which characterized the discourse of decline concerned some aspect of the economics of theatre. These complaints, though often exaggerated, collectively suggest that the fundamental problems for theatre were material ones, and that the economic condition of Russia was not yet strong enough to support so many artistic enterprises, especially in the provinces.

The sense of disillusionment among the cultural intelligentsia over the artistic and material consequences of commercial theatre was more keenly felt because of a persistent adherence to the notion that a serious, educative theatre could 'civilize' the masses. Writers and theatrical commentators continued to insist on the social importance of theatre. 'In the cultural development of every people,' wrote the journalist D. Kolchugin in 1883, 'theatre undeniably has enormous value. The stage is the transmitter to the popular masses of bright ideas, humane views.' He recalled Catherine the Great's view of theatre as a school for the people, and proclaimed that 'the actor is a teacher of the crowd'.[27] Alexander Pleshcheyev, introducing his new theatrical journal in 1884, stated that 'we will constantly be guided by the idea that the stage should have as its purpose not the amusement of an idle crowd with a weakness for spicy shows and tawdry brightness, but the moral training of the masses'.[28] In an article entitled 'Theatre As a School of Public Morals' – which focused on provincial theatre on the grounds that it was directly dependent on audiences for survival – another writer claimed that some of the tasks of theatre were 'to ennoble tastes, to develop a habit for association, to make people appreciate the pleasure of awakening ideal desires, to raise the person of the crowd above his humdrum, dull reality, to reveal to him the better, higher aspects of life, not being deceptive about their reality, to arouse an interest in public issues, to develop a sense of civic duty'.[29]

Furthermore, there was a widespread conviction among members of the intelligentsia that theatre, together with literature, could help to overcome the cultural divide between the elite and the people and foster a unified national culture. The problem was how to realize such aims in the context of a highly commercial entertainment market that appeared largely unconcerned with such matters. The economic dilemmas that many described as decline meant that impresarios were primarily concerned with attracting ticket-buying crowds rather than staging plays intended to enlighten and edify. For the cultural intelligentsia, and others, the solution was to be found in the idea of subsidized 'people's theatres', which would have the dual merit of targeting the *narod* while ensuring that commercial considerations remained secondary to the task of raising the cultural level of the masses.[30]

The intelligentsia's resilient faith in the transformative power of theatre was now increasingly expressed in calls for accessible people's theatres for the education of workers and peasants. People's theatres (*narodnye teatry*) were distinct from those which were simply popular with mass audiences (*obshchedostupnye teatry*, or generally accessible theatres) in that they had the express aim of educating the lower orders or training them to behave in particular ways.[31] The intelligentsia, for instance, viewed them as a means of transmitting elite culture to the masses, while the authorities, although ambivalent about the potential consequences of mass entertainment, regarded them as a possible way of instilling discipline among the ordinary people of urban Russia and diverting them from the temptations of the tavern and other vices.

As we have seen, the idea of theatre as a tool for educating the people had its roots in the eighteenth century. After the emancipation of the serfs in 1861, the issue of popular education became more urgent. Now that peasants were free to move and were increasingly drawn to urban centres, thoughts of how to 'civilize' them preoccupied the intelligentsia and the authorities to an unprecedented degree. Because of the low rates of literacy, theatre was regarded as a means of acculturating the new urban population. Hence, as noted in chapter 3, Trepov's proposal in 1868 for a people's theatre. At that time, however, the authorities were still uneasy about any schemes to educate the masses, especially in the capitals, and nothing came of the plan.

Despite growing interest in the idea of people's theatre from the 1860s onwards, practical results remained limited. Vasily Malafeyev received permission to organize a people's theatre at the St Petersburg Manufacturing Exposition in 1870, and Alexander Fedotov mounted a similar venture at the Moscow Polytechnical Exposition in 1872, but these were exceptional and were permitted only because, crucially, they were temporary. During the 1880s, however, the issue of a people's theatre acquired renewed urgency, especially now that the abrogation of the Imperial Theatre monopoly had removed the main legislative obstacle to the organization of alternative entertainments. Two of its leading proponents were Nikolai Popov and Ivan Shcheglov. Popov, a dramatist and director from the merchant estate, was primarily interested in improving the artistic standard of theatrical fare available to ordinary people, as opposed to organizing specially designed didactic entertainments. But he was convinced that commercial theatre was incapable of improving standards and believed that the task should be undertaken by local government and the state.[32] Shcheglov, a writer of many tracts about theatre for the people, argued in contrast to Popov that melodrama and vaudeville should retain their places in the repertoire, as their very popularity made them useful for moral instruction.[33] Common to Popov and Shcheglov, however, was the conviction that theatre should be more broadly accessible.

Hopes were raised by the opening of Lentovsky's Skomorokh in 1882, since it expressly aimed to attract ordinary people. But the Skomorokh also exposed a latent dilemma. It was a theatre for the people, but it was also a commercial enterprise. This meant that its repertoire was designed primarily to entertain audiences rather than preach to them, in keeping with Lentovsky's theatrical philosophy. The cultural intelligentsia expressed disdain at the lack of seriousness in the Skomorokh's repertoire. The implicit question was raised: if people's theatre was to be educative, could it also be commercial? This, of course, was tantamount to saying that the people were incapable of deciding for themselves what constituted appropriate entertainment.[34]

The Skomorokh and its aims initially met with approval from theatrical commentators. Four months after it opened, Kolchugin wrote, 'The idea of giving ordinary people useful, pleasant and even educational entertainment is an excellent one.' The new theatre had clearly attracted an appreciative audience, mainly composed of working people, despite the fact that its fifteen-kopek seats had doubled in price as a consequence of ticket speculation, itself an indication of the Skomorokh's popularity.[35] When Lentovsky's enterprise was relaunched in November 1886, the journal *Theatre and Life* declared, 'We consider the creation of this theatre and its opening an event of great public importance.' Its *narodnost'* lay in its accessibility for the masses:

A moderately priced theatre for all the public is essential as one of the most powerful methods for the spiritual development of the masses, as one of the instruments for delivering an ennobling artistic impression to the masses. Theatre is a higher school, a rostrum from which the best geniuses and talents of Russia, in their artistic and poetic works, teach us goodness and truth, [but] until now it was only a luxury, accessible to the prosperous classes of our urban population. With the opening of Lentovsky's theatre, this 'luxury' becomes available to all. From today, for only five, ten kopeks, thousands of people every day get the opportunity to become acquainted for the first time with the artistic works of our poets and writers!! Henceforth Pushkin, Turgenev, Ostrovsky and other glorious names among our gifted writers for the stage, and their wonderful works that speak to the spirit and the heart of the Russian man, will cease to be empty, obscure names, empty sounds, for the popular masses of our capital!![36]

Others were less optimistic about the venture, questioning the suitability of the repertoire. A reviewer for the *Russian Gazette* who witnessed a performance of Dmitriev's *Evil Stepmothers* at the Skomorokh asked,

Why are such plays staged at a 'people's' theatre? . . . How is the people's spirit realized in such plays? . . . The question arises, what can such plays develop in audiences? Evidently nothing except senseless scoffing, indeed merely a taste for 'buffoonery' [*'skomorosh'ikh' vkusov* – here the reviewer is making a play on the theatre's name, calling to mind its less respectable medieval meaning]. It is also evident that the humour of such plays is indistinguishable from the humour of balagans on Devichy Field.[37]

Theatre and Life responded to the attack by contending that the repertoire of the Skomorokh included works by leading playwrights and that productions such as *Evil Stepmothers* were necessary for a people's theatre, as evidenced by their success with audiences. It also retorted that the Skomorokh was a moderately priced theatre, and only in that sense was it 'for all the public'. It was not the task of the Skomorokh to create a special repertoire for the people, especially as the people's theatre issue was 'still a vexed question'.[38] For others, however, a play's popularity could not be the measure of its suitability for mass consumption. In 1895, Popov attacked Cherepanov's stewardship of the Skomorokh. Under Lentovsky's tutelage, he argued, it had functioned as a genuinely accessible theatre, and decent, well-executed productions gave spectators with low incomes access to 'intelligent entertainment'. Cherepanov, however, had taken the theatre down to the level of a 'bad balagan', discouraging the 'intelligent public of modest means'. Its repertoire, insisted Popov, had become 'insufferable'.[39]

From the early 1880s, awareness of the difficulties faced by people's theatres in staging the 'right' sort of repertoire while remaining both financially viable and affordable to audiences gave rise to calls for a state-subsidized network of people's theatres. Subsidies would mean that the repertoire could be chosen with higher artistic-educational aims in mind, rather than likely box-office takings. They would also ensure that, if audiences were smaller as a result, tickets could remain inexpensive. Within a short space of time, a wide network of people's theatres was established. Most of them, however, were created not at the prompting of the cultural intelligentsia, but through the realization of industrialists and temperance organizations that theatricals could assist them in their efforts to combat drunkenness and raise productivity. While this was not irrelevant to intelligentsia concerns about raising the cultural level of the masses by exposing them to serious plays, it was motivated by a more precise set of aims.

Initially, subsidized people's theatres were organized during the 1880s and 1890s not by the state but by factory owners. They included the Vasilevsky

Ostrov Workers' Theatre, established in St Petersburg in 1887. By the mid 1890s factory theatres were common in most industrial areas of Russia. As Nikolai Popov reported in 1896,

A number of facts, which have demonstrated clearly enough the significance of these entertainments for the factory owners themselves, have inspired the largest factories to set up theaters and organize *narodnye gulian'ia*, while the factory folk, having discovered the possibility of spending holidays out of the tavern, have thus lessened the number of post-holiday absences and in this manner have begun to return with interest what their employers have spent on the organization of entertainments. This mutual benefit, naturally, causes other factory owners to join the new current.[40]

Factory theatres were soon followed by people's theatres organized by the state-funded Guardianships of Popular Temperance. In 1899 alone they were responsible for 1,332 performances throughout the empire.[41] People's theatres grew rapidly from ninety-seven in the empire in 1901 to 150 in 1904. Government-subsidized temperance theatres numbered 361 by 1905.[42] A small number were organized by wealthy philanthropists. The most prominent, the Ligovsky People's House established in St Petersburg in 1903 by Countess Sofia Panina, had as director Pavel Gaideburov, who gave priority to a serious and didactic repertoire replete with the classics of the Russian and non-Russian dramatic canon.[43]

The idea of an educative theatre was thus powerfully reasserted in the subsidized people's theatre movement. The intelligentsia had supported this idea as a means of circumscribing the potential pitfalls of purely commercial ventures. As E. Anthony Swift argues, 'The movement to create theaters for the people was an elite attempt to civilize the people by offering them an improved substitute for commercial fare: a people's theater with a systematic repertoire oriented toward art rather than profit.'[44] In practice, however, the majority of such theatres were motivated primarily by the more prosaic aim of diverting the urban population from destructive vices. If in the process they became acquainted with the achievements of literary theatre, so much the better.

Although the tsarist authorities funded the efforts of temperance societies to develop a network of people's theatres, they remained fundamentally ambivalent about the consequences of mass entertainment. The success of the Skomorokh, in its second incarnation from 1886, alerted them to the potentially subversive influence of popular theatre. Konstantin Pobedonostsev was particularly alarmed in early 1887 by the news that Lentovsky planned to stage Tolstoy's *The Power of Darkness*, which he regarded as a work of 'coarse realism'.[45] Claiming that the Skomorokh exercised a 'harmful influence on the morals of the poor', he persuaded the tsar to ban Tolstoy's play. This was despite the fact that the censor had recently approved *The Power of Darkness* for a performance at the Alexandrinsky, which now had to be cancelled.

Pobedonostsev was chiefly concerned to prevent the Skomorokh staging Tolstoy's play, but his intervention resulted in a general ban. This led to the decision to introduce a separate censorship regulation for popular theatres a year later, in early 1888.[46] Since 1865, censorship in the Russian empire had been carried out by the Chief Administration for Press Affairs, part of the Ministry of Internal Affairs. All plays had to be approved by its drama section before they could be performed by any theatre in the country.[47] In connection with the introduction of special regulations for popular theatres, Minister of Internal Affairs Dmitry Tolstoy expressed the following concerns:

In examining plays the censor has in view the more or less educated public that attends theater performances, but not exclusively any one social class. Due to his level of mental development, his outlooks and conceptions, the common man will often interpret in an utterly wrong sense something that would present no temptation for a somewhat educated person, and thus a play containing nothing blameworthy from a general point of view may be unsuitable and even harmful for him. Since the theater unquestionably has an important educational significance, it would seem necessary to ensure that the people receive from it sober and beneficial impressions and nothing that would promote their moral corruption.[48]

Under the new regulation, the censors were required to be mindful of both the content of plays and the audiences for whom they would be performed. Whereas the imperial or private theatres could mount a production of any play that appeared on the lists of approved works drawn up by the Ministry of Internal Affairs, popular theatres were obliged to seek special permission to stage them.

The obvious problem was how to determine what constituted a popular theatre. Not all theatres which attracted large numbers of ordinary workers were actually called 'narodnyi'. The Skomorokh was a case in point, having altered its latest subtitle in February 1888 from 'Theatre of Popular [*narodnyi*] and Accessible Performances' to 'Theatre of Melodrama and Diverse Performances', an evident attempt to circumvent the new censorship regulations then being introduced.[49] The authorities evaded the issue of terminology by deciding to be guided by ticket prices. It was assumed that if tickets were inexpensive, audiences were more likely to consist of members of the ordinary working classes. It was further assumed that such audiences were more impressionable than the regular patrons of the imperial or private theatres, and therefore had to have their entertainments carefully selected and monitored. The head of the Chief Administration for Press Affairs, P. N. Durnovo, informed Lentovsky that if he wanted the Skomorokh to stage as broad a range of productions as possible, he would have to raise ticket prices in order to remove his venture from the category of popular theatre.[50]

Apart from the obvious fact that educated or unimpressionable people might comprise the majority of an audience even where tickets were inexpensive, the new regulation revealed a breathtaking condescension on the part of the authorities towards people of low income. After all, lack of resources or formal education did not necessarily mean that spectators were unintelligent or more likely to misinterpret a performance. The regulation also underlined official confusion about the stage. Theatre was meant to initiate the masses into the civilized culture of the educated elite, but how could this task be accomplished if access to some of that culture was prohibited?

The special regulation did not contain specific criteria for the assessment of a play's suitability for popular consumption. Nevertheless, a pattern of forbidden categories gradually emerged. They included works depicting rulers or clergy, works depicting rebellion or oppression, works satirizing authorities, works inciting class envy, and works depicting crime or sex, considered morally inappropriate.[51] An example of a play that was approved by the censor (after initial difficulties relating to the proposed Skomorokh production in 1887) for all theatres except those considered popular was Tolstoy's *The Power of Darkness*. This was somewhat ironic, given that Tolstoy wrote the play with the people's theatre in mind. The five-act drama depicts a series of tragic and barbaric events which take place in a peasant household. Nikita, a farm labourer, is having an affair with Anisya, the wife of his employer, Pyotr. With the help of Nikita's mother, who covets Pyotr's money, Anisya poisons her husband and marries Nikita. The latter soon becomes violent and starts an affair with his stepdaughter, Akulina (Pyotr's daughter from a previous marriage). When Akulina has Nikita's baby, Anisya and Nikita's mother persuade him to murder the child. The play ends when the tormented Nikita confesses to all the hideous crimes that have been committed in the household and is taken away by the police. In considering *The Power of Darkness* for translation into Latvian in 1899, the censor wrote, 'If the stage representation of such vile crimes creates, and it must create, disagreeable feelings for educated theatre audiences, then for uneducated audiences especially such scenes must create a really debauched image.'[52] Another play that was banned from popular stages only was Beaumarchais' *The Marriage of Figaro*, on the grounds that it was 'spotted with witty escapades against the nobility'.[53]

The special regulations remained in force until 1917. Not everyone felt reassured, however. In 1902 one provincial landowner, in terms reminiscent of Adlerberg, expressed the fear that people's theatre would create 'the thorns of free-thinking, discontent, and a critical opinion of everything that Russia lives by'.[54] Of course, from the point of view of the authorities it was not only popular theatre audiences that were at risk. After the Korsh Theatre production in November 1892 of Ibsen's *A Doll's House*, which deals with a wife's rebellion against the stultifying authority of her husband and was widely regarded (despite Ibsen's protestations) as an appeal for women's rights, Pobedonostsev wrote to the censor, 'This summer I re-read [Ibsen's] plays out of curiosity and became convinced that if they are propagated on the stage they will produce a harmful effect on minds.'[55] There were no immediate consequences, however, and Ibsen continued to be staged from time to time.

Thus, during the 1880s and 1890s, the much-anticipated proliferation of theatres had resulted in a certain sense of disillusionment among the cultural intelligentsia, as expressed in a discourse of decline, and a certain sense of trepidation on the part of the authorities. Commercial entertainment, unfettered by state interference (with the exception of censorship), had failed to produce the kind of serious, educative theatre that had been advocated for so long. The turn to subsidized people's theatres constituted a tacit admission that civil society – in the sense of self-supporting, non-state public associational activity – was largely unable or unwilling to create the type of theatre envisaged by the intelligentsia. The major exceptions, such as the enterprises of Korsh, Mamontov, Suvorin and to some extent Lentovsky, rather proved the rule. Meanwhile, as the authorities looked warily on, commercial theatres continued to entertain with the *krylovshchina* and the ubiquitous melodrama, vaudeville and operetta.

One of the unexpected consequences of the spread of commercial entertainment was a temporary revival in the reputation of the Imperial

Theatres. During the 1870s they had been heavily criticized for adhering to bureaucratic routines and outmoded traditions. It was claimed that the artistic development of Russian theatre was being held back by the directorate's monopoly, such arguments being partly responsible for the abolition of the monopoly in 1882. Now that freedom of the theatres had arrived in the capitals, however, and the artistic results, with a few notable exceptions, were seen to be unimpressive, many writers and critics began to look to the Imperial Theatres to set and maintain a standard. The word that was often used to describe them was *obraztsovyi*, meaning model or exemplary, the standard which others might seek to emulate. Where the state theatres were considered to fall short of model standards, they were nevertheless expected to aspire to those standards.

One writer argued that the imperial stage 'ought to be a model for all private (particularly provincial) theatres, since it possesses material and artistic resources such as are not available to private entrepreneurs'.[56] The dramatist A. I. Palm claimed in 1883 that the Imperial Theatres were beyond competition because their resources liberated them from the pursuit of 'narrow commercial aims'. This, he asserted, must remain the case for the foreseeable future, given that the standard of private theatres was dependent on that of the imperial stages, presumably because the former would seek to compete with the latter for audiences and critical plaudits. This did not mean, of course, that the Imperial Theatres were faultless. Palm also suggested that a national theatre was still required in order to give a 'general tone and direction to stage art in Russia'.[57] In practice, however, the example that the government stage could set for private theatres beyond the capitals was limited. This was not just a matter of geography. Although stars of the imperial stages regularly toured the provinces, it was normally as individuals. It was even rumoured that tours by whole troupes or parts of troupes were forbidden, and that the rule had been introduced to satisfy the greed of Malyi Theatre artists who wanted to reap all the benefits of a lucrative tour.[58]

This is not to suggest that the Imperial Theatres were regarded unanimously as the ideal institutions in an increasingly diverse theatrical landscape. Many artists rejected their traditions, believing the serious private enterprises of the capitals to be better suited to the development of their craft. During the 1880s and 1890s, the administration of the Imperial Theatres was dominated by men whom Vorontsov-Dashkov had appointed from among his old regimental colleagues. One theatre official observed that 'The period of the eighties and nineties was called by the press at that time the epoch of second lieutenants, since the Minister of the Imperial Court, Count Vorontsov-Dashkov, was kindly disposed towards the Finnish Life Guards regiment, and when appointed minister in 1881 shoved into theatre posts the poorest officers who had served in the Turkish campaign of 1877–8.'[59] For many actors, this climate was incompatible with the pursuit of creativity. The popular actor Vladimir Davydov spent two years at the Korsh Theatre (1886–8) in a break from his career at the imperial Alexandrinsky, where he appears to have been dissatisfied with the roles assigned to him. In a letter to the writer and poet Alexei Pleshcheyev, he wrote, 'I dislike having anything to do with the second lieutenants and sergeant-majors who are now ruling and filling the government stages and theatres.'[60]

Ultimately, however, most artists were unable to resist the lure of the imperial stages because they possessed unequalled resources and offered pensions. As one observer noted, this meant that private theatres would never be in a position to compete with them for the best talents,[61] and despite the grumblings of many who regarded the Imperial Theatres as being too attached to the government or languishing in a state of artistic stagnation, they continued to attract the leading performers. Indeed, in many respects the status of the Imperial Theatres was guaranteed during the 1880s and 1890s by the rich galaxy of stars that appeared on their stages.

The Moscow Malyi was home to the most important actors of the period, several of whom continued to demonstrate the capacity of thespians to articulate and represent constituencies of idealism and ideology in Russian society. Vladimir Nemirovich-Danchenko, one of the future founders of the Moscow Art Theatre (see chapter 7), wrote that the Malyi actors 'enjoyed the affection of the public and even greater trust than the authors' and that it was 'easy to understand that this was an epoch of the true kingdom of actors'.[62] Supreme among them was Maria Ermolova (1853–1928). Although she initially trained for the ballet, Ermolova was given an opportunity to perform in drama in 1870 when she was asked to stand in for Glikeriya Fedotova in the title role of Lessing's *Emilia Galotti*. Although her performance was well received by the critics, for the next few years Ermolova was confined to secondary parts. But she soon emerged as the leading actress of the Malyi and became the idol of progressive youth. Instrumental in this transformation was her benefit performance of March 1876, when she took the part of Laurencia in Lope de Vega's *Fuente Ovejuna*, which depicts a popular uprising. According to Boris Varneke, 'The actress managed to find for this [role] shades and feelings akin to the moods of the progressives in the audience. The performance turned into a political demonstration, and for this reason the piece was soon forbidden for a long time to come.'[63] Ermolova's portrayal of Laurencia established her reputation among the Moscow public as an actress with radical sympathies, and in her many roles (including Joan of Arc and Mary Stuart) she emphasized 'renunciation of personal well-being and happiness for the sake of serving higher ideals'.[64]

Other actors at the Malyi who enjoyed high public profiles included Glikeriya Fedotova (1846–1925), Alexander Lensky (1847–1908), Alexander Sumbatov-Yuzhin (1857–1927), Mikhail Sadovsky (son of Prov, 1847–1910) and his wife Olga Sadovskaya (1849–1919). These were only the most influential stars in a strong company that perpetuated the Malyi's tradition, established by Shchepkin, of playing a prominent role in public life. As young people were reputed to remark, 'We studied at the University, but we were educated at the Maly Theatre.'[65] In St Petersburg, the Alexandrinsky provided less of a focus for progressive youth and in general was regarded as more conservative. This was a function of its geographical proximity to the court and the government and the fact that its audience tended to comprise officialdom to a greater extent than the Malyi. Observers often drew attention to the notable presence of merchants at Malyi performances, although the Alexandrinsky audience also contained many merchants.[66] The Alexandrinsky nevertheless boasted stars such as Maria Savina (1854–1915), Vladimir Davydov (1849–1925) and the popular comic actor Konstantin Varlamov (1848–1915). Savina's popularity and consequent authority was such that she held almost complete sway at the Alexandrinsky. A humorous sketch in a satirical journal depicted the plan of a new theatre designed for her future benefit nights – the auditorium was so vast that trams and trains were used to convey people across it, and the spectators at the back observed the performance through telescopes and listened to the action on telephones connected to the stage.[67]

None of this meant that the Imperial Theatres could afford to be complacent, and their managers were alert to the potential implications of the new environment. In St Petersburg, until the appearance of Suvorin's enterprise in 1895, serious theatre-goers had little to entice them away from the Imperial Theatres. In Moscow, however, the Korsh Theatre quickly established itself as a legitimate drama stage, and in 1887 the writer and dramatist M. V. Karneyev even claimed that it was starting to draw audiences away from the Malyi.[68] The management of the state theatres responded to the appearance of private theatres by endeavouring to reassert their status as the leading theatrical institutions. Early in 1886, for example, Ostrovsky was appointed artistic director of the Malyi, although he was not to live long enough to register an impact. In 1892 the directorate joined the theatrical periodical bandwagon when it began to publish the lavish *Yearbook of the Imperial Theatres* to provide an 'illustrated account of the work of the Imperial Theatres'.[69] The early yearbooks were dominated by information about the repertoires, officials and artists of the state theatres, and eschewed critical articles. This objective character was designed to convey an image of aloof superiority, of institutions which sat above the theoretical bickering that surrounded other theatrical journals. Later volumes, however, contained articles on theatre history, and under the editorship of Nikolai Drizen (1909–15) the *Yearbook* became essentially another theatrical journal, appearing as seven or eight issues a year and publishing critical articles which reflected lively debates about the stage.[70]

In 1882, after a protracted campaign for freedom of the theatres, the legal framework for the organization and development of private theatres in the capitals was finally put in place. During the 1880s and 1890s, however, ideals clashed with realities. In the eyes of the cultural intelligentsia, commercial theatre appeared incapable of delivering a 'school for the people'. Civil society and the market could not be trusted to improve the cultural level of the masses. As a consequence, the attention of many cultural activists turned to the authorities. Subsidized stages were thought to hold the key to reversing the perceived decline of theatre, and it is no coincidence that the Imperial Theatres temporarily returned to fashion among many members of the intelligentsia. Impresarios continued to pursue their private ventures, but for the time being they lost some of their status as saviours of the national stage.

Chapter 6

POVERTY AND PROFESSIONALIZATION

The most significant contribution made by theatre to the development of civil society in Russia emanated from attempts to address the problem of poverty among artists. Material difficulties had always afflicted the vast majority of artists, especially in the provinces, but the problem of thespian indigence was increasingly conspicuous now that the number of theatrical enterprises had proliferated. During the 1880s and 1890s, determined efforts were made to address this problem, resulting in the creation of the Russian Theatre Society (Russkoe teatral'noe obshchestvo, or RTO) in 1894. In the process of representing the interests of theatre people and seeking to alleviate their impoverishment, the RTO gradually fashioned itself into a fully fledged professional association and symbolized the extent to which many artists now regarded themselves as professionals.

The term 'acting profession' has wide currency, but is often used to refer generally to the work of actors. In the stricter historical sense used here, a profession is an organized and credentialed occupation founded on a special expertise and claiming to work disinterestedly to the benefit of the community (the classic professions are medicine, law and teaching).[1] 'Professionalization' occurs when occupational groups assert their status by articulating a common identity on the basis of their expertise – for instance, by organizing national associations and conventions.

Historically, professionalization has served a variety of purposes, including the need to exchange specialist knowledge more effectively, or to control access to a field that contains an overabundance of practitioners. In Russia, until the second half of the nineteenth century, specialist personnel were trained by the state in its technical institutes and assigned to positions in the civil service or the army. Associations and congresses for (increasingly self-styled) professionals appeared only after the 'great reforms' of the 1860s and 1870s, which had resulted in the rapid expansion of the numbers of trained experts.[2] The political and social circumstances of tsarist Russia meant that the burgeoning professional groups lacked autonomy and were often defined officially – if they were acknowledged as occupations with a collective identity at all – as 'estates' (*sosloviia*).[3] For the members of such groups, there was no inherent conflict between estate identity and their self-image as professionals, and indeed some members of occupational groups aspired to *soslovie* status, as, in theory, it acknowledged their collective significance.[4] The major driving force behind the formal organization of Russian professionals (those, at least, that have been researched) was evidently altruistic rather than self-serving. According to one observer, 'Political obstacles to doing one's work effectively, rather than economic issues or social status, seem to have been the strongest spur to professionalization [in Russia], although these other issues at times played a role.'[5]

Theatre people attempted to define their work as a profession during the 1890s and the early years of the twentieth century in the mistaken belief that professional status would act as a bulwark against the effects of the market. The professions are traditionally contrasted with the entrepreneurial classes because they are assumed to be concerned primarily with the application of scientific knowledge rather than the pursuit of profit. While scholars have shown that the distinction between professional and entrepreneurial ideals obscures the extent to which most professions are inextricably bound up with the market,[6] historically certain occupational groups have regarded the distinction as meaningful. Although theatre people could never escape the market – after all, without ticket-buying audiences they would be bereft of purpose and income – they nevertheless came to view professionalism as a potential guarantee against financial misfortune. Professionalization was not conceived as a strategy to establish entertainment monopolies or to restrict access to scarce resources (though some artists expressed concern about this issue). On the contrary, while the specific individuals who initiated theatre professionalization (mainly Imperial Theatre celebrities, but also a few jurists and publishers with theatrical interests) already enjoyed material security and social prestige, the evidence suggests that they acted primarily to improve the material and working conditions of provincial artists, the most numerous and vulnerable members of the occupational group, rather than to protect their own interests in the face of an expanding industry – indeed they promoted its further expansion. Such altruism does not necessarily preclude a preoccupation with self-interested internal occupational stratification, but there is little indication that this was a significant motive. Rather, the apparent purpose behind the cultivation of the notion that theatre people were members of a profession was to render them worthy of the esteem considered necessary to promote the social acceptance and attract the governmental support that might help to alleviate their unenviable material circumstances. Theatre people invoked professionalism as the antithesis of commercialism for an additional and related reason: theatre was allegedly being debased by speculators, whose entrepreneurial ethos was damaging Russian culture. They anticipated that, by establishing theatre work as a profession, the nefarious profit motive would be removed, to the benefit of both art and artists.

Theatre people encountered a variety of obstacles in their efforts to assert their professional identity, above all the difficulty in agreeing what, if any, formal qualifications were necessary for a career on the stage and how to credential them. Yet the professionalization of Russian theatre people was real enough. The organizational history of Russian theatre in the 1890s reflects several of the standard features of professionalization, notably the appearance of a national regulatory association and the convening of national congresses. Moreover, Russian theatre people increasingly described themselves as members of a profession (*professiia*) with a disinterested role to play in public life. In examining professionalism, we will consider four topics: poverty among artists; the work of the association that was formed to look after their interests, the Russian Theatre Society; the manner in which theatre people attempted to assert their professional identity at national congresses; and finally, the relationship between the Russian Theatre Society and the state, and its significance for professionalization.

The history of the theatre is replete with stories about impoverished thespians. In Russia, one of the earliest surviving documents relating to actors is a petition to Tsar Alexei from the students of Johann Gottfried Gregory's theatre class, set up in 1673 to train actors for the new but short-lived court theatre. The petition from Vaska Meshalkin and his twenty-five colleagues claimed that the students received no salary, had worn out their clothes and boots, and had nothing to eat or drink. It concluded by asking the tsar for a 'salary for sustenance . . . so that we, your slaves, being in the business of comedy, do not die of starvation'.[7] The plea was successful, and the students were granted a daily allowance. As Boris Varneke points out, the petition was the first of a 'boundless number of both oral and written requests from actors tormented by hunger and poverty'.[8]

It is impossible to calculate the number of actors employed in Russian theatres at this time with any degree of certainty. Probably about thirty actors were involved in the average enterprise,[9] suggesting that over six thousand worked in the 216 provincial theatres recorded for 1899. When the unknown but no doubt considerable numbers involved in the touring circuits, club stages and capital theatres are taken into account, then the total most likely exceeds ten thousand. By 1917, the Russian Theatre Society had six thousand members, but many artists were not affiliated to it.[10] Nor do any of the above estimates include the (smaller) numbers of people like set designers and régisseurs who were covered by the contemporaneous term 'theatre people'. What *is* certain is that the number of theatre people was growing rapidly towards the end of the nineteenth century, and that most of them worked in small provincial theatres in unpredictable economic circumstances.

Tales of actors suffering from economic deprivation, cold and hunger were commonplace from the early nineteenth century.[11] The expanding numbers of theatre people during the latter half of the century, however, made the various dilemmas more conspicuous. The problem was particularly acute in the provinces, where stage work afforded few benefits or material rewards. Theatrical work was seasonal, and actors and actresses had a particularly difficult time during Lent, when Russian drama was prohibited and theatres were used by travelling foreign troupes. A cartoon from 1884, entitled 'Metamorphoses in the Life of a Provincial Actor', shows six stages of an actor's year. The first scene, 'During the Theatre Season', depicts a feted actor on stage receiving garlands, bowing slightly in acknowledgement of the recognition. The second scene, 'In Butter Week', shows the actor devouring a well deserved meal. The third scene, 'At the Beginning of Lent', has him well-dressed and confident, chatting to a lady in the street. In the fourth scene, 'At the End of Lent', the actor is selling (or perhaps pawning) some of his clothes and other possessions. 'At Easter', the fifth scene, shows him performing in a fairground puppet booth. In the final scene, 'During the Summer', he is pictured as a tramp, huddled under a bridge.[12]

The publisher and sometime provincial actor Nikolai Leikin described his experiences in a diary that he kept during Lent. The manager of his troupe had complained of making only forty-five rubles from a performance. He invited the actors to visit him at home to discuss their wages, but when they arrived he had already left town. The actors therefore asked the local governor if they could stage a performance in order to raise enough funds to see them through

1 The Free Russian Theatre on Tsaritsyn Meadow, St Petersburg.

2 Denis Fonvizin.

НЕДОРОСЛЬ,

КОМЕДІЯ

ВЪ ПЯТИ ДѢЙСТВІЯХЪ.

Представлена въ первый разъ

ВЪ САНКТПЕТЕРБУРГѢ

Сентября 24 дня 1782.

продается у Клостермана, противъ адмиралтейства, въ домѣ мещанскаго клоба. No. 106.

Въ Санктпетербургѣ,

Печатана въ вольной типографіи у Шнора,

1783

3 Frontispiece of the 1783 edition of *The Minor*.

4 Alexander Shakhovskoi.

5 Expulsion of a French actress from Moscow during the war with Napoleon.

6 Nikolai Sheremetev.

7 The theatre at Ostankino.

8 Mikhail Shchepkin.

9 Vasily Karatygin.

10 Pavel Mochalov.

11 Vissarion Belinsky.

12 Ivan Sosnitsky and Pyotr Karatygin (brother of Vasily) in *Woe from Wit*.

13 Bolshoi Theatre, Moscow, during a coronation gala performance.

14 'The First Step of Freedom of the Theatres in Petersburg.' The sketch depicts the
Imperial Theatre monopoly as a rotten oak tree whose collapse has enabled the
mushrooming of new, if undistinguished, theatres, including operetta and variety venues.
The growth of the 'desired mushroom', people's theatre, is hindered by the large stone.

15 Fyodor Korsh.

16 Mikhail Lentovsky.

17 'Apropos the Resumption of the Benefit System.' The sketch depicts artists of the
Alexandrinsky Theatre squeezing money out of the public, a comment on the ubiquity
of benefits. Ticket speculators are shown fishing for some of the proceeds.

18 'The Dramatic Condition of the Russian Private Actor during Lent.' Until 1907 Russian language performances were restricted during Lent, especially in St Petersburg and Moscow, resulting in temporary unemployment for many actors. The sketch depicts an actor being assailed by creditors, including a cobbler, a butcher and a money-lender. The insets show the kind of 'Lenten entertainments' that were permitted.

19 Meeting room of the council of the Russian Theatre Society.

20 Russian Theatre Society's refuge for aged theatre people.

Lent. Under the rules, he could permit only a 'concert with *tableaux vivants*', which the troupe agreed to produce:

> It was decided to stage the scenes as quickly as possible in order to entice the public; the actresses were persuaded to bare as much of their chests as possible. Aglaeva will portray Bacchante and Rastupov a satyr. Tenerifova will sing 'When Your Husband Suddenly Feels Like Doing It' [*Kogda suprug zakhochet vdrug*] from *Elena* [Offenbach's *La Belle Hélène*], and in the second part will portray a bathing nymph.

In the event, the proceeds from the show were poor because the circus was in town. Consequently, one member of the troupe went to perform conjuring tricks in taverns for 'inebriated merchants', while another sang in out-of-town restaurants. Leikin himself went to the circus, which was obviously drawing the Lenten crowds, and applied, unsuccessfully, to be a clown. To make ends meet, he pawned his collections of Ostrovsky, Shakespeare and Molière.[13] And the problem of unpaid wages was not only a provincial one. In Moscow, for example, K. O. Shcherbinsky dissolved his short-lived theatrical enterprise in 1885 without paying the actors.[14]

At a congress of theatre people held in Moscow in 1897, stories about the woeful condition of provincial artists abounded. The veteran Imperial Theatre actress Nadezhda Medvedeva addressed the audience as follows:

> You are all, dear people, familiar with the life of the contemporary Neschastlivtsev [a wandering player, practically indistinguishable from a vagabond, in Ostrovsky's play *The Forest*], you all know that after a weakly performed drama on the stage, there, in the wings, between scenery that is dusty and full of holes, they frequently get carried away by those 'dramas behind the stage' which wear out the very heart of a man, bring glistening tears to the hardest eyes.[15]

At the same gathering, Evtikhy Karpov, by then a régisseur at the Imperial Theatres after his short spell at Suvorin's, sketched a general picture of theatre in the provinces:

> A poorly heated and dimly lit, cramped theatre, dirty and ragged scenery ... broken furniture ... shabby costumes ... poor properties ... a cheap, randomly assembled troupe, playing ad lib, hurriedly, not knowing the roles.

A repertoire powdered with farces and fairytale melodramas, fighting 'for an improvement in the takings' ... 'Touring artists' performing *King Lear* and *Shylock* [*sic*] after one rehearsal with an unfamiliar troupe ... The lack of takings, the hunger of actors, the flight of the impresario or 'manager of the company', the miserable, involuntary end-of-the-season turn to credit, to the cost of twelve kopeks per ruble ... Almost universal discontent, complaints about the hard labour of the provincial actor, about the absence of an audience ... Here is the usual, typical picture of provincial theatre in our time.[16]

At a second congress of theatre people, held in Moscow in 1901, one delegate spoke of the 'oppression' that the provincial actor was forced to endure, and claimed that there were two 'castes' in the 'artistic family': the 'well-known artists living in clover' (i.e. Imperial Theatre stars) and 'artists in the provinces, living a pitiful existence'.[17]

One of the most common causes of poverty among actors, and therefore a perennially urgent issue for them, was the inefficient or crooked impresario, notorious for maltreating theatrical troupes. As the number of theatre people grew, this problem was brought to the attention of the government, as evidenced by a classified (and awkwardly phrased) circular sent from the Ministry of Internal Affairs to all local governors early in 1886:

From information in the possession of the Ministry of Internal Affairs, it is evident that, in recent times, impresarios of private theatres, having assembled troupes of actors, very often find themselves completely bankrupt [and are unable] to pay them the agreed salary, and the actors, arriving from some town, from more or less remote districts, not only lack the means to return to [their] previous residences, but fall into destitution and thus increase the number of people who find themselves under the care of the government and public institutions. Such a situation shows that theatrical presentations are being embarked upon without the sufficient resources to guarantee the fulfilment by impresarios of the obligations they have taken upon themselves.[18]

The circular concluded by instructing governors to ensure that the local police were satisfied that impresarios possessed sufficient funds before granting permission to open theatres. The persistence of the problem, however, suggests that this measure had minimal impact, and the government did little else to address thespian impoverishment.

It was therefore left to theatrical artists themselves to seek to alleviate their dire material circumstances. Yet although hardship and exploitation had always accompanied provincial theatrical life, the political and social circumstances of imperial Russia meant that effective action began only in the 1890s. Earlier in the century, serf actors were for the most part in no position to complain about their circumstances, even where they were fortunate enough to receive payment for entertaining their masters in private or local ticket-buying audiences in public. For artists in other provincial troupes, social hostility made it largely impossible to exert any influence over employers. Some theatre people must have had access, where absolutely necessary, to the varieties of poor relief that were available. Social welfare boards, set up in 1775, were 'the major providers of medical and charitable aid in preemancipation Russia'; but they were not considered effective.[19] The Imperial Philanthropic Society and its branches, as well as independent charitable associations, tried to tackle poverty, but they were relatively few in number until the 1870s. There is evidence of twenty-eight independent charitable associations existing during the reign of Alexander I, with a further twenty established under Nicholas I.

During the reign of Alexander II, however, as a consequence of the 'great reforms', associational activity increased massively, including the creation of 753 new charitable associations.[20] Associations designed specifically to address the problems of theatre people date from this period, and the timing of their appearance is therefore explained by the twin effects of growth in the theatre industry and the more favourable climate for associational activity. But it was the Russian Theatre Society that first made a significant impact on the lives of theatre people. Formed in 1894 in the midst of another upsurge in associational activity across the empire – statistics from the Police Department show that between 1890 and 1896 a total of 2,176 new associations were formed[21] – the new society turned out to be more than a charity: it led theatre people in a bid for full professionalization.

The formation of the Russian Theatre Society constituted the first serious manifestation of many artists' ambitions to pursue professionalization.[22] It emerged from smaller charitable associations devoted to the needs of poverty-stricken thespians. The earliest was the Russian Artists' Mutual Assistance Society, founded privately in St Petersburg in 1877.[23] This was succeeded in 1883 by the Society for the Benefit of Indigent Stage People, established on the initiative of the Imperial Theatre actress Maria Savina. Its other leading figures were the Imperial Theatre stars Vladimir Davydov and Nikolai Sazonov, the writer Dmitry Grigorovich, and the publisher and editor Andrei Kraevsky. In 1894, that organization was reformed as the Russian Theatre Society (henceforth RTO), on the grounds that, according to one observer, the desperate state of Russian theatre, especially in the provinces, demanded more 'urgent intervention'.[24] Although the creation of the RTO marked an organizational break from the society established in 1883, the earlier association came to be regarded as an integral part of the RTO's history. In 1903, for example, the RTO's council observed its 'twentieth anniversary'.[25] The charter of the RTO named its founders as Kraevsky, Savina, Davydov, Sazonov, Grigorovich, Vsevolozhsky (director of Imperial Theatres), E. N. Zhuleva (Imperial Theatre actress), V. P. Gaevsky (literary and music critic), A. A. Potekhin (playwright), F. A. Burdin (Imperial Theatre actor), and D. M. Leonova (Imperial Theatre opera singer). The fact that Burdin and Gaevsky died in 1887 and 1888 respectively indicates that the charter included the founders of the RTO's 1883 predecessor. It is noteworthy that Savina, Sazonov and Davydov – three of the RTO's most prominent supporters – all had backgrounds in provincial theatre, perhaps partly explaining why the society devoted so much attention to the needs of provincial theatre people.

Whereas Savina's original society had confined its aims to philanthropic work, the RTO, according to the opening line of its founding charter, aspired to assist the 'all-round development of theatre affairs in Russia'.[26] In pursuit of this broad aim, the RTO set itself three main tasks: 'representation before administrative and public institutions of the needs of theatre affairs in Russia and of the interests of Russian theatre people'; 'mediation between the supply and demand of theatrical-artistic labour in all its forms'; and 'material help of any kind for theatrical enterprises in general and indigent stage people in particular'. It would pursue these aims by working with other 'liable institutions' on issues regarding 'theatrical welfare', by founding a 'pension or old-age insurance fund', by organizing congresses of theatre people, by appointing agents to represent the society's interests in the provinces, by opening an informational-statistical bureau (to collate data on all aspects of Russian theatre, and to mediate in the theatrical labour and property market, which would include helping stage people to find work), by publishing a periodical specialist theatre organ, by taking on the responsibility of representing the authorial rights of dramatists in private theatres, by issuing financial assistance and loans to its members, and by helping to set up private theatres.

The formal structure of the RTO consisted of a council and a general assembly of all members. The general assembly elected members of the council by secret ballot, for a period of three years. Each year a third of the council's members were replaced or had to be re-elected. The council met at least once a week to administer the society's main tasks. All matters were decided by a simple majority vote, a casting vote being made by the chairman in the event of a tie. General assemblies met annually and for special purposes. All members of the RTO had the right to vote at the assemblies, and all issues were again decided by simple majority vote, with some exceptions. The exclusion of a member, amendments to the charter, and closure of the society required majority votes of no less than two-thirds of all members in attendance. For amendments to the charter, at least half of all members residing in St Petersburg (where general assemblies took place) needed to be in attendance. Membership was open to all adults, of both sexes, and of any rank or status. The annual membership fee was 'no less than five rubles', and a one-off contribution of 'no less than one hundred rubles' secured life membership. Honorary membership for those who rendered a particular service to the society and its aims could be granted by secret ballot of the general assembly.[27]

Interest in the society spread rapidly. In 1898 it already had 1,461 members, and by 1902 that number had almost trebled to 4,444, although this was still less than half of the likely total number of people working in Russian theatre at the time.[28] Given that few artists would have been unaware of the RTO's existence by 1902, why did so many remain outside? First of all, not all theatre people would have been able or willing to part with the minimum annual membership fee. Secondly, where at least one actor in a particular troupe was a member, others may have felt that this was sufficient representation (even though membership was meant to be on an individual rather than collective basis). Thirdly, some wandering players, who spent much of the year travelling from town to town seeking work, may never have encountered an opportunity to join the RTO. And finally, it is possible that some impresarios dissuaded artists from joining the society because they regarded it as a threat to their interests. Nevertheless, the size of the RTO's membership was unusually large by comparison with other contemporaneous associations. According to Stepansky, the 'typical pre-revolutionary public organization' had a 'maximum of several hundred members'.[29]

The RTO successfully implemented much of its programme, financing its work largely from membership dues, interest on its capital and loans, income from its property, special performances and, from 1900, government subsidies. To help indigent artists, it made loans available to individuals who had been working in theatre for no less than five years and who had been members of the RTO for no less than two years (although members of the RTO who were also members of the loans-savings banks attached to the Mariinsky and Malyi theatres were not eligible for society loans). Loans were intended either for personal needs or for expenses related to theatre work. Whole troupes of artists could apply for a loan, chiefly for expenses related to the work of the company (so long as at least two-thirds of the troupe had been members of the RTO for at least two years). Individuals could receive no more than three hundred rubles, and for no more than six months. Troupes could receive no more than six hundred rubles, and for no more than three months. For these purposes, the RTO defined 'theatre people' quite broadly to include not only drama, opera and ballet performers, but also scenery painters, scenery shifters, prompters, régisseurs and their assistants, conductors and their assistants, and the musicians of permanent theatre orchestras – in other words, all those directly involved with the creative side of theatre.[30] The society also made small grants available to artists. The weekly meetings of the council were mainly concerned with the distribution of financial aid. The amount of money that it spent on the society's 'charitable missions' steadily increased during the early years of its existence, reflecting its rising membership rather than any sudden deterioration in the overall fortunes of artists:

1898	9,591 r. 85 k.
1899	11,633 r. 70 k.
1900	14,281 r. 39 k.
1901	19,907 r. 93 k.
1902	32,964 r. 40 k.
1903	46,412 r. 06 k.[31]

The records of the council also indicate that while the number of loans and grants increased substantially at the turn of the century, they decreased in 1904 and 1905. This was a consequence of straitened economic circumstances rather than fewer applications for assistance. In May 1904, the council chairman, A. E. Molchanov, reported that the society's material wellbeing had been adversely affected by 'grave events' (the Russo-Japanese War), but a request for a larger government subsidy ('in view of the growth of the society and the expansion of its activity') was rejected.[32]

Loans and grants were not the only form of assistance offered by the RTO.

For several years it helped to house elderly artists in rented apartments, before finally opening its long-planned refuge for aged theatre people in 1902 on Petrovsky Island in St Petersburg,[33] and in the same year the society opened an orphanage for artists' children.[34] Like many associations that represented the interests of occupational groups in late imperial Russia, the RTO also looked to the government to promulgate legislation that would lessen the hardship experienced by its members. For example, following a resolution at the 1901 congress of theatre people, the society's council agreed to ally itself with other associations by petitioning the Ministry of Finance for theatre people to be included among the 'toilers' eligible for state insurance, then under consideration by the government.[35]

The RTO made impressive strides in its endeavour to become the country-wide hub of the Russian theatre business. In November 1896, it opened its informational-statistical bureau in Moscow. This acted as an agency for the hiring of theatre people, providing a more formal way for artists, especially those from the provinces, to seek employment, and for impresarios to find employees.[36] It should be noted that the RTO's informational-statistical bureau was not the first office to act as an intermediary between artists and impresarios. A theatrical agency that fulfilled similar functions was established in Moscow in 1892 by E. N. Rassokhina and lasted to 1917. Rassokhina was known to artists as 'Elizaveta I, Queen of the Actors'.[37] Karpov recalled that when he was working as a régisseur at Suvorin's Theatre, he had approached Rassokhina's agency to find actors for the troupe, and that although it responded quickly, only three or four artists from a list of about one hundred currently seeking a position were suitable.[38]

The RTO established a large network of agents (*upolnomochennye*) to act on its behalf throughout Russia, and their numbers jumped from 84 in 1898–9 to 650 in 1904.[39] The social profile of the agents lends weight to the view that those who led the professionalization process for theatre people already enjoyed certain material and social advantages. Most appear to have held positions of authority or status in provincial Russia, judging by the way they defined themselves for the society's records. For instance, one of the Vologda region's agents was a land captain (*zemskii nachal'nik*), who also happened to be involved in a local artistic circle. The agent for Penza was a branch manager of the Moscow International Commercial Bank. Most of the others held an official rank, though there was one editor and one 'artist'. Indeed, the evidence shows that many artists were at least volunteering to become agents at about the same time as the initial list of agents was produced.[40]

The trebling of the society's membership between 1898 and 1902 is a further indication that the RTO was becoming the organizational focus for artists. Even in cases where it had no direct authority, it became the acknowledged intermediary between theatre people and the relevant official bodies. For example, Jewish actors wishing to travel to Moscow to secure new contracts could now contact their local RTO representative, who would pass the request to the council which in turn would request permission for travel rights from the Moscow governor on behalf of the actors.[41] All this suggests that the RTO quickly established itself as an organization with structures that increasingly enabled it to communicate with provincial artists. These structures also gave a growing number of theatre people the means to express a collective occupational identity.

At the same time, the RTO aimed to consolidate and extend its authority in all spheres of theatre activity. In the summer of 1898, for instance, the council chairman, V. S. Krivenko, spoke of the need for the society to support the general development of 'fairgrounds, theatres and other useful and sensible amusements for the people'.[42] In March 1899, the council effectively acquired the right to prohibit individuals from forming troupes and opening theatres if it considered them 'in this respect unreliable' (though it would require the backing of the Ministry of Internal Affairs).[43] In January 1900, the council resolved to petition the Ministry of Internal Affairs to grant the RTO 'the right of real control over theatre affairs in Russia'.[44] It is unclear whether a petition was sent to the ministry, but the resolution was made at a time when the state was beginning to take a greater interest in the work of the society, notably by providing an annual subsidy.

As the RTO's activities grew, so did its bureaucratic apparatus. For example, in October 1898 it decided to create another information bureau attached to the council in St Petersburg, though subordinate to the one in Moscow. The new office helped the council to discharge its duties and issued information to members, and others, about the activities of the society. Other functions included ensuring that membership dues were paid in good time; dealing with foreign theatrical agencies; mediating between artists and impresarios; dealing with petitions, chiefly from provincial members, about censored plays, and offering help for the production of 'complex historical plays, translations of foreign plays and so forth'; and running a library.[45] By the time of the 1905 revolution, however, the growth of the RTO's apparatus had led to accusations that it was becoming too bureaucratic (see chapter 7).

In a short space of time, the RTO had become recognized as the official, authoritative association representing the interests of theatre people. Most of its work involved attempts to alleviate hardship among its members, but it was a multi-purpose organization, and its efforts to establish itself as a general regulatory body for the theatre industry gave it the characteristic of a professional association. It should also be noted that the RTO was one of the earliest successful actors' associations in the world. Although the Union of German Theatre People had been founded as early as 1871, in the United States the Actors' Equity Association did not appear until 1913, and the British equivalent, Equity, was not established until 1929, although both were preceded by other, less successful attempts at organization.[46]

The growing organizational strength of the RTO was evident in the two congresses of theatre people it convened in Moscow in 1897 and 1901. Unlike its general assemblies, which, for geographical reasons, ordinarily comprised only members of the RTO residing in St Petersburg, the congresses were designed to bring together artists from all over the empire. Their success in doing so indicated that, under the leadership of the RTO, Russian theatre people were beginning to regard themselves as members of a country-wide collective. The idea of a gathering of theatre people had been in circulation for some time. Anatoly Kremlev, for example, a lawyer with an active interest in theatre, had proposed such a gathering in 1889 for consideration of matters germane to Russia's thespians.[47] Inspired by organizational developments in other occupational groups, the RTO had from its inception regarded congresses as a means of discussing theatrical affairs and associated problems, as well as achieving other aims of the society as set out in its charter.[48] In October 1896, an organizing commission elicited the views of artists by issuing twelve thousand copies of a circular calling on those interested to say what issues they regarded as most urgently requiring discussion. The commission received no more than sixty responses from 'all ends of Russia'.[49]

More than one thousand delegates attended the first congress, while approximately five hundred attended the second. The proceedings of the congresses highlight the various ways in which, in addition to associational activity, Russian theatre people were asserting themselves as a profession.[50] Three particular issues stand out: the alleged threat to theatre's social value from commercialism; whether to regulate entry to the occupational group by means of a recognized qualification; and the internal regulation of working conditions, notably through the use of contracts between artists and impresarios.

Speakers at both congresses, especially the first, emphasized theatre's social value and the consequent importance of theatre people. Professions normally bid for social, economic and political status by claiming expertise and responsibility for tasks considered essential to the country. As one historian of the Russian example has written, 'Professors claimed a special responsibility for the higher education system, physicians for public health, lawyers for the legal basis of the state, and engineers for economic and technical progress.'[51] Members of the artistic intelligentsia had long believed that they bore a special responsibility for popular enlightenment, and the notion that theatre had social and educational utility was nothing new. But now that mass entertainment had arrived, these ideas were invoked as a particular response to the effects of the market. Several speeches at the 1897 congress alluded to the perceived significance of theatre beyond mere entertainment. Kremlev reiterated the well-established view that theatre was a recognized educational tool, while asserting theatre's role as a fusion of the arts:

> To speak of the social mission of the actor is to speak of the social mission of art. Stage art is really a synthesis of all the others: in stage art, all the most original attributes of art in general are expressed more clearly, and no other art has as powerful an influence on society as stage art.

Consequently, 'The actor, with the resources of his art, performs a high educational mission.'[52]

But some at the congress expressed profound concern that this 'mission' was threatened, or had already been eclipsed, by commercial interests. The playwright Alexei Potekhin repeated the old concern that the educational function of theatre was increasingly being pushed aside by economic necessities. He observed that the Imperial Theatres had always been protected, unlike provincial stages. With the development of 'education and civilization', the need for theatre had grown, as had the number of people wishing to devote themselves to artistic endeavours.

> Is it not strange that, in these conditions, theatre has become a sacrifice of speculation and mercantilist enterprise, that it has lost its educational meaning and has become an industrial venture, and the contingent of genuine theatre people has become overwhelmed by people without any relation to art, who look upon it only as a means of existence?

Theatre, he said, had slowly lost its 'educational and moralizing mission', as businessmen turned it into an 'amusement arcade' subject only to mercantilist concerns and the caprice of majority taste.[53] At the same congress, the writer P. D. Boborykin emphasized the educational importance of theatre and the impoverishment of theatre people: 'In our country, almost more so than anywhere in western Europe, it is possible to view theatre as one of the most motive and attractive instruments and manifestations of the development of society.'[54] Theatre, he argued, must fulfil its 'artistic-educational mission' chiefly in the provinces, but its artistic quality could not be separated from the economic conditions of the actor's life: 'It is sad, but a stage proletariat does exist.'[55]

In a contribution to a debate about whether Imperial Theatre troupes from St Petersburg and Moscow should be prohibited from touring the provinces because they deprived provincial artists of opportunities to work, the (provincial) actor T. N. Selivanov argued that the real problem with such tours was that they were devoid of educational objectives. Moving on to another point, he argued that the difficulties of Russian theatre derived not from the absence of impresarios, as another speaker had suggested, but from their 'material bankruptcy'. He concluded, 'Free competition should not be allowed. The principle of *laissez faire, laissez passer,* has had its time in both economic science and state law; it is time to renounce it in the theatre business.'[56] A certain P. V. Panin blamed the low standards of the repertoire on the material motives of impresarios. Like several others, he was prepared to acknowledge that the poor state of provincial theatre was partly caused by talentless artists. But, he argued, general improvement would occur only when such people were guaranteed economic security.[57] This sentiment was widely expressed at the 1897 congress, and one of its final resolutions called for the introduction of a minimum wage for theatre people, recommended to be at least twenty-five rubles per month.[58] The congress almost unanimously supported the argument that town administrations and *zemstva* should assume responsibility for provincial theatre. This was partly to ensure the extension of theatre to areas of the country where it was currently absent or lacked the financial resources to survive, but it was also conceived as a strategy to protect theatre from the effects of the market.

A certain Alexander Kolyupanov, for example, suggested that if local authorities rather than private enterprise ran Russia's theatres, they could reallocate any profits to struggling theatres in other towns.[59] In such circumstances, contended the actor Dmitry Karamazov, the need to speculate would be removed.[60] Kremlev insisted that theatres should be organized by local authorities since only they could act 'disinterestedly'.[61] Likewise, another actor, V. V. Nikulin, observed that theatre could play a leading role in provincial public life, but first had to cease being a 'commercial under-taking'.[62] In order to justify the plea for greater local authority involvement in theatre, a certain Basmanov once again expressed the perceived link between the low artistic standards of the repertoire and the material insecurity of actors, which compelled theatre managers to defer too much to audience taste: 'The golden age for theatre art will begin when the government comes to the aid of theatre people.'[63]

The first congress appears to have raised the morale of some theatre people, who believed they were now taken more seriously by society. Reflecting on its impact, the actor N. I. Sobolshchikov-Samarin wrote, 'I, a theatrical down-and-out, for the first time felt like a human being and a citizen.'[64] Opening the second congress, Molchanov described the gathering as 'a significant occurrence in the history of the Russian stage, indicating how unshakably and firmly has been consolidated the view of the cultural and public significance of the actor's work'. He also reflected on the importance of the first congress:

> For the first time, the actor was acknowledged and felt himself to be a public figure, worthy of such attention and gratitude as the people of other professions. This is the result of the tireless struggle of many generations of Russian actors, of the best representatives of native theatre – something of which they so recently were unable to dream. One should recall the sad time when the actor was regarded as a kind of pariah, and only the noble voices of Gogol, Belinsky [and Sergei] Aksakov were raised in defence of the actor, striving to show society that the actor is not a buffoon summoned forth for the amusement of the crowd, but a loyal servant of the motherland in its age-old movement towards light, truth and love.[65]

While it is unlikely that the wider social impact of the congresses was as considerable as such comments suggest, many theatre people clearly believed in the public value of their work, and the congresses produced formal articulation of it within their occupational group. Moreover, the close juxtaposition of anti-commercial rhetoric and the notion of actors' value and dignity in congress speeches was not coincidental. By insisting that theatre had a vital public mission that was increasingly distorted by the market, speakers were making the case for the government support that would free the stage from the problem. What made the argument so compelling for so many artists was the impoverishment that commercial theatre seemed to entail. This is not to suggest that artists were being insincere when they spoke of the theatre's public mission and its declining standards. But when such language is placed in the context of the RTO's efforts to address hardship among artists, it is quite clear that the pejorative effects of commercial theatre were widely felt, and that the assertion of professionalism was perceived as a solution.

Another aspect of professionalization evident at the two congresses was the issue of regulating entry to the occupational group by means of a qualification. The Imperial Theatres already maintained their own schools to ensure a steady supply of talented performers, and most of their artists received school training. But with the exception of ballet such training was not essential for a career on the imperial stages, as the case of Maria Savina, the leading actress at the St Petersburg Alexandrinsky in the late tsarist period, demonstrates. Without any formal training, Savina became an accomplished provincial actress, and was then talent-spotted while performing in a St Petersburg club.[66] From the 1870s, private drama classes organized by enthusiasts began to appear, mainly in the capitals, but they were not necessary for theatre work.[67] Konstantin Stanislavsky cast doubt on the usefulness of the existing theatre schools, recalling that 'The majority of the so-called professors of dramatic art were charlatans, as they have remained till the present day; and prominent individual actors were in the possession of some fundamentals which they either worked out themselves, or received as a heritage from the great actors of the past generations.'[68] (Presumably his co-founder of the Moscow Art Theatre, Nemirovich-Danchenko, who taught drama at the school of the Moscow Philharmonic Society, was an exception.) The vast majority of ordinary theatre people worked at the lower levels of the entertainment industry, mainly in the provinces, where anyone could audition to join a theatrical troupe, regardless of wealth or status, and where natural aptitude and perseverance, rather than formal training, often accounted for success.

Demands for an entry qualification that would enable credentialed individuals to be formally recognized as theatre artists appear to have been motivated by a concern for artistic standards, but they also betrayed a preoccupation with the social status of theatre people, testifying to the widely held sentiment that the purported seriousness of the vocation should be acknowledged by some degree of difficulty in gaining access to it. There was a general consensus that artists should be educated. A resolution of the 1897 congress advocated the establishment of permanent theatre schools in the capitals and the provinces, and the provision of free courses for actors and régisseurs, but stopped short of calling for obligatory attendance.[69] Some speakers favoured a more formal system of certification by diploma,[70] and one even suggested that the Moscow Solodovnikovsky Theatre, recently purchased by the RTO, be transformed into a central institution where all actors would be required to make their debuts in return for a diploma granting them the right to join a troupe.[71] But while the first congress agreed in principle that some type of qualification was required 'in view of the appreciable influx into the artists' milieu of people without the qualities necessary for the maintenance of the best artistic standards and moral ideals of theatre art',[72] it deferred a recommendation on what form this should take until the next congress.

At the 1901 gathering, speakers articulated a much closer connection between the low social status of theatre people and the absence of a means of certifying that artists were suitably qualified for their vocation. Despite Molchanov's positive remarks about the improving image of theatre people, many felt that their social status remained unchanged. A certain Fokhts, at the beginning of a discussion about an entry qualification, claimed that the term 'artist' was a 'swear word' and was often used to describe 'rogues' and 'thieves'. Another speaker was optimistic that this would change with the passage of time because the 'degradation' of the term 'artist' was rooted in the fact that, in the past, most theatre people had been serfs. Yet another thought the explanation to be that too many people were casually pursuing a stage career because they could do nothing else: 'It is essential to shut the doors of the Theatre Society to such characters, where only the real "priests" of art should be.' The régisseur Yu. M. Ozarovsky argued, to much disapproval, that all art required a 'preparatory school', and theatre was no exception – without 'school discipline' it was 'impossible to produce a real professional [*professional*]'. A certain I. E. Veldeman suggested that the RTO petition for all actors to be recognized as 'esteemed' (*pochetnyi*), since the 'priest of art' is a 'popular teacher and public figure'. But, he insisted, the right to such a title would have to be based on an educational qualification.[73] Like all such proposals, however, there was little indication of what might constitute an appropriate education for theatre people.

Many expressed opposition to the idea of an entry qualification. The playwright Vladimir Nemirovich-Danchenko reminded delegates to the 1897 congress that theatrical talent often manifested itself in people with little formal training.[74] In the opinion of V. I. Nikulin, speaking at the 1901 congress, an artist required only 'intuition', and if any qualification was to be imposed it should be for 'the régisseur who teaches the actors'. Alexander Kugel, also addressing the 1901 gathering, argued that the establishment of an entry qualification would be impossible, and that 'the door should be open to all', although he conceded that a 'qualification of recognition' (*tsenz priznaniia*) might be required in order to ascertain 'who is an actor and who is not'. Such a qualification, however, should be established only by theatre colleagues, and only by ballot.[75] The final resolutions of the 1901 congress reflected the lack of consensus on the question of a qualification. No 'obligatory conditions' for stage employment were to be established in the meantime, but in future membership of the RTO was to be dependent on a ballot and references from other artists, unless the applicant had worked in theatre for three years.[76]

Theatre people thus confronted a dilemma in their bid for professional status – how to establish a formal, credentialed entry route to a vocation where the requisite skills were largely instinctive and, in contrast to those entailed in other professions, were successfully acquired by many practitioners without any training, let alone in a clearly defined corpus of knowledge. (Stanislavsky's famous 'system', in so far as it might be considered a more methodical approach to training actors, crystallized somewhat later, from about 1910 onwards.)[77] Nevertheless, discussions about the need for better-educated actors and an entry qualification, conceived as ways to improve artistic standards, indicated how seriously theatre people expected to be taken. There is little evidence that congress delegates were concerned primarily by market saturation and were seeking to regulate access to the stage for economic reasons. Although a few delegates to the 1897 congress drew attention to the material disadvantages of having two troupes in a thinly populated town, most resisted any tendency towards local monopolies, insisting on the beneficial effects of such competition on artistic standards. Consequently no prohibitory measures were recommended.[78] The only explicit attempt to exclude people from theatre work was related to the separate issue of antisemitism. At the 1901 congress, the actress Polina (or Pelageia) Strepetova was applauded by some when she spoke against general residency rights for Jewish artists, claiming that too many people were already competing for places in Russian theatres. Kugel, who was Jewish, then reminded the auditorium that it had applauded him when he had argued that 'the door should be open to all'.[79]

The third significant aspect of professionalization manifested at the congresses was seen in proposals to regulate the working conditions of theatre people. Historically, the process of professionalization has entailed efforts by occupational groups to regulate their own affairs, including the knowledge-base of their work, conditions of access, and internal relations between members. The principal objective for Russian theatre people in seeking to regulate their internal relations was to alleviate the hardships caused by managerial exploitation. Impresarios had long been notorious for failing to honour contracts, where they existed, often paying artists less than the agreed fee or absconding without paying them at all.[80] Moreover, contracts did not conform to any recognized standard (both Rassokhina's agency and the RTO's informational-statistical bureau used a variety of contracts),[81] tended to be weighted in favour of impresarios, and had no legal force. Olenina cites two examples from Kazan: in 1870, employment regulations for the Kazan theatre were drawn up, but were written from the perspective of the impresario, and in 1880, V. I. Bibin produced a brochure on how to organize a theatrical artel, but it was concerned mainly with financial matters rather than with defining the rights and obligations of artists.[82] In her address to the 1897 congress, Medvedeva articulated the general consensus among delegates that theatre, 'like any business that entwines the interests of a large number of toilers, must be regulated to a certain extent'.[83] Consequently, a new standard contract for theatre people was proposed, one that, in the view of A. D. Lavrov-Orlovsky, would place theatre affairs 'on a foundation of justice and duty'.[84]

Suggestions about what should be contained in the new contract provide further glimpses of the problems encountered by theatre people in their relations with impresarios. Karamazov, for example, argued that fines should be imposed only where artists had breached 'clear professional obligations' such as learning their roles properly and arriving on time for rehearsals. Misdemeanours of a 'moral character' should be the remit of the courts, not theatre managers. Practices detrimental to an actor's health, such as having to rehearse 'without a coat and galoshes in a cold theatre', should not be obligatory.[85] The special committee that drafted the new contract during the congress emphasized the need for contractual specificity about such issues as the duration of an agreement between artist and impresario, or the designation of an actor's *emploi*, time of arrival at work, salary, and number of performances per month.[86] The basic principles of the standard contract were agreed upon, although it was another six years before it came into force. The issue was revisited by the 1901 congress, by the RTO general assembly in October of the same year, and by a commission which convened in March 1902, when, as Molchanov observed, the breaching of contracts had taken on 'an epidemic, threatening character'.[87] The standard contract finally became operative in January 1903.[88]

Theatre people also pursued other ways of dealing with untrustworthy managers. Claiming that the relation of an artist to an impresario stood 'outside the law', Selivanov advocated the establishment of an arbitration tribunal to settle disputes. He also proposed that impresarios who failed to pay salaries should be banned from running theatres in the future.[89] By 1903, the RTO had introduced a compulsory system of monetary deposits (*zalogi*) for impresarios, who were required to submit a signed declaration and a sum of money to the society's informational-statistical bureau as a guarantee of payment to artists. The deposit was used to remunerate the artists if the enterprise failed or if the impresario disappeared.[90] Although *zalogi* appear to have been used in some parts of Russia before 1903 – Karamazov mentioned them at the 1897 congress and called for them to be made obligatory for all impresarios[91] – it took the emergence of the RTO as an increasingly effective regulatory association to make them a general requirement.

It is worth noting that the efforts to regulate the working conditions of artists served to enhance the status of the RTO. The special committee that formulated the standard contract insisted that only members of the RTO would be required to adhere to its provisions.[92] In other words, the legal protection that theatre people demanded would be conditional upon joining the society, which would work to enforce contracts. As Olenina has pointed out, this meant that the standard contract had a 'half-hearted character' for provincial actors as not all of them were members of the RTO.[93] Moreover, when the congresses resolved that it was necessary to petition the government about a particular matter, it was assumed that the RTO would do so on behalf of theatre people.

Like other associations in late imperial Russia, the RTO had its work monitored by the government. For example, its charter had to be approved by the Minister of Internal Affairs, an annual account of its expenditure and activities had to be submitted to the same ministry, and the St Petersburg governor could close the society if deemed necessary on the basis of 'information regarding disorders or violations of the charter'.[94] Yet the RTO's leadership did not consider government supervision incompatible with its aims. On the contrary, it actively sought its support and welcomed the (usually nominal) involvement of senior government and court figures in its business. Forging links with the government made financial sense, in that an association of impoverished artists would never be in a position to raise enough funds on its own to rectify the often desperate material condition of its members, and indeed the RTO succeeded in persuading the government to subsidize its activities. From 1895, it received five thousand rubles per annum to assist aged and infirm theatre people,[95] and from 1900 it received ten thousand rubles per annum from the State Exchequer to support its general work.[96] Symbolic links with the tsarist state were also forged. In December 1895, the RTO was brought under the official patronage of the tsar, described in the council records as a 'joyous event for the society'.[97] It further courted the favour of the state by granting honorary membership to influential figures, including the Minister of the Imperial Court Baron Frederiks, the Minister of Finance Count Witte, Grand Duke Sergei Alexandrovich, Grand Duke Konstantin Konstantinovich, and Prince A. P. Oldenburgsky.[98] Sergei Alexandrovich also accepted an invitation to be 'most august patron' of the 1897 congress,[99] and Grand Duke Sergei Mikhailovich was named president of the society in July 1900.[100]

While the benefits of close cooperation between the RTO and the government are obvious from the society's point of view, the state's apparent readiness to support commercial theatre, using the RTO as a conduit, is less explicable. Some government officials believed in the educational potential of theatre, or at least viewed it as a convenient distraction for ordinary people. The governor of St Petersburg favoured establishing *balagany* as permanent features of city life because they might distract people from the taverns.[101] Kugel recalled that Prince N. V. Shakhovskoi, a government official and, from 1901 to 1906, head of the Chief Administration for Press Affairs, remarked to him in early 1897, 'I think theatre is an ally of the government, since it diverts minds from sharp political issues.' Kugel claimed that this view was widely held (though he personally regarded it as an 'illusion').[102] This kind of attitude might explain the financial largesse bestowed on the RTO, even though, as we have already seen, particularly with regard to popular theatre, officialdom was simultaneously concerned about the potential of the stage, whether by design or default, to foment unrest.

Arguably, therefore, the apparent loyalty of the RTO's leadership made the society a politically useful association through which the government could supervise, albeit indirectly, Russia's commercial theatres. There is a certain amount of evidence that lends weight to this interpretation. In February 1899, after an evening performance at a St Petersburg theatre, V. S. Krivenko, then chairman of the RTO's council, had a conversation with Tsar Nicholas II during which, in addition to thanking the tsar for the annual subsidy that had recently been promised to the society and answering his questions about its work, Krivenko 'also explained the efforts of the society to do what it can to help the government, in the interests of the expedient organization of theatre affairs in Russia'. The tsar, according to Krivenko's account, remarked that he loved the theatre, was 'certain of its beneficial educational significance', and asked the chairman to convey his gratitude to members of the society for their 'effort to serve the state in the field of the good ordering of theatrical spectacles and the expedient organization of artists'.[103]

In November 1900, Grand Duke Sergei Mikhailovich informed the Assistant Minister of Internal Affairs, P. N. Durnovo (former head of the Chief Administration for Press Affairs), that the RTO was a 'reliable assistant of the government' in its endeavour to place the organization of private theatre on a firmer footing.[104] In January 1904, the society was granted permission to use the title 'Imperial' in recognition of the 'successful results' of its work.[105] In making this decision, the government was guided by the assessment of the deceased Minister of Internal Affairs, D. S. Sipiagin. Before he was assassinated in April 1902, Sipiagin, in a paper to the tsar that suggests close familiarity with the views of Sergei Mikhailovich cited above, had remarked that the RTO 'is, in the matter of the regulation and correct development of the Russian private theatre, a reliable assistant of the government'.[106] The number of public organizations and societies entitled to bear the title 'Imperial' could be counted in the tens. According to Stepansky, 'Imperial' societies were 'not officially regulated', could appeal to the tsar, and received subsidies and other privileges.[107] While the RTO already enjoyed most of these benefits, its new title confirmed the trust that the government appeared to place in its leadership. For some, however, it signified the extent to which the society was becoming part of the establishment.

Although government support helped the RTO to address some of the material difficulties experienced by theatre people, and the title 'Imperial' implied a degree of privilege, state patronage had little impact on the social status of the majority of artists. For example, many theatre people wanted their occupational group to be recognized as a *soslovie*, something which, in the absence of civil rights, might offer some occupational guarantees or privileges. At the 1897 congress, A. Z. Serpoletti claimed that it would improve the fortunes of theatre, and urged the RTO to petition the government on the issue.[108] A draft programme for the second congress included, as a high priority, the question of creating a *soslovie* (obligatory for all stage people) or a 'union' (voluntary).[109] But theatre people were never granted such recognition. In 1902, a certain N. N. Emelyanov asked the council if the formal title (*zvanie*) of artist or a *soslovie* of artists existed in Russia, but the council replied that, as far as it was aware, neither existed.[110] Although the 1876 version of the 'Statute on the Prevention and Suppression of Crimes' refers to performing artists as a *soslovie*, the use of the term in this context appears to have been informal, since artists were never an official estate.[111] The only formal recognition ever accorded to artists was the granting of the status of honorary citizenship to a few artists of the Imperial Theatres in 1839.[112]

In its efforts to establish theatre as a profession during the late tsarist period, the Russian Theatre Society enjoyed mixed success. Some of the core attributes of the traditional professions, such as an entry qualification based on rigorous training, remained elusive, and it is by no means evident that the growing self-respect of artists was accompanied by an improvement in the broader social perception of them. Nevertheless, the RTO successfully established itself as the authoritative representative of theatre people, who were able, through its work, to express a collective occupational identity for the first time. Using the society as an intermediary, theatre people increasingly spoke the language of a profession, confirming that, at the very least, the aspiration to professional status was strong.

The drive to establish theatre work as a profession was a direct response to mass impoverishment among artists. Late imperial Russian theatre was predominantly commercial (partial exceptions were the Imperial Theatres and subsidized people's theatres) and the interests that led to the country-wide organization of its workers were material ones. But while professionalization was embraced as the antithesis of commercialism, artists did not seek to manipulate the market for their trade as such; they were endeavouring, rather, to address its consequences. The experience of theatre people in late imperial Russia therefore accords with Terence Johnson's observation that, even where the 'class orientation' of an occupational group is paramount, 'the ideological weapons of professionalism may be of great value in justifying their cause'.[113] In perceiving the advantages of professional status, theatre people represented, or at least anticipated, what might be called the democratization of the professional ideal – its diffusion among occupational groups not traditionally classified as professions.

More broadly, the experience of the Russian Theatre Society is further testimony that the relationship between state and civil society in late tsarist

Russia was not necessarily antagonistic. Associational activity did not inevitably entail a struggle to escape the authority of the state; it was also a method of alerting it to a specific problem and seeking its assistance. Despite certain limits on the power and achievements of the Russian Theatre Society and its congresses, it managed to function as a meaningful intermediary between state and society. Thus, if Russian theatre was a 'school for the people', it was increasingly evident by the end of the nineteenth century that one of the principal lessons it had imparted, at least to its practitioners and employees, was the value of associational activity as a way of mobilizing their occupational group. Joseph Bradley has perceptively concluded that 'Under autocracy, voluntary associations not only gave civil society meaning, they made an essential contribution to the process by which Russian subjects were becoming citizens.'[114] The foregoing discussion suggests that this observation could be applied to Russian theatre people and their associational activity with much justification. And as the revolutionary upheavals of the early twentieth century drew nearer, the issue of citizenship became ever more urgent.

Chapter 7

THEATRICAL REVOLUTIONS

Between 1898 and 1905, Russian theatre witnessed two 'revolutions', one primarily artistic – the radical innovations of the Moscow Art Theatre – the other sociopolitical – the growing opposition to the tsarist regime that resulted in the 1905 revolution. There is an implicit assumption in many studies of Russian theatre that both developments stemmed from one common epochal spirit of rebellion. Thus, Sergei Danilov argues that during the early years of the twentieth century, as the revolution approached, there occurred an intensification of 'progressive-democratic tendencies' in the theatre. This was especially evident in the repertoires of certain theatres, which appeared to reflect the growing radical mood in the country.[1] The Moscow Art Theatre, in particular, was closely associated with the apparent radicalization of the repertoire, and has been described by a Soviet historian as 'the most prominent exponent of the progressive requirements of the national theatrical culture'.[2] Moreover, in its efforts to revive and reform the aspirations of Shchepkin and Ostrovsky for a naturalistic style of acting and a national stage, the Art Theatre reaffirmed the notion that the stage could fulfil an important social and even didactic role.

In certain respects, it was the Art Theatre's association with Anton Chekhov and more especially Maxim Gorky that sealed its reputation not only for artistic reform but for political radicalism. Yet the contemporaneous meaning of these associations should not be misread. Stanislavsky conveniently referred in his memoirs to the 'revolutionary aims' of the new theatre, but he was alluding, of course, to an artistic revolution.[3] The founders of the Art Theatre rebelled against what they saw as the outmoded production techniques of the Imperial Theatres. Their dedication to mounting naturalistic productions based on carefully crafted ensembles, as opposed to hastily staged, routine performances serving as vehicles for 'star' actors, meant that it was somewhat inevitable they would be attracted to the plays of Chekhov and that, on his advice, they would persuade Gorky to write for them. The techniques of the Art Theatre resulted in acclaimed productions of the two playwrights' work, and this guaranteed the new drama a higher profile than it might otherwise have enjoyed. Thus, artistic motives served to restore Kliuchevsky's 'incomparable mirror', but the world it reflected seemed more politically restless than before.

Politics entered the theatres more directly during the 1905 revolution. As the situation in the country became increasingly tense, a range of anxieties about public order and political direction were expressed by artists and audiences. The authorities responded in predictable ways – mainly by attempting to ensure that the theatres functioned as normally as possible, a tricky task during the key moments of the revolution, notably Bloody Sunday (9 January 1905) and the general strike (October 1905). The course of the revolution also revealed how far artists' professional aspirations had advanced, together with their understanding of how to achieve them. If Russian theatre of the *fin de siècle* was beginning to reassert its Enlightenment mission, it was also more attuned to the means by which it might be fulfilled. This chapter develops these themes by looking more closely at the two 'revolutions'.

The early history of the Moscow Art Theatre provides an important reminder that, amidst all the talk of decline and the apparent preoccupation with material issues, artistic matters remained at the forefront of what many theatre people were trying to achieve. The Moscow Art Theatre – or MKhT, from its Russian acronym – set out to challenge the dominant conventions of the Imperial Theatres at the end of the nineteenth century. In the process, it demonstrated once again that a private theatre could also be an artistically accomplished one. Although its early success was not as complete as is often assumed – finances remained precarious and audiences tended to drift off after the initial excitement of a premiere – the MKhT staged several critically acclaimed productions which, in the longer term, served to revolutionize theatrical practice, not only in Russia but throughout the world. In order to appreciate the magnitude of the achievement, it is necessary to illustrate the kind of production conventions against which the Art Theatre rebelled. The chief repositories of these conventions were the Imperial Theatres. Although they boasted a galaxy of stars, they were by no means at the cutting edge of modern staging; and although they were looked upon as 'model' and 'exemplary' institutions – often more in hope than in expectation – they remained, for the most part, tenaciously resistant to innovation until the Art Theatre compelled them to contemplate reform. In their memoirs, the founders of the Art Theatre largely ignored the innovative achievements of the Korsh, Mamontov and Suvorin theatres, especially in the realm of scenic authenticity and attention to historical detail. By comparing their artistic ambitions with Imperial Theatre routines, they appeared more revolutionary than they actually were. The subsequent renown of the Art Theatre should not obscure the fact that it built on foundations laid by other ventures.

Complaints about formulaic, unimaginative and unnatural staging in the state drama theatres date from at least the middle of the nineteenth century. The following account of the stage sets at the Alexandrinsky in the 1860s provides a glimpse of the problem:

> For decorating the walls there are only two paintings, one of the Aleksandra Waterfall and the other of the repentant Mary Magdalen. These were an eyesore for audiences who were forced to contemplate them three or four times a week. As for the remainder of the furnishings, for example the door curtains and window hangings – either dark red or green – these are generally soiled, faded and discoloured as well as unspeakably crumpled. They have no fixtures – usually a piece of metal is stuck up and a curtain unceremoniously suspended from it. The less said about the furniture the better – three changes (one green and two red) totally inadequate.[4]

Nikolai Drizen, editor of the Imperial Theatre yearbook between 1909 and 1915, proffered similar comments in his memoirs:

> Furniture was put on stage according to a pre-established order – contrary to that of any house: for instance, two arm chairs on one side of the stage, a table in between, and two chairs on the other side, a sofa in the background and a table next to a wall. No real pictures, decorations, ornaments or curtains were hung on the walls: they were all painted on sets. There was no period style. Court salons were always Gothic, a drawing room in a wealthy house had murals like those in a Venetian palace, and a poor man's room was as large as the stage. Costumes were classified as Italian, Spanish, and French, Louis XV or Henry IV – but the actors did marvels.[5]

The founders of the Art Theatre also reacted against the formulaic acting of the 'stars', many of whom were highly adept at a given *emploi* but often seemed incapable of capturing the essence of a character. This was due not to any deficiency in talent; it was simply an unquestioned tradition. The co-founder of the MKhT, Vladimir Nemirovich-Danchenko, described the acting and the sets of the 'old theatre' thus:

> There were the same people the public had so often seen, the same attractive individualities of Savina, Varlamov, Dalmatov, Strapetova [*sic*], and the rest, in their inspired theatrical mood. A new wig and a new mode in dress did not change the *human being*. Quite apart from this, there were the same green decorations representing the village – a garden which the public had seen yesterday in quite another play and would see to-morrow in a third play; the same diffused greenish electric illumination, which the public had grown accustomed to consider as lunar light, though there was nothing about it remotely resembling the moon. There were the same immense pavilions, which but yesterday were supposed to represent merchants' mansions, while to-day they were but the small, cosy rooms of a farm-house.[6]

The Art Theatre placed renewed emphasis on realism in acting, seeking to restore the apparently forgotten achievements of Shchepkin, and the Stanislavsky 'system' of acting later emerged as a result. The MKhT also rebelled against the lack of central direction in theatrical productions, becoming a major pioneer of the régisseur's theatre. Prior to the foundation of the MKhT, stage régisseurs worked in the government theatres but they did not perform the central role with which they came to be associated. Rather, the régisseur was usually an official without much inclination for the artistic side of the business. As Nemirovich explained, with some exaggeration, in regard to the Moscow Malyi,

> At the head of the administration were not literary men, but government officials. Prior to his appointment as chief, the manager had not the least contact with the theatres; he was an officer of the Guard, a position he had gained through his wife. The rôle of stage director was a very modest one; it had neither a creative nor a pedagogic content. Actors listened to him merely out of politeness.[7]

In certain respects, the all-powerful régisseur was the Art Theatre's most important innovation. It established the idea, now taken for granted, that productions should be governed by a 'single will'. This was how Nemirovich understood the import of the new theatre: 'In this, then, lies the first and most significant difference between the new and the old theatre: a single will reigns in our theatre.'[8] There was, however, an unintentional irony in that statement, as the Art Theatre often had to contend with the clashing wills of its co-founders.

The most famous of the two founders was Konstantin Alekseyev (1863–1938), who adopted the pseudonym 'Stanislavsky' in 1885. He was born into a wealthy Moscow merchant family, whose connections enabled him to form acquaintances with leading merchant patrons of the arts, including Pavel Tretyakov, Savva Mamontov and Alexei Bakhrushin. A keen participant in amateur dramatics, he organized the 'Alekseyev circle' to pursue his extra-curricular interests in the stage. His first experience as a stage director came in 1888, when he established the Moscow Society of Art and Literature together with the drama teacher and régisseur Alexander Fedotov (organizer of the temporary people's theatre at the Moscow Polytechnical Exposition in 1872) and the opera singer Fyodor Komissarzhevsky (father of the equally well-known Fyodor and Vera). The society initially mounted productions at the old Pushkin Theatre, where Anna Brenko's enterprise had been based. Nemirovich witnessed several performances and claimed to have been impressed, particularly by Stanislavsky's contribution.

A key early influence on Stanislavsky's ideas about staging was exercised by the theatrical company of Georg II, Duke of Saxe-Meiningen, whose stage director was Ludwig Cronegk. The company performed in Russia in 1885 and 1890. Stanislavsky attended several performances during the Meiningen's second tour, and was impressed both by the attention to historical detail, and by the general atmosphere with which the productions were imbued. The influence of the Meiningen troupe on Stanislavsky was later evident, for example, in the Society of Art and Literature's production of *Othello* in 1896, one critic writing that the Meiningen had left a 'very deep trace' in Stanislavsky's memory. In terms of scenery and costumes, he claimed, Moscow had never before witnessed a Shakespeare play produced to this quality.[9] Encouraged by his successes and growing fame as an amateur actor and régisseur, by early 1897 Stanislavsky was considering ways of establishing a new full-time theatre to which he could devote all his energy.[10]

Vladimir Nemirovich-Danchenko (1858–1943) was a playwright of some distinction, as well as a writer of stories and journalism for various periodicals. In 1896 he was awarded the coveted Griboyedov prize for one of his works, *The*

Price of Life, although he himself felt that the accolade should have been given to Chekhov for *The Seagull*. Nemirovich penned a total of eleven plays between 1881 and 1901, all of which were staged, mainly at the Moscow Malyi.[11] From 1891, on the recommendation of the Malyi actor Sumbatov-Yuzhin, he taught drama at the school of the Moscow Philharmonic Society, where his pupils included the future MKhT actors Vsevolod Meyerhold and Ivan Moskvin.

Notwithstanding the regular success of his plays on the imperial stage, Nemirovich was acutely aware of the shortcomings of the Malyi's production techniques. Consequently, during the summer of 1897, he submitted a reform proposal to Pavel Pchelnikov, manager of the Moscow Imperial Theatres from 1882 to 1897. On 21 June Nemirovich had an audience with the manager to learn his response, and it was immediately clear that Pchelnikov was unimpressed. As if anticipating this reaction, Nemirovich had already arranged to meet Stanislavsky later the same day. He was now convinced that thoughts of reforming the Imperial Theatres were futile, and he would share his ideas about a new theatre with Stanislavsky instead. Famously, the two met at the Slavyansky Bazaar restaurant in central Moscow at 2 p.m. They did not finish talking until 8 a.m. the following day, by which time they had agreed to establish a theatre based on innovative production principles.[12]

The new company was formed mainly from members of Stanislavsky's Society of Art and Literature (fourteen artists) and pupils from Nemirovich's drama class at the Moscow Philharmonic Society (twelve artists). A number of others were invited, forming a troupe of thirty-nine artists.[13] None of the artists was offered a contract. Nemirovich explained this as follows: 'In my own case, I have never entered into an agreement with anybody, my experience being that, if an actor wants to break away, then it isn't worth retaining him. Anyone working for the theatre is of interest to it in so far as, and just so long as, he is himself enriched by the theatre.'[14] The RTO's standard contracts were still a few years away, but it is nevertheless curious that the Art Theatre, progressive in so many ways, neglected this aspect of its affairs.

The question of funding the new theatre was vital. Since the end of the state theatre monopoly, it had become evident that serious theatres could survive only with the support of a wealthy patron. Lentovsky's experience indicated that, even with a popular repertoire, it was not possible to guarantee the financial wellbeing of an enterprise. Stanislavsky was a scion of a wealthy manufacturing dynasty, but his wealth was tied up in the business. According to Nemirovich, Stanislavsky's personal fund was reserved for his children.[15]

There was another reason why he was unwilling to bankroll the theatre, which was to ensure that it was taken seriously. Stanislavsky feared that if the new project was funded from the capital of a single merchant, it would be regarded as a purely commercial venture, designed primarily to make money, and not devoted to serious art. His preferred method of financing the theatre was through a joint stock-holding company. As he explained in a letter to Nemirovich in August 1897,

> Moscow will label my participation in a private scheme – witness Mamontov – cheap commercial tyranny. Whereas the creation of a limited company and, what is more, a popular price theatre, will endow me with the merit – that is what they will call it – of being an educator, of serving an artistic and educational charity. I know the businessmen of Moscow. In the first instance they will boycott the theatre *on principle* and in the second, *on pure principle* they will stump up a pile of money to support *something they have created.*[16]

Thus, Stanislavsky and Nemirovich set out to establish the Art Theatre on the basis of a joint stock-holding company by attracting outside investors. The majority of theatres in the Russian empire were organized along similar lines, although in most cases the investors were the artists themselves, rather than external supporters, and the rationale was purely financial, not artistic. It has been calculated that in 1893 about 90 per cent of theatrical troupes working in provincial towns were organized as joint stock-holding companies.[17] For the Art Theatre, there were thirteen initial investors, the major investor being Savva Morozov, the wealthy merchant and sponsor of revolutionary parties.

Stanislavsky and Nemirovich also appealed to the Moscow city duma for a contribution. They claimed that the new theatre would be 'generally accessible' (*obshchedostupnyi*), intended for spectators of modest means, including students and poorer members of the intelligentsia. As Nemirovich explained, indicating yet another way in which the Art Theatre intended to break with tradition,

> we wanted to provide cheap places in the neighbourhood of the most expensive ones. Thus, for example, the first four rows were to be for very well-to-do people at four rubles a seat. This was more expensive than in other theatres; but immediately behind them there were to be seats for a ruble and a half and even for less, while the front rows of the first balcony,

usually the best places in all theatres, were scheduled at a ruble a seat; as for the boxes of the first balcony, we would not charge for them the usual price of ten or twelve rubles, but only six.[18]

The duma's response, however, was to ignore the request for a whole eighteen months, by which time the Art Theatre had already opened under other arrangements.

The appeal for a duma contribution on the basis of the theatre's intended accessibility might seem like a ruse to attract government funding, as only an accessible theatre would be deemed worthy of support. Yet there is some evidence to suggest that the ambition was sincere. When the artists of the new company gathered for their first rehearsals at Pushkino, outside Moscow, in the summer of 1898, Stanislavsky delivered a speech in which he declared that their aim was 'to bring light into the lives of the poorer classes, to give them a few moments of beauty in the darkness that surrounds them. We are,' he continued, 'trying to create the first rational, moral public theatre.'[19] Everything else about the genesis of the Art Theatre, however, indicates quite categorically that Stanislavsky and Nemirovich were motivated by artistic considerations and little else.

During their famous meeting at the Slavyansky Bazaar, the Art Theatre's founders had elaborated the principles on which the new theatre would be organized. Nemirovich's comments illustrate how he and Stanislavsky understood the difference between the old theatre and the new, and they are worth quoting at length:

The working out of a plan in all its details was not difficult, because the organized forms in the old theatre had grown decrepit to such a degree that they seemed to implore a change to new forms.

For example: the office should yield precedence to the demands of the stage. The theatre exists for that which happens on the stage, for the creativeness of the actor and author, and not for those who manage them. The office must resiliently accommodate itself to all the curves, unexpectedness, collisions, which fill the atmosphere of artistic labour. This very simple truth was in the old theatre submerged under official staffs, injunctions, procedures, protectionism, career-hunting, routine in all interrelations – so submerged, indeed, that the official form became more important than the art content. . . . It was impossible to introduce the slightest reform on the stage if it necessitated some insignificant change among the desks of the office.

Another example: every play must have its own setting, i.e. its own decorations, furniture, and properties, all suited to the particular play, and costumes especially made to suit the various rôles. . . . The old theatre had its 'garden', its 'wood' – as the officials themselves contended, 'of the most approved verdure'; it had a reception-room with soft-lined chairs and a tall lamp in the corner with a yellow shade eminently suited for a comfortable love passage; a larger reception-room with pillars, painted of course; a middle-class room with red mahogany furniture. In the storeroom of decorations there were 'Gothic' and 'Renaissance' properties for 'classical' plays, as all costume-plays were called by the director, even though they were written by contemporary authors. They had, correspondingly, chairs with high backs, a black carved table, and a curule chair, which the director stubbornly persisted in calling the 'culture' chair. All these properties were used now in one play, now in its successor. Every actor had his own wardrobe and acquired it according to his taste. He did not even find it necessary to take counsel with the director. Actresses talked it out among themselves in order not to repeat the colour of the dresses. Of a monolithic spectacle, in which all parts were harmoniously merged, no one ever thought.[20]

In order to achieve the desired artistic effect, several innovations were necessary. For the first time in Russian theatre history, there would be lengthy rehearsals, as well as dress rehearsals for all productions. (According to Nemirovich, the first dress rehearsal in Russian theatre took place in 1894.)[21] There would be no benefit nights, and the emphasis would be on ensemble acting, coordinated by the stage director who would ensure the artistic unity of productions. The greater amount of time to be devoted to preparation meant that the MKhT would sacrifice quantity for quality in the repertoire. Whereas the Imperial Theatres were accustomed to staging plays with only a few days of rehearsal, relying on formulaic *mise-en-scène* and the attraction of individual 'stars', the MKhT would devote months to preparation and rehearsal. Its inaugural production, *Tsar Fyodor Ioannovich*, was rehearsed an unprecedented seventy-four times, and *The Seagull* twenty-six times.[22] The result was that, whereas the Imperial Alexandrinsky staged a total of 394 plays between 1900 and 1917, the Moscow Art Theatre produced approximately seventy between its inception and 1917.[23]

The theatre opened on 14 October 1898 as the Moscow Art-Accessible Theatre, based initially in the building of the Hermitage gardens theatre (not to be confused with Lentovsky's Hermitage, which was a separate enterprise at a different location). Its inaugural performance of *Tsar Fyodor Ioannovich*, which had been premiered at the Suvorin Theatre in St Petersburg only two days earlier, was a considerable success, in part because the play had previously been banned. Suvorin had persuaded the authorities to remove the ban, and St Petersburg and Moscow audiences were seeing the play in performance for the first time. Audiences for subsequent Art Theatre productions fell away. But it was a magnificent debut which, in its preparation and staging, signalled the seriousness of the new enterprise. During 1898, for example, Stanislavsky made three visits to provincial towns in order to gather material for the production. In Rostov-Suzdal he even spent the night in an old palace by candlelight in order to prepare himself for working on the production. In Nizhny-Novgorod he purchased old items from a disused monastery, including clothing and kitchen utensils.[24] The authentic historical detail and atmosphere, as well as the ensemble acting, ensured a stunning performance – no doubt something of a collective relief after seventy-four rehearsals. The achievement of naturalism and historical accuracy was endorsed by the historian Vasily Kliuchevsky – just as he had regarded Fonvizin's *The Minor* as a realistic insight into the Russia of the 1780s – and he implored his students to see *Tsar Fyodor Ioannovich* at the Art Theatre in order to see 'what he was like'.[25]

The most important success of the first season was Chekhov's *The Seagull*. The play suffered a dismal failure at its premiere at the Alexandrinsky in 1896, whose production principles and 'star' system were wholly unsuited to it. The imperial company approached it as a conventional comedy and staged it for the benefit of Elizaveta Levkeyeva, a popular comic actress. The actors struggled to understand their parts, and the perplexed audience reputedly laughed in all the wrong places. Chekhov, already having doubts about his aptitude as a dramatist, was present, and was distraught at the audience's response. He disappeared for several hours, reputedly roaming along the Neva embankment in a biting wind. He departed the city unannounced, writing of the premiere to his family, 'In the theatre there was a heavy atmosphere of depression, perplexity and humiliation. The actors played abominably, stupidly. The moral: one should not write plays.'[26] Who was to blame? The artists? The playwright? The audience? The problem lay in the unusual originality of Chekhov's play. It was unlike anything the actors had performed before, and it required protracted preparation, something that was not provided by the Alexandrinsky. The founders of the Art Theatre, on the other hand, especially Nemirovich, recognized the originality of *The Seagull* and, crucially, understood how to produce it: with a proper ensemble, carefully coordinated by a professional stage régisseur. *The Seagull* premiered at the MKhT on 17 December 1898 in an auditorium that was 'by no means full'.[27] Whereas the St Petersburg audience had laughed at the play – it is, after all, described as a 'comedy' – the Moscow spectators sensed its melancholic mood, which was emphasized by the Art Theatre production. When the curtain was lowered, the audience sat in complete silence, making the actors nervous, but an agonizing pause soon gave way to thunderous applause. The Art Theatre went on to premiere Chekhov's next plays, which he wrote especially for it: *Uncle Vanya* (1899), *The Three Sisters* (1901) and *The Cherry Orchard* (1904).

The MKhT's first season was a resounding critical success, but a financial failure, the theatre ending the season with debts amounting to forty-five thousand rubles.[28] From its third season, 1900–1, it was known as the Moscow Art Theatre, the word 'accessible' having been dropped from its title. 'Accessible' suggested that the MKhT expected to attract popular audiences and this, as the authorities pointed out to Nemirovich, made it liable to the special censorship regulations for popular theatres. Stanislavsky and Nemirovich expressed interest in reaching out to popular audiences (and they allocated some tickets to factory workers), but they were motivated chiefly by artistic ambition and refused to have their repertoire restricted to works approved for the *narodnyi* stage.[29] The change to the theatre's name was also related to the need to raise ticket prices in order to address the venture's financial problems, as prices were raised to a point where the theatre could no longer be considered 'generally accessible'.[30] In the event, the theatre was saved from certain ruin only by Savva Morozov, who paid off all the debts it had accumulated during its first few years and bankrolled its move to new state-of-the-art premises, the reconstructed theatre in the Lianozov House, where Korsh had started out in 1882, and which became the MKhT's permanent residence. Thus, despite Stanislavsky's concerns, the Moscow Art Theatre ended up being supported by a wealthy patron in all but name. Indeed, from November 1901 Morozov was the major shareholder (together with Stanislavsky and Nemirovich), having bought out the other investors, although other shareholders were soon introduced, mainly from among the actors.[31] When Morozov committed suicide for reasons unrelated to his theatrical affairs in the spring of 1905, the Art Theatre's financial future became uncertain once again. In early 1906, the company undertook a fundraising tour of western Europe, which was, like its first season, a critical success but a financial failure.[32] The theatre would survive the last years of tsarist Russia, to be taken under the wings of the Soviet government.

What of the Art Theatre's reputation as a politically radical institution? Soviet historians made much of the fact that it gave its inaugural performance in the same year that the Russian Social Democratic Labour Party (RSDRP) was founded, and that Savva Morozov donated money to both, implying that the two developments were part of the same upsurge in radical activity. But the vastly different concerns of the RSDRP and the MKhT indicate that the timing of their appearance was largely a coincidence. Nemirovich claimed that most of the artists were uninterested in politics, although a few appeared to harbour radical political sympathies.[33] From the government's point of view, the fact that the most important private theatre to date emerged at a time of growing revolutionary ferment automatically made it suspect. In 1903, in connection with an application for permission to create a loans-savings bank for Art Theatre employees, the *okhrana* (secret police) reported to the Moscow chief of police D. F. Trepov (better known as the governor-general of St Petersburg at the time of the 1905 revolution) that, with the exception of G. S. Burdzhalov, one of the original actors of the MKhT, there was no 'unfavourable' political information about the founders. It nevertheless considered that 'the whole troupe of artists of this theatre does not inspire confidence in its political loyalty', as most of them had connections with 'unreliable' types like Gorky and Leonid Andreyev. The report recommended that the application be refused. Trepov added to the report the following resolution: 'The troupe of this theatre constitutes a centre to which the whole of the unreliable element of Moscow clings, and under favourable circumstances this centre could easily turn into a seat of revolutionary activity, and for these reasons the application should be declined.'[34]

The wider perception that the Art Theatre was a haven of radicalism derived to a large extent from the links that it forged with Maxim Gorky. The Art Theatre was the first theatre to produce his major plays: *The Petty Bourgeoisie* (1902), *The Lower Depths* (1902) and *Children of the Sun* (1905). The fact that *The Lower Depths* was banned from the Imperial Theatres threw into relief the MKhT's perceived radicalism in staging it. Following the success of the Art Theatre's production in 1902, Vladimir Telyakovsky, director of Imperial Theatres, decided to stage *The Lower Depths* at the Alexandrinsky, but his plans met with opposition from the Minister of Internal Affairs, Vyacheslav von Plehve. Although the play had been approved for the private theatres, it was regarded as unsuitable for the imperial stages. Telyakovsky failed to see the logic of this, commenting, 'if such plays really are dangerous, then they are dangerous to all theatres'. The Minister of the Imperial Court, Baron Frederiks, informed Telyakovsky that the tsar had been consulted about the issue and had allegedly remarked that 'once Gorky has been placed under police surveillance, his surname has no place on an Imperial Theatre playbill'.[35] The impact that productions of Gorky's plays had on the political image of the Art Theatre was evidenced most clearly at the time of the premiere of *Children of the Sun* in October 1905. Danilov has suggested that although the production did not enjoy as much success as that of *The Lower Depths*, it strengthened the MKhT's status as 'the leading progressive-democratic Russian theatre'.[36] There were rumours that the performance would be broken up by gangs of the right-wing Black Hundred group. During the last act of the play, there is a scene in which a crowd sets upon a professor, and the professor's wife brandishes a revolver in front of the crowd. In what was an unwitting tribute to the realism of the Art Theatre, the audience mistook the scene for a Black Hundred invasion of the stage and a commotion broke out in the auditorium as spectators scrambled for the exits.[37]

Thus, while political radicalism was attributed to the Art Theatre, it did not inhere within it to any significant degree. As an institution, it was for its time artistically radical, pioneering the realistic, ensemble production to which the new drama of Chekhov and Gorky was particularly suited. Meanwhile, as the authorities looked on suspiciously, the innovations of the MKhT began to reverberate across the theatrical community, even causing the Imperial Theatres to reflect on their role.

In explaining their reasons for establishing the Moscow Art Theatre, both Stanislavsky and Nemirovich had emphasized the artistic backwardness of the Imperial Theatres and, in Nemirovich's case, the difficulty in persuading their officials to contemplate the idea of reform. Indeed, over the years, several artists – such as Anna Brenko and, temporarily, Vladimir Davydov – had abandoned the government stage in order to escape from its routines and discover better environments for creativity. Yet it would be inaccurate to conclude that the Imperial Theatres were entirely lacking in reform-minded individuals. It is noteworthy that, at the very time Stanislavsky and Nemirovich were planning the Art Theatre, the prominent Malyi actor Alexander Lensky was preparing to open a filial of the Malyi and the Bolshoi, the so-called Novyi Theatre (1898–1907). Pchelnikov had recently been replaced as manager of the Moscow Imperial Theatres by Vladimir Telyakovsky, later director of the entire Imperial Theatre system (1901–17), who was more inclined to countenance artistic experiments. Most notably, as director Telyakovsky later employed the radical stage régisseur Vsevolod Meyerhold for the Imperial Theatres. In the meantime, he granted Lensky the use of the Shelaputin theatre building on Moscow's Theatre Square, where he staged drama and opera. Lensky was, like Nemirovich, critical of the Malyi's production techniques, and at the Novyi he endeavoured to create productions characterized by artistic unity. It was a sign that the Imperial Theatres were not entirely averse to trying new things.

In general, however, relatively few practical changes were introduced into the way the state theatres operated. The principal response of the Imperial Theatres to the rise of private theatres and in particular the MKhT was to clarify their theoretical status. In 1899 Vladimir Pogozhev, manager of the St Petersburg Imperial Theatres (1882–1900), declared that the directorate – and by implication the group of theatres over which it presided – was a 'state institution which, by means of clear artistic methods, fulfils some of the general educative tasks of the government'.[38] During 1899–1900, Pogozhev chaired a commission charged with producing a new statute on the administration of the state theatres. The commission comprised officials of the directorate and the Ministry of the Imperial Court.[39] A draft of the statute, three volumes of regulations and statistics, was published in 1900, and its introduction, written by Pogozhev, addressed the issue of the Imperial Theatres' status in the reformed theatrical landscape:

> The reform of 1882 had huge consequences both for the Imperial Theatres in particular and for Russian theatre in general. The availability of private enterprise in the capitals summoned forth a whole series of theatres in St Petersburg and Moscow, the best artistic talents of the provinces were drawn to the capital . . . [and] for the first time the Imperial Theatres had to reckon with private competition. . . . In the end, the Imperial Theatre lost its historical physiognomy of the grandest of the landowner theatres and already a second decade [after the end of its monopoly] it awaits elucidation of the principles of its existence, definition of the precise terms of its activity, and their systematic legislative consolidation.[40]

What, then, was the purpose of the government stage, and how could it justify the annual subsidy of four million rubles which it received from the Ministry of the Imperial Court and the State Exchequer?[41] Article 1 of the draft statute asserted that 'The Imperial Theatres function as an academy of all types of stage art in Russia and, as such, constitute a state institution fulfilling the general educative tasks of the government by means of model productions.'[42] Pogozhev argued that a theatre can fulfil one of three functions: it can be a purely commercial undertaking, where the principal objective is to make a profit; it can be purely for entertainment, bowing to public taste without regard for artistic quality or monetary gain; or it can be an institution with 'higher educative tasks', in which the primary concern is the quality of the repertoire.[43] Without doubt, Pogozhev contended, the Imperial Theatres were intended to fulfil the third function: 'The choice of the third principle set out above, in all its purity, is prompted by the logic of the state structure of the great Russian monarchy, by the history of the Imperial Theatre itself, and by its undoubted services to the education of Russian society.'[44] Thus, while the Imperial Theatres remained emphatically of the state (*gosudarstvennyi*), the Pogozhev commission represented an effort to reassert their wider public (*obshchestvennyi*) importance. This was, in a sense, an attempt to reclaim for the government stages the idea of the 'higher educative tasks' of theatre, which the intelligentsia had spoken about for so long and which, in recent years, had invigorated many of civil society's theatrical ventures.

Notwithstanding Lensky's project at the Novyi Theatre and Pogozhev's idealism, it is normally assumed that the artistic development of the Imperial Theatres continued to be hindered by the fact that they were administered by officials who had little feeling for art. One historian of the Alexandrinsky wrote that the bureaucracy that presided over it 'frequently paralyzed any reform initiatives, and condemned the imperial stage to routine and conservatism'.[45] Another wrote of 'bureaucratic red tape and a formal hierarchy, which undermined the Imperial Theaters'.[46] And a third has written that the MKhT 'was conceived as an alternative to government-run theaters, which were top-heavy with bureaucracy and short on innovative spirit'.[47] But such assessments should be balanced against recognition of the Imperial Theatres' achievements, as well as the fact that they did manage to introduce a degree of reform. Their last director, Telyakovsky, commanded a reasonable amount of respect, given that he had no artistic training whatsoever. A typical assessment was offered by the set designer Alexander Golovin: 'A soldier by education, he was, however, "in his place" in the role of leader of the Imperial Theatres. Perhaps he lacked specialist knowledge, but he had, at any rate, good taste, which often helped him out.'[48] Under Telyakovsky, artists were relatively free to create the productions they wanted to, and the directorate interfered relatively little in artistic matters. And although many of the same sets were used over and over again for markedly different kinds of drama, it is not entirely accurate to say that no investment was made in new sets. Stage directors at the Imperial Theatres, such as Pyotr Gnedich and Alexander Sanin, were increasingly influenced by the Art Theatre; Sanin had even worked there. Following the success of *The Seagull* at the Art Theatre, Telyakovsky resolved that the Imperial Theatres should learn from its techniques.[49] Thus, the degree of stagnation in the Imperial Theatres and their reluctance to change in the wake of the Art Theatre's artistic revolution should not be exaggerated.[50]

Revolutions are crowded and complex events, but they also serve to illuminate the problems from which they stem, exposing latent social conflicts and political anxieties. The 1905 revolution in Russia was a classic example. Long-standing social and political grievances were brought to a head by the country's disastrous performance in the Russo-Japanese War. From the autumn of 1904, increasingly bold liberal organizations began to demand political reforms. The crisis of 1905 began when peaceful demonstrators were gunned down by troops outside the Winter Palace in St Petersburg on 9 January, a day that came to be known as Bloody Sunday. It culminated in the general strike of October, which compelled the government to concede a measure of political reform, including the formation of a national duma and a relaxation of press censorship.

The government's long-standing wariness of theatre's public role now seemed justified by a series of incidents that reflected the tense situation in the country. Theatrical performances began to prompt political demonstrations, the first occurring in the theatre of Vera Komissarzhevskaya in St Petersburg. In 1896, after three years on provincial stages, Komissarzhevskaya (1864–1910) joined the troupe of the Alexandrinsky, but in 1902, frustrated by its routines, she left for the provinces, where she remained until 1904. She then returned to St Petersburg and set up her own theatre. Producing the works of Gorky, Chekhov and Ibsen, it attracted a democratic following, notably from among the student population of the city, and quickly established a reputation as a progressive theatre, in many ways the St Petersburg equivalent of the Moscow Art Theatre. Performances at Komissarzhevskaya's theatre were often transformed into political demonstrations, the first of which took place on 10 November 1904 during the premiere of Gorky's *Summerfolk*.[51] On the very same evening, a 'scandal' occurred in the Mikhailovsky Theatre, not far from Passazh, where Komissarzhevskaya's theatre was initially located. It involved an actress of the French troupe, Eliza Balletta, who was intimately involved with the Grand Duke Alexei Alexandrovich. Prior to the Russo-Japanese War, the grand duke had been an influential figure in the Russian Navy, and it was rumoured that millions of rubles assigned to the navy had in fact gone to Balletta. Smarting under the early catastrophes of the war, audiences met Balletta with hostility. On the evening of 10 November, when she appeared on stage someone stood up and declared to the audience, 'This is where our navy is! On every finger of this woman there is a battleship!'[52]

The next flashpoint occurred at the time of Bloody Sunday, 9 January 1905. The St Petersburg Imperial Theatres commenced their performances as normal, but the performance at the Alexandrinsky was disrupted by protesters, who regarded it as deeply insensitive to proceed with such frivolities on that day. The Imperial Theatres closed for three days as a result, reopening on 13 January.[53] After Bloody Sunday, the governor-general of St Petersburg, D. F. Trepov, ordered that Gorky's *Summerfolk* be removed from theatrical repertoires in view of its political undertones. (The play addresses the issue of the intelligentsia's relations with ordinary workers and peasants, and urges the intelligentsia to work in the interests of the *narod*. It was later revived in the autumn of 1905.)[54] Then in February 1905, the composer and professor of music at the St Petersburg Conservatory Nikolai Rimsky-Korsakov added his signature to a letter published in the liberal newspaper *Our Days* demanding artistic freedom and other reforms in Russia. The following month, he attacked the lack of democracy at the Conservatory, and was immediately sacked. His students protested by staging a performance of Rimsky's *Kashchei the Immortal* at Komissarzhevskaya's theatre, which led to yet another political demonstration in the auditorium.[55] Trepov reacted to these events by instructing Telyakovsky 'not to permit for some time the public performance of Rimsky-Korsakov's work', in view of the opposition to his dismissal and the fear that 'undesirable demonstrations' might be provoked by performances.[56] There were widespread protests about Rimsky's dismissal in the press. As Lynn Sargeant has argued, the 'scandal served as a surrogate for broader debates over the relationship between educated society and the autocratic state' because it was regarded by liberals as 'a miniature example of the repressive policies that were strangling Russia's civic, cultural, and political development'.[57]

In the midst of the unrest and the general crisis of authority, the government determined that the theatres would remain open, in order to convey an impression of normality. Four days after Bloody Sunday, the manager of the Moscow Imperial Theatres, N. K. von Bohl, assured Telyakovsky that, although strikes were breaking out across the city, he intended to ensure that performances were unaffected, noting that 'the police defence of the theatres has, at my request, been significantly strengthened'.[58] On at least one occasion, the authorities intervened to pre-empt a demonstration. The police uncovered a plan by unidentified radicals to disrupt a performance of Sophocles' *Antigone* at the Alexandrinsky on 15 February. According to the police report, the intention was 'to use the content of this play for the organization of an anti-government demonstration'. Lines spoken by the character King Creon such as 'in my land, I alone reign' and 'the land belongs to he who reigns over it by right' were to be met with shouts of 'Down with the autocracy!' As a result, the Minister of the Imperial Court, Baron Frederiks, ordered the removal of the play from the repertoire of the imperial stage.[59] When *Antigone* was restored to the Alexandrinsky repertoire in 1906, its potential to spark a protest had not disappeared. Nikolai Khodotov, the actor who played Haemon, Creon's son, recalled that when he spoke the line 'a free land cannot belong to one person', there was an 'outburst of enthusiasm among the audience'.[60] Following the declaration of the October Manifesto (17 October) there was another series of incidents in the playhouses of Russia. During the performance of Ostrovsky's *Not Always Shrovetide for a Cat* at the Alexandrinsky on 18 October, several renditions of the national anthem were demanded from sections of the audience as an expression of loyalty to the tsarist regime. Someone responded by shouting 'Down with the autocracy!', causing a commotion and a temporary interruption of the performance.[61] These incidents indicated the manner in which theatre as public space provided a location for the expression of political opinions and anxieties throughout the course of the revolution.

The events of 1905 also demonstrated how advanced many theatre people's professional aspirations had become, as had their understanding of the extent to which the realization of those aspirations depended on wider reform. On 12 February 1905, the newspaper *The Word* printed a statement entitled 'The Needs of the Russian Theatre', which, in Danilov's words, was testimony to 'the extent to which the public-political consciousness of Russian theatre people had grown by 1905'.[62] According to the Soviet theatre encyclopedia, the statement was prepared by members of the Russian Theatre Society,[63] though none of the RTO's leaders appeared among the 189 signatories, most of whom are unknown to the annals of Russian theatre history. One of the signatures was 'Yablochkina': this might have been the prominent Malyi Theatre actress Alexandra Yablochkina, although it is possible that it was her less famous sister

Evgeniya, also an actress. Other reasonably well-known signatories included Evtikhy Karpov, Vera Komissarzhevskaya, Alexander Kugel and Nikolai Khodotov. Addressing the condition of theatre in Russia, the statement began by reiterating what was by now a standard refrain: 'Theatre is both a temple of art and a school for the people. Theatre enlightens and instructs the people and, at the same time, gives artistic pleasure, softening manners, developing in people a sense of mutual relations.' In an allusion to the congresses of 1897 and 1901, however, the statement pointed out that the economic condition of theatre and theatre people was woeful, and that theatre stood 'outside any legal protection and firm principles of legality'. It went on to highlight the issue of censorship, which, it argued, was more severe for the stage than for the printed word and hindered the theatre in its mission of directly addressing contemporary issues. It also criticized administrative and police arbitrariness in the running of theatres (for example, in determining performance times or the number of free seats to be distributed for performances).

Material insecurity and administrative oppression, continued the statement, hindered theatre in its enlightening and social mission.

> The many needs of the theatre were expressed at two congresses of stage people, but the most essential and urgent of them, till now, have not found fair satisfaction. One of the most important needs of the stage world must be deemed the formation of a union of stage people on the basis of a self-governing corporation.

In what appears to be a reference to Pogozhev's commission, the statement noted that 'The importance of theatre for the state was recognized by a royally established commission for the review of theatrical legislation.' But what the theatre required was a 'general legal order', including 'The abolition of special dramatic censorship, freedom of the press, unions and assemblies, the inviolability of the individual, freedom of conscience, freedom of movement, responsibility of officials before the law for measures taken by them'. These were the 'necessary conditions in which the theatre, having provided itself with general civic freedom of existence and action, can confidently devote itself to its peaceful, cultural business, prospering on behalf of the country and giving the requisite scope to the talents of its workers'.[64]

A month later, a similar statement was issued on behalf of Russian dramatists, attacking censorship and calling for the establishment of a legal order. Referring to theatre as a 'factor in public life', the statement lambasted the arbitrariness of officialdom (while conveniently overlooking the fact that most other major theatrical centres in Europe were still constrained to an extent by some form of censorship):

> The situation in the realm of theatre serves as a sharp indicator of the country's cultural level, its progressive growth or its disintegration. Nowhere at the present time is theatre experiencing such a cheerless condition as in Russia. The immediate cause of this is the contemporary condition of Russian dramaturgy. No branch of literature, not even journalism, suffers from administrative arbitrariness as does dramaturgy. While in the West theatre stands at the head of a free literary-social movement, Russian theatre has its hands and feet constrained. A few officials control all the great business of contemporary Russian dramaturgy, changing at their discretion the plots of plays, misrepresenting their thoughts, twisting their fundamental ideas, discolouring their very appearance, prohibiting any mention of a whole range of phenomena in public life. But in such disfigured form, the dramatic work is by no means secure from further arbitrariness: at any given moment, it might be prohibited for separate localities and even suddenly removed from the repertoire at the demand of any department, or even simply because the public dared to applaud certain sentences. Upon which exact law the controllers of Russian dramaturgy's fate rely, no one has ever considered it necessary to tell us, the dramatists. It is clear that the name of this law is unlawfulness, that the lever moving the whole mechanism is individual arbitrariness. The only way out of the present agonizing situation, in our view, is . . . the renovation of Russia on the basis of a state founded strictly on the rule of law.[65]

The forty-nine signatories of this statement, not all of them dramatists, included B. S. Glagolin, Evtikhy Karpov, Alexander Kugel and Alexander Sumbatov-Yuzhin. Similar sentiments and demands were expressed on 20 October, when a large meeting of theatre people took place in the Panaev Theatre in St Petersburg. It produced the following resolution:

> Theatre people consider necessary the abolition of all laws and orders which practically hinder the realization of the liberties indicated in the manifesto: 1) the abolition of capital punishment; 2) an amnesty for political criminals; 3) the urgent convocation of a constituent assembly on the basis of direct,

secret, equal and universal suffrage for the drawing up of regulations regarding the structure of the state.[66]

In addition to calling for civic rights, theatre people demonstrated their growing political confidence by demanding a greater level of self-regulation and autonomy. These demands surfaced in two contexts, one of which was the Russian Theatre Society. During 1905, when the majority of educated society seemed radicalized against the tsarist regime, the close links between the RTO's leadership and the state were called into question. The boundaries between government involvement and self-regulation had never been clearly defined, and this created an underlying tension within the RTO about the extent of its relations with the state.

The RTO remained committed to helping indigent theatre people during the revolution. In February–March 1905, its annual general assembly considered a proposal to curtail RTO expenditure in view of its financial difficulties. But the chairman of its council, A. E. Molchanov, argued that, on the contrary, the society's charitable work had to be extended on account of the crisis afflicting the country in general and theatre people in particular, a view endorsed by the majority of delegates.[67] A 'Committee for the Salvation of Actors' was formed in the summer of 1905 to examine the extent of the crisis and how to address it,[68] reporting two months later that there were both general and particular causes, that its extent could not be established, and that the committee was reinventing itself as the 'Committee for the Organization of Self-Help Among Theatre People'.[69] Meanwhile, the council had agreed that, in view of the 'stock-exchange prices' in the country, the RTO would have to draw upon its emergency funds to see itself through the difficult period.[70]

While all this was going on, the RTO's leadership remained loyal to the tsarist state, and in this sense it appears to have been quite unusual. Harley Balzer has noted that 'At least until 1905, leadership of virtually all Russian professions was in the hands of radical activists inculcated with intelligentsia values.'[71] This was particularly evident immediately prior to the 1905 revolution. Professional groups were instrumental in the formation of the Union of Liberation in 1903, which demanded liberal reforms, organized a political banquet campaign, and called upon 'members of the liberal professions' to form unions, or 'intelligentsia unions'. In May 1905 they coalesced into the (political) Union of Unions, which went on to play a major role in organizing the general strike of October 1905.[72] Many theatre people contributed to the growing clamour for change, as exemplified by 'The Needs of the Russian Theatre'. Yet this was not the work of the RTO's leadership, which seemed reluctant to express support for the opposition movement, perhaps being anxious to avoid jeopardizing the society's subsidies and status.

The more established it became, the more the RTO was regarded by many of its ordinary members as a bureaucratic tool of the government, increasingly detached from their interests. Kugel claimed that two conflicting tendencies had emerged within the society, one that promoted greater regulation of theatre affairs, another that aspired to 'cast off the yoke of bureaucracy and live a free public life'.[73] The latter surfaced at the general assembly of February–March 1905, where several of the society's members, no doubt emboldened by the wider climate of subversion in Russia as the revolution gathered pace, criticized the council severely. The actor B. S. Glagolin claimed that the society was 'trying to become a kind of branch of the Ministry of Internal Affairs', while a certain M. B. Gorodetsky claimed that 'the bureaucratic tendency of the council is impeding the advance of Russian theatre and the Russian actor'.[74] The Alexandrinsky actor N. Kh. Pashkovsky alleged that the council was neglecting many of its duties, 'limiting its work almost exclusively to philanthropy'.[75] In response to these attacks the council resigned *en masse*, but it was reinstated shortly afterwards, probably because, as Kugel observed, the majority of theatre people ultimately accepted the need for the greater regulation of theatre work that the council had pursued over the years, regarding this as 'the way to defend the interests of labour from the pressure of capital and entrepreneurial exploitation'.[76] Claims that the council was not fulfilling the aims of the society as elaborated in its charter seem harsh. Yet the charge that, in pursuing the RTO's aims, the council had become more bureaucratic and closely linked to the state appears incontestable. (Similar accusations were made against the Imperial Russian Musical Society during 1905, which claimed to be the voluntary association of its members but increasingly behaved like a government agency.)[77] The momentary challenge to the RTO's close association with the state indicated that some members no longer believed that the society's interests were best served by working with the authorities, providing a glimpse of a civil society that was increasingly confident and assertive.

The problems that confronted the RTO led, in 1906, to the formation of a Union of Theatre People (Soiuz stsenicheskikh deiatelei). The union was not, however, conceived as a rival organization (and it does not appear to have been connected to the Union of Unions). It was established as an autonomous branch of the RTO, and its members were required to belong to the society.

The creation of a union had been a long-standing objective. The idea was mentioned as early as the 1897 congress,[78] and one of the principal tasks of the second congress had been to discuss its draft charter. The union was not, therefore, merely an improvised response to the crisis of February–March 1905, even though it was mentioned in 'The Needs of the Russian Theatre'. But its formation appears to have been expedited by the financial difficulties that beset the RTO during 1904 and 1905, and it is unlikely that the revolutionary turmoil of 1905 and the criticisms of the council were merely coincidental. In February 1905, an auditing commission stated that the function of the RTO was to promote the 'public initiative of theatre people, developing in them the spirit of free competition and friendly assistance' and, on these grounds, it proposed that 'the only opportune and at the same time completely reliable way of renovating the work of the Theatre Society and strengthening its financial position is the urgent establishment of a Union of Theatre People'.[79] The report commented that the moment was appropriate, in view of current events and the widespread demands for self-government.

The apparent purpose of the union was to deal more efficiently with the various interests that fell under the auspices of the RTO. The revised charter of the society included the following new aim: 'to unite its members, on the basis of self-government and mutual aid, into special unions, namely theatre people, playwrights and composers, theatre orchestra musicians, and others'.[80] Judging by the union's founding charter, approved in June 1906, its key aims replicated several of the RTO's. While its stated goal was 'The improvement of theatre affairs in Russia and the improvement of the condition of theatre people', its specific functions betrayed a primary concern for the financial security of its members, seen, for example, in the setting up of a loans-savings fund and insurance schemes for unemployment, illness and so forth, funded chiefly from membership dues and donations.[81]

The union's emphasis on the material interests of its members suggests that it was more like a trade union than a professional association.[82] This raises the question whether the RTO was essentially a surrogate trade union prior to 1906, when trade unions were legalized in Russia. Yet while the RTO clearly performed certain 'trade union' functions, notably representing the interests of industry workers, its efforts to regulate as many aspects of theatre affairs as possible mark it out as a professional association.[83] Moreover, it is worth noting that the distinction between a trade union and a professional society was not recognized in late imperial Russia. The word 'union' (*soiuz*) was used to describe a variety of associations and was largely devoid of the class connotations it had elsewhere, even though in the context of the 1905 revolution it came to represent the independent public activity that the tsarist government feared.[84] Notwithstanding misleading terminological impressions, the Union of Theatre People served to re-emphasize one of the most prominent, if not exclusive, original aims of the RTO, namely to look after the material needs of artists.

The second context for demands for greater self-regulation and autonomy in theatre during 1905 was the Imperial Theatres. During the revolution, artists of the government stages momentarily identified with civil society rather than the state that employed them. Although the involvement of some of the imperial stars in the RTO demonstrated a commitment to activity and philanthropy that overlapped with organizations of civil society, by and large the state theatres had remained aloof from such activity. The first signs of tension between the directorate and its troupes arose in connection with the artists' uneasiness about performing when the political situation was so precarious and demonstrations were ubiquitous, although this was more a matter of safety than of political sympathy. In St Petersburg, some artists announced their unwillingness to perform on 13 October. Telyakovsky favoured closing the theatre temporarily, but Frederiks believed that this would demoralize the population, and that if the artists feared an incident the police presence in the theatres should be strengthened.[85]

Tension was increased by the fact that private theatres had already shut down and by the news that the governor-general of Moscow had deemed it wise to close the Malyi (14–27 October).[86] Telyakovsky came under more pressure from Alexandrinsky artists to close the theatres, but was told by Trepov 'If the artists don't want to act, force them.' If necessary, he added, 'take a revolver in your hand, then they will listen!'[87] On 16 October Frederiks sent a telegram to Telyakovsky ordering him to keep the theatres open and expressing the hope that 'the artists of the Imperial Theatres will perform their duty and assist in the calming of the capital'.[88] According to Telyakovsky, Trepov also believed that the normal functioning of the Imperial Theatres would help to maintain an appearance of calm in St Petersburg.[89]

In the midst of this uncertainty, the artists of the Alexandrinsky, inspired by the October Manifesto, formulated demands for autonomy from the directorate. A meeting of the troupe took place on 18 October, at which the general mood was one of loyalty to the government. The leader of the troupe, Pyotr Gnedich, composed an address from the troupe to the tsar in which, in addition to describing the October Manifesto as a 'patriotic act' and themselves as 'free artists', they declared that, in their eyes, recent events meant that they now had the opportunity to assert their artistic independence from the directorate.[90] The means by which the artists were to be given the greater degree of self-administration they requested was a repertoire council, to be elected by members of the troupe. The directorate had established a repertoire council in 1903, but its seven members were all appointed by the administration and it was only consultative. In consequence, Savina had refused to collaborate with it, and the council was disbanded. The directorate attempted to resurrect the idea in late 1905 and to give the council a greater role in decision making. Some of the artists demanded a body that would effectively carry out the major tasks currently fulfilled by the directorate itself, including full control over the repertoire and the hiring and firing of artists, while others preferred the status quo.[91]

Although a new repertoire council was elected at the beginning of 1906, demands for autonomy quickly disappeared from the Imperial Theatres. This suggests that they were largely inspired by the widespread spirit of rebellion and demands for self-administration of 1905, rather than an innate desire for radical change. Most of the Imperial Theatre elders were opposed to such demands, and the majority were disinclined to press the issue lest they forfeit their privileged positions. Self-administration would serve to distance them from the government and its bureaucracy, the very source of their relative material security and prestige.

In many respects, the two 'theatrical revolutions' of the 1898–1905 period were the logical culmination of Russian theatre's discovery and development of its public role during the nineteenth century, both as an industry and as an idea. In the Moscow Art Theatre, the cultural intelligentsia had at last identified a sustainable private enterprise that was dedicated to a serious, educative repertoire but was not hidebound by bureaucracy. After all the doubts of the 1880s and 1890s, civil society appeared still to be capable of producing a theatrical institution of wider import (and vice versa). The government, for its part, never quite reconciled itself to the proliferation of entertainments and continued to regard private theatres as potentially seditious. During 1905, the authorities banned a range of plays for fear that they would provoke further disorder. Even at the Imperial Theatres, the artists displayed uncharacteristic signs of rebelliousness, albeit fleetingly, as the government struggled to maintain a semblance of public normality.

But for all its concern, these were not the fundamental issues, even for theatre people. As the government fretted about censorship and demonstrations, it became evident that a quieter but more fundamental theatrical revolution had occurred. The end of the state theatre monopoly and the development of a theatrical civil society, together with the continued growth of regional theatre, had gradually cultivated a sense of citizenship among many artists, which built on a longer-standing belief in the worth of their vocation. This was a result of the organizational experience gained in the struggle against low social status and material hardship. The events of the 1905 revolution demonstrated that the professional aspirations of theatre people had developed to the point where they were articulated in the same breath as demands for wider civic freedoms. To be sure, there was a sense in which theatre people were merely caught up in the euphoria of the moment and were simply repeating the political mantra of other organized occupational groups. But seen from the perspective of the nineteenth century, particularly the concerns that led to the emergence of the Russian Theatre Society, the radical demands of artists look less spontaneous. The 'school for the people' had turned out to be more of a 'school for citizens' for theatre people themselves, although Russia's experience of the twentieth century made the practical application of that lesson more problematic than might have seemed possible in 1905.

EPILOGUE

Theatre made an important contribution to the development of civil society in imperial Russia, notably through the creation of new cultural enterprises and an energetic representative association. None of this occurred in isolation from wider circumstances, of course; it was facilitated by the social and economic changes experienced by Russia from the middle of the nineteenth century onwards. Yet it is important to emphasize that the creation of new theatres and the urge to organize theatre people as a profession were born of a widespread conviction amongst educated Russians that the stage, as a public forum, had a vital didactic role to perform. And therein lay the source of a fundamental ambivalence towards the state that was manifest among many theatre people. The campaign for freedom of the theatres was firmly rooted in a belief that civil society should play a greater part in the production of Russia's national culture, yet it quickly became apparent that, notwithstanding a few prominent exceptions, commercial freedom was highly unlikely to deliver the kind of serious, educative stage advocated by the intelligentsia, nor was it likely to ensure material security for the vast majority of theatre people.

The consequence was a gradual, often tentative, recognition that the theatrical aims of the cultural intelligentsia could not be achieved without some level of state involvement. Hence the assertions of the 1880s and 1890s that the Imperial Theatres, with substantial government resources at their disposal, ought to act as models, and hence the Russian Theatre Society's pursuit of state subsidies and influential allies within the administration. During 1901, false rumours circulated that the government planned to take control of theatrical enterprises throughout the provinces, yet the response was by no means universally hostile. One writer, echoing sentiments expressed at the congresses of theatre people held in 1897 and 1901, welcomed the plan on the grounds that Russian theatre urgently required material support, and that it was a duty of governments to assist the development of cultural activity. State involvement, the writer insisted, would serve to revitalize a stagnant theatrical scene.[1] The state, for its part, entered cautiously into an alliance with the theatrical branch of civil society. It subsidized people's theatres and welcomed the efforts of the Russian Theatre Society to organize and regulate the acting profession; but it remained profoundly uneasy about the rapid growth of the entertainment industry, and at times appeared reluctant to support further expansion – the Moscow duma, for instance, declined to subsidize the Art Theatre. For the state, the fundamental dilemma was how to prevent theatre, increasingly available to a mass audience, from undermining the prevailing social and political order. This was an almost constant concern from the premiere of Fonvizin's *The Minor* onwards, even though the burden of evidence since 1782 indicated that the subversive potential of the stage *per se* was somewhat exaggerated. For civil society, the fundamental dilemma was how to define and delimit the role of the state in theatrical culture, an issue that finally surfaced during the 1905 revolution. These dilemmas remained unresolved until after the collapse of tsarism and the rise of the Bolsheviks in 1917.

During the early years of the twentieth century, Russian theatre entered a period of creative brilliance that lasted into the mid 1920s. A group of innovative and experimental avant-garde directors, foremost among whom were Vsevolod Meyerhold, Nikolai Evreinov and Alexander Tairov, spearheaded an artistic revolution against the naturalistic ideals of the Moscow Art Theatre. Valery Briusov, in a well-known article from 1902 entitled 'Unnecessary Truth', argued that the task of theatre was not to mirror reality but to convey ideas and feelings in a self-consciously theatrical manner.[2] Vyacheslav Ivanov, writer and symbolist theoretician, argued for a 'collective theatre' that would return the stage to its 'ancient prototypes', such as classical tragedy or medieval mystery plays.[3] Even Stanislavsky experimented with symbolism in the Art Theatre Studio.[4] The preoccupation with formalism perhaps reflected the post–1905 disillusionment with politics and public life evinced by some members of the intelligentsia, yet many continued to adhere to the idea of a realistic theatre. In 1908 the conflicting views about the relative merits of symbolism and realism were represented in two influential collections of essays: *'Theatre': A Book about the New Theatre* and *The Theatre Crisis*. Subsequently, during the Russian civil war and the early 1920s, the artistic radicalism of the avant-garde experimentalists intensified, deriving further inspiration from the belief that a new kind of society was imminent.

Russian theatre people generally welcomed the demise of the tsarist regime in February 1917, since it heralded an end to censorship and new opportunities to accomplish artistic and civic goals. Even the artists of the former Imperial Theatres – now called State Theatres – proved eager to cooperate with the Provisional Government and to mount gala performances in its honour. In return they expected full autonomy from the government while continuing to receive generous subsidies. From May 1917, each State Theatre was run by an elected committee that was responsible for the management of artistic and financial affairs. Government appointees monitored the committees, however, and it proved impossible to consolidate autonomy during the months before October 1917.[5] The Bolsheviks initially concentrated on establishing their authority over the theatres; the systematic use of the pre-revolutionary stage for propaganda was instituted at a later date, although in the meantime a plethora of new amateur theatres was used for political purposes. The civil war period witnessed something of a theatre epidemic. By 1920, for example, there were 1,210 theatres and 911 drama groups attached to the Red Army alone.[6]

During the early years of the Soviet regime, a fierce debate took place among cultural activists about the fate of pre-revolutionary theatres. Some comrades regarded them as bourgeois institutions which had to be entirely destroyed in order that resources could be lavished on establishing new proletarian theatres. Supporters of this approach included, for a while, Meyerhold and Platon Kerzhentsev, author of the influential pamphlet *The Creative Theatre.*[7] Others, including Lenin, argued that the cultural accomplishments of the pre-revolutionary era must be preserved for posterity. Anatoly Lunacharsky, the Bolshevik Commissar for Enlightenment, with responsibility for the country's theatres, endeavoured to steer a steady course between these two extremes, encouraging the radicals but protecting the traditional stages. Hence, while activists in the Proletarian Culture movement (Proletkult) organized theatricals for ordinary workers, attacked bourgeois theatre and endeavoured to create a new proletarian repertoire, the State Theatres – which now included former prominent private ventures such as the Moscow Art Theatre – were able to continue their traditions in an atmosphere of relative cultural pluralism.[8]

Lunacharsky fervently believed that the traditional theatres would choose to adapt their repertoires to conform with the ideology of the Soviet regime.

Indeed, from the early 1920s the repertoires of the State Theatres began to include adaptations of the classics designed to emphasize their radical aspects. Ostrovsky's works, regarded in the tradition of Dobrolyubov, proved most suited to the task. In 1923, Lunacharsky, increasingly impatient with the formalists, issued the plea 'Back to Ostrovsky!' on the centenary of the dramatist's birth. Huntly Carter, a journalist and critic who made several theatrical pilgrimages to Moscow during the 1920s, described the works of Ostrovsky as 'a godsend to the New Theatre with its stated aim of exhibiting anything that truthfully and ruthfully exposes the assinine stupidity, the offensive pretension, the self-degradation of the official class'.[9] Some accomplished plays from the new Soviet dramaturgy appeared by the second half of the 1920s. Notable among them was Konstantin Trenev's civil war drama *Lyubov Yarovaya*, which proved a major success at the Moscow Malyi.

The Sovietization of the repertoire during the 1920s was not entirely voluntary, but the extent of state direction prior to the 1930s should not be exaggerated. The process of subjugation occurred gradually. In August 1919 the Soviet government nationalized all theatrical property in Russia and established Tsentroteatr, an organ that oversaw a main theatre department and a separate State Theatre department. Theatres were required to submit repertoire plans for approval, but there was little attempt to direct repertorial content. This largely remained the case from 1923, when the government augmented its presence in the State Theatres with appointed managers, and a new Chief Repertoire Committee (Glavrepertkom) was put in charge of theatrical censorship.

The turning point for theatre came in May 1927, when the Central Committee agitprop department convened a conference on theatrical affairs in Moscow. Cultural radicals were in the ascendancy, and Lunacharsky was attacked by several delegates for allowing the traditional theatres to function with relatively little interference and not doing enough to Sovietize the stage. The result was growing pressure on the pre-revolutionary theatres to overhaul their repertoires. The conference marked the overture to socialist realism in theatre, complete state control of the stage, and the imposition of a propagandistic repertoire. Nikolai Gorchakov, who witnessed this process, later insisted that the seemingly healthy condition of Soviet theatre during the 1930s was entirely illusory. Immense resources were lavished on all theatres, but they were required to serve the aims of the state. More theatres than ever were established across the country, and all actors found employment, but they were deprived of creative freedom.[10] In a sense the dilemmas of the early twentieth century were finally resolved. The state had taken complete control and transformed the stage into a political tribune. In the post-Stalin years, theatre regained much of its status among the intelligentsia as a potentially significant force for the social and political reformation of the country, but that story belongs to another study.

APPENDIX OF TITLES

The following list provides the Russian titles of plays, operas and ballets cited in translation in the text.

Antigone	*Antigona*
The Bankrupt	*Bankrot*
The Bigamist	*Dvumuzhnitsa*
Boris Godunov	*Boris Godunov*
The Brigadier	*Brigadir*
The Cherry Orchard	*Vishnevyi sad*
Chicanery (or The Slanderer)	*Yabeda*
Children of the Sun	*Deti solntsa*
The Comedy of the Russian Nobleman Frol Skobeyev	*Komediia o rossiiskom dvorianine Frole Skobeeve*
Contrabandists (The Sons of Israel)	*Kontrabandisty (Syny Izrailia)*
The Dark Coniferous Forest	*Temnyi bor*
The Death of Tarelkin	*Smert' Tarelkina*
Dmitry Donskoi	*Dmitrii Donskoi*
Dmitry Kalinin	*Dmitrii Kalinin*
Doctor Moshkov	*Doktor Moshkov*
A Doll's House	*Nora*
Don't Get Into Someone Else's Sleigh	*Ne v svoi sani ne sadis'*
The Drinks Vendor	*Sbiten'shchik*
Egmont	*Egmon*
Emilia Galotti	*Emiliia Galotti*
An Enemy of the People	*Doktor Shtokman (or Vrag naroda)*

Enough Stupidity in Every Wise Man	Na vsiakogo mudretsa dovol'no prostoty
Ermak	Ermak
Ermak Timofeeich	Ermak Timofeeich
Evil Stepmothers	Likhodeiki-Machekhi
The Fashion Shop	Modnaia lavka
The Forest	Les
The Fruits of Enlightenment	Plody prosveshcheniia
Fuente Ovejuna	Ovechii istochnik
The Ghosts of Fortune	Prizraki schast'ia
The Government Inspector	Revizor
Guilty Without Guilt	Bez viny vinovatye
Hamlet	Gamlet
The Hand of the Almighty Saved the Fatherland	Ruka vsevyshnego otechestvo spasla
Hannele	Gannele
The Heart Is Not a Stone	Serdtse ne kamen'
The Hump-Backed Horse	Konek-gorbunok
Ilya the Bogatyr	Il'ia Bogatyr'
It's a Family Affair	Svoi liudi – sochtemsia
Ivan Susanin	Ivan Susanin
Ivanov	Ivanov
Izmail	Izmail
The Jacobites	Iakobity
Kashchei the Immortal	Kashchei bessmertnyi
Kuteikin's Betrothal	Sgovor Kuteikina
Kuzma Minin the One-Armed	Kuz'ma Minin Sukhorukii
A Lesson to Coquettes, or The Lipetsk Spa	Urok koketkam, ili Lipetskie vody
Liberated Moscow	Osvobozhdennaia Moskva
The Liberation of Moscow in 1812	Osvobozhdenie Moskvy v 1812 godu
A Lie Stands Only until the Truth Is Known	Lozh do pravdy stoit
The Living Corpse	Zhivoi trup
The Lower Depths	Na dne
Lyubov Yarovaya	Liubov' Iarovaia
Madame Sans-Gêne	Madam San-Zhen
Manfred	Manfred
Marfa-Posadnitsa	Marfa-Posadnitsa

The Marriage of Figaro	Bezumnyi den', ili Zhenit'ba Figaro
A Marseille Beauty	Marsel'skaia krasotka
Mary Stuart	Mariia Stiuart
The Matchmaker	Svakha
The Merchants	Kuptsy
The Miller, the Sorcerer, the Deceiver and the Matchmaker	Mel'nik, koldun, obmanshchik i svat
The Minor	Nedorosl'
Misfortune from a Carriage	Neschast'e ot karety
Mitrofanushka in Retirement	Mitrofanushka v otstavke
Natalya the Boyar's Daughter	Natal'ia, boyarskaia doch'
The New Sterne	Novyi Stern
Not Always Shrovetide for a Cat	Ne vse kotu maslenitsa
The Petty Bourgeoisie	Meshchane
Poverty Is No Vice	Bednost' ne porok
The Power of Darkness	Vlast' t'my
Pozharsky	Pozharskii
The Price of Life	Tsena zhizni
Recollections of the Battle of Borodino	Pamiat' borodinskoi bitvy
Riurik	Riurik
Rusalka	Rusalka
Ruslan and Liudmilla	Ruslan i Liudmila
The Sailor	Matros
The Scarlet Rose	Alaia roza
The Seagull	Chaika
Semira	Semira
The Snow Maiden	Snegurochka
The Sorcerer	Charodeika
The Storm	Groza
Sumbeka, or The Decline of the Kazan Kingdom	Sumbeka, ili Padenie Kazanskogo tsarstva
Summerfolk	Dachniki
Talents and Admirers	Talanty i poklonniki
Tatyana Repina	Tat'iana Repina
The Three Sisters	Tri sestry
Tsar and Grand Duke of All Rus, Vasily Ivanovich Shuisky	Tsar' i velikii kniaz' vseia Rusi, Vasilii Ivanovich Shuiskii
Tsar Fyodor Ioannovich	Tsar' Fedor Ioannovich

Uncle Vanya	*Diadia Vania*
Vadim of Novgorod	*Vadim Novgorodskii*
Vaniushin's Children	*Deti Vaniushina*
Velzen, or The Liberation of Holland	*Vel'zen, ili Osvobozhdennaia Gollandiia*
Voyage to the Moon	*Puteshestvie na lunu*
Woe from Wit	*Gore ot uma*
Wolves and Sheep	*Volki i ovtsy*
A Woman's Jest	*Zhenskaia shutka*

BIBLIOGRAPHY

ARCHIVAL MATERIALS

Gosudarstvennyi tsentral'nyi teatral'nyi muzei imeni A. A. Bakhrushina (GTsTM):

Fond 1	A. A. Bakhrushin
Fond 39	A. A. Brenko
Fond 58	I. A. Vsevolozhskii
Fond 123	F. A. Korsh
Fond 144	M. V. Lentovskii
Fond 280	V. A. Teliakovskii
Fond 532	Sobranie nauchnykh rabot

Rossiiskii gosudarstvennyi arkhiv literatury i iskusstva (RGALI):
Fond 641	Russkoe teatral'noe obshchestvo

Rossiiskii gosudarstvennyi istoricheskii arkhiv (RGIA):
Fond 472	Kantseliariia ministerstva imperatorskogo dvora
Fond 481	Iuristkonsul'tskaia chast' ministerstva imperatorskogo dvora
Fond 497	Direktsiia imperatorskikh teatrov
Fond 652	Vsevolozhskie

NEWSPAPERS AND PERIODICALS

Birzhevyia vedomosti
Ezhegodnik imperatorskikh teatrov
Khudozhestvennaia gazeta
Khudozhnik
Literaturnaia gazeta
Moskovskie vedomosti
Moskovskii dnevnik zrelishch i ob"iavlenii
Novosti dnia
Oskolki
Panteon
Peterburgskaia gazeta
Pravitel'stvennyi vestnik
Repertuar i panteon
Repertuar russkogo i panteon vsekh evropeiskikh teatrov
Russkaia stsena
Russkii arkhiv
Russkii kur'er
S.-Peterburgskiia vedomosti
Severnaia pchela
Slovo
Sufler
Syn otechestva
Teatr
Teatr i iskusstvo
Teatr i zhizn'
Teatral
Teatral'naia Rossiia/Teatral'naia gazeta
Teatral'naia zhizn'
Teatral'nyi i muzykal'nyi vestnik
Teatral'nyi mirok
Teatral'nyia izvestiia
Teatry i p'esy
Vestnik Evropy
Zhizn' iskusstva

PRINTED PRIMARY AND SECONDARY SOURCES

Abalkin, N. (ed.), *Malyi Teatr, 1824–1974*, vol. 1: 1824–1917 (Moscow, 1978).

Alekseev, A. A., *Vospominaniia aktera* (Moscow, 1894).

Alexander, John T., 'Catherine the Great and the Theatre', in Roger Bartlett and Lindsey Hughes (eds.), *Russian Society and Culture and the Long Eighteenth Century: Essays in Honour of Anthony G. Cross* (Münster, 2004), pp. 116–30.

Altschuller, Anatoly, 'Actors and Acting, 1820–1850', in Robert Leach and Victor Borovsky (eds.), *A History of Russian Theatre* (Cambridge, 1999), pp. 104–23.

Ambler, Effie, *Russian Journalism and Politics, 1861–1881: The Career of Aleksei S. Suvorin* (Detroit, 1972).

Arenzon, E. R., *Savva Mamontov* (Moscow, 1995).

Arkhiv direktsii imperatorskikh teatrov, vypusk 1, 1746–1801 gg., otdel 2 (St Petersburg, 1892).

Aseev, B. N., *Russkii dramaticheskii teatr ot ego istokov do kontsa XVIII veka* (Moscow, 1977).

Bailes, Kendall E., 'Reflections on Russian Professions', in Harley D. Balzer (ed.), *Russia's Missing Middle Class: The Professions in Russian History* (Armonk, N.Y., and London, 1996), pp. 39–54.

Baker, Michael, *The Rise of the Victorian Actor* (London, 1978).

Bakhrushin, Iu. A., *Vospominaniia* (Moscow, 1994).

Balmuth, D., *Censorship in Russia, 1865–1905* (Washington, D.C., 1979).

Balzer, Harley D., 'Introduction', in Harley D. Balzer (ed.), *Russia's Missing Middle Class: The Professions in Russian History* (Armonk, N.Y., and London, 1996), pp. 3–38.

Balzer, Harley D. (ed.), *Russia's Missing Middle Class: The Professions in Russian History* (Armonk, N.Y., and London, 1996).

Belinskii, V. G., *O drame i teatre*, 2 vols. (Moscow, 1983).

Benedetti, Jean, *Stanislavski: A Biography* (London, 1988).

Benedetti, Jean (ed. and trans.), *The Moscow Art Theatre Letters* (London, 1991).

Bertensson, Sergei, 'The Premiere of "The Inspector General"', *Russian Review*, 7 (1947–8), no. 1, pp. 88–95.

Beskin, E., *Krepostnoi teatr* (Moscow and Leningrad, 1927).

Bill, Valentine T., *The Forgotten Class: The Russian Bourgeoisie from the Earliest Beginnings to 1900* (Westport, Conn., 1959).

Binyon, T. J., *Pushkin: A Biography* (London, 2002).

Borovsky, Victor, 'Russian Theatre in Russian Culture', in Robert Leach and Victor Borovsky (eds.), *A History of Russian Theatre* (Cambridge, 1999), pp. 6–17.

Borovsky, Victor, 'Theatre Administration at the Court of Catherine II: The Reforms of Ivan Elagin', *Theatre Research International*, 24 (1999), no. 1, pp. 42–53.

Borovsky, Victor, *A Triptych from the Russian Theatre: An Artistic Biography of the Komissarzhevskys* (London, 2001).

Bowlt, John E., 'The Moscow Art Market', in Edith W. Clowes, Samuel D. Kassow and James L. West (eds.), *Between Tsar and People: Educated Society and the Quest for Public Identity in Late Imperial Russia* (Princeton, 1991), pp. 108–28.

Bowlt, John E., 'Two Russian Maecenases: Savva Mamontov and Princess Ternisheva', *Apollo*, December 1973, pp. 444–53.

Bradley, Joseph, 'Russia's Parliament of Public Opinion: Association, Assembly, and the Autocracy, 1906–1914', in Theodore Taranowski (ed.), *Reform in Modern Russian History: Progress or Cycle?* (Washington, D.C., and Cambridge, 1995), pp. 212–36.

Bradley, Joseph, 'Subjects into Citizens: Societies, Civil Society, and Autocracy in Tsarist Russia', *American Historical Review*, 107, no. 4 (October 2002), pp. 1094–123.

Briusov, Valerii, 'Nenuzhnaia pravda', in Valerii Briusov, *Sobranie sochineniia*, vol. 6 (Moscow, 1975), pp. 62–73.

Brooks, Jeffrey, *When Russia Learned to Read: Literacy and Popular Literature, 1861–1917* (Princeton, 1985).

Burgess, Malcolm, 'The Early Theatre', in R. Auty and D. Obolensky (eds.), *An Introduction to Russian Language and Literature* (Cambridge, 1977), pp. 231–46.

Burgess, Malcolm, 'The First Russian Actor-Manager and the Rise of Repertory in Russia during the Reign of the Empress Elizabeth Petrovna', in L. R. Lewitter and A. P. Vlasto (eds.), *Gorski Vijenats: A Garland of Essays Offered to Professor Elizabeth Mary Hill* (Cambridge, 1970), pp. 57–84.

Burgess, Malcolm, 'The Nineteenth- and Early Twentieth-Century Theatre', in R. Auty and D. Obolensky (eds.), *An Introduction to Russian Language and Literature* (Cambridge, 1977), pp. 247–69.

Burgess, Malcolm, 'Russian Public Theatre Audiences of the 18th and Early 19th Centuries', *Slavonic and East European Review*, 37 (1958–9), pp. 160–83.

Buturlin, M. D., 'Teatr grafa Kamenskogo v Orle v 1827 i 1828 godakh', *Russkii arkhiv*, 1869, no. 10, columns 1707–12.

Carr-Saunders, A. M., and P. A. Wilson, *The Professions* (Oxford, 1933).

Carter, Huntly, *The New Spirit in the Russian Theatre, 1917–28, and a Sketch of the Russian Kinema and Radio, 1919–28, Showing the New Communal Relationship Between the Three* (London, 1929).

Chernukha, V. G. (introduction) and I. A. Murav'eva (ed.), *Aleksandr Tretii: vospominaniia, dnevniki, pis'ma* (St Petersburg, 2001).

Clowes, Edith W., 'Social Discourse in the Moscow Art Theater', in Edith W. Clowes, Samuel D. Kassow and James L. West (eds.), *Between Tsar and People: Educated Society and the Quest for Public Identity in Late Imperial Russia* (Princeton, 1991), pp. 271–87.

Clowes, Edith W., Samuel D. Kassow and James L. West (eds.), *Between Tsar and People: Educated Society and the Quest for Public Identity in Late Imperial Russia* (Princeton, 1991).

Conroy, Mary Schaeffer, 'Civil Society in Late Imperial Russia', in Alfred B. Evans Jr, Laura A. Henry and Lisa McIntosh Sundstrom (eds.), *Russian Civil Society: A Critical Assessment* (Armonk, N.Y., 2005), pp. 11–27.

Cooper, Joshua, *The Government Inspector and Other Russian Plays* (London, 1990).

Cross, Anthony, 'Mr Fisher's Company of English Actors in Eighteenth-Century Petersburg', *Newsletter of the Study Group on Eighteenth-Century Russia*, 4 (1976), pp. 49–56.

Cross, Anthony, *By the Banks of the Neva: Chapters from the Lives and Careers of the British in Eighteenth-Century Russia* (Cambridge, 1997).

Cross, Anthony, 'The English Embankment', in Anthony Cross (ed.), *St Petersburg, 1703–1825* (Basingstoke, 2003), pp. 50–70.

Cross, Anthony (ed.), *St Petersburg, 1703–1825* (Basingstoke, 2003).

Custine, Astolphe, Marquis de, *Empire of the Tsar: A Journey through Eternal Russia*, foreword by Daniel J. Boorstin, introduction by George Kennan (New York, 1990).

Danilov, S. S., 'Materialy po istorii russkogo zakonodatel'stva o teatre', in S. S. Danilov and S. S. Mokul'skii (eds.), *O teatre. Sbornik statei* (Leningrad and Moscow, 1940), pp. 177–200.

Danilov, S. S., *Ocherki po istorii russkogo dramaticheskogo teatra* (Moscow and Leningrad, 1948).

Danilov, S. S., 'Revoliutsiia 1905–1907 godov i russkii teatr', *Teatr*, 1955, no. 7 (July), pp. 116–26.

Danilov, S. S., *Russkii dramaticheskii teatr XIX veka*, vol. 1 (Leningrad and Moscow, 1957).

Danilov, S. S., and M. G. Portugalova, *Russkii dramaticheskii teatr XIX veka*, vol. 2: *Vtoraia polovina XIX veka* (Leningrad, 1974).

Davydov, V. N., *Rasskaz o proshlom* (Leningrad and Moscow, 1962).

Dianina, Katia, 'Passage to Europe: Dostoevskii in the St Petersburg Arcade', *Slavic Review*, 62 (2003), no. 2, pp. 237–57.

Dixon, Simon, *Catherine the Great* (London, 2001).

Dmitriev, Iu. A., *Mikhail Lentovskii* (Moscow, 1978).

'Dnevnik naslednika tsesarevicha velikogo kniazia Aleksandra Aleksandrovich. 1880 g.', *Rossiiskii arkhiv*, 6 (1995), pp. 344–57.

Dobroliubov, N. A., 'Luch sveta v temnom tsarstve', in G. I. Vladykin (ed.), *A. N. Ostrovskii v russkoi kritike: sbornik statei* (Moscow, 1953), pp. 197–284.

Dobroliubov, N. A., 'Temnoe tsarstvo', in G. I. Vladykin (ed.), *A. N. Ostrovskii v russkoi kritike: sbornik statei* (Moscow, 1953), pp. 43–196.

Dolgov, N., *Dvadtsatiletie teatra imeni A. S. Suvorina* (Petrograd, 1915).

Donskov, A., *Mixail Lentovskij and the Russian Theatre* (East Lansing, Mich., 1985).

Dramaticheskii slovar' (Moscow, 1787).

Dreiden, S., 'Teatr 1905–1907 godov i tsarskaia tsenzura', *Teatr*, 1955, no. 12 (December), pp. 104–9.

Drizen, N. V., 'Liubitel'skii teatr pri Ekaterine II', in *Ezhegodnik imperatorskikh teatrov. Sezon 1895–1896 g.g. Prilozheniia*, book 2 (St Petersburg, 1897), pp. 77–114.

Drizen, N. V., *Materialy k istorii russkogo teatra* (Moscow, 1905).

Drizen, N. V., *Stopiatidesiatiletie imperatorskikh teatrov* (St Petersburg, c. 1906).

Du Quenoy, Paul, 'Harlequin's Leap: Performing Arts Culture and the Revolution of 1905 in Saint Petersburg' (unpublished Ph.D. dissertation, Georgetown University, 2005).

Dynnik, Tat'iana, *Krepostnoi teatr* (Moscow, 1933).

Eberly, Don E., *The Essential Civil Society Reader* (Oxford, 2000).

Eklof, Ben, John Bushnell and Larissa Zakharova, *Russia's Great Reforms, 1855–1881* (Bloomington, 1994).

Falkus, M. E., *The Industrialisation of Russia, 1700–1914* (London and Basingstoke, 1972).

Frame, Murray, *The St Petersburg Imperial Theaters: Stage and State in Revolutionary Russia, 1900–1920* (Jefferson, N.C., and London, 2000).

Freeze, Gregory L., 'The *Soslovie* (Estate) Paradigm and Russian Social History', *American Historical Review*, 91, no. 1 (January 1986), pp. 11–36.

Frieden, Nancy Mandelker, *Russian Physicians in an Era of Reform and Revolution, 1856–1905* (Princeton, 1981).

Fülöp-Miller, René and Joseph Gregor, *The Russian Theatre, Its Character and History, with Especial Reference to the Revolutionary Period*, translated by Paul England (Philadelphia, 1929).

Galai, Shmuel, *The Liberation Movement in Russia, 1900–1905* (Cambridge, 1973).

Gauss, Rebecca B., *Lear's Daughters: The Studios of the Moscow Art Theatre, 1905–1927* (New York, 1999).

Gellner, Ernest, *Conditions of Liberty: Civil Society and Its Rivals* (London, 1996).

Gertsen [Herzen], Aleksandr, 'Po povodu odnoi dramy', in A. I. Gertsen, *Sobranie sochinenii v tridtsati tomakh*, vol. 2 (Moscow, 1954) (originally published in *Otechestvennye zapiski*, 1843, no. 8, part 2), pp. 49–72.

Giliarovskii, V. A., *Moi skitaniia. Liudi teatra* (Moscow, 1987).

Glama-Meshcherskaia, A. Ia., *Vospominaniia* (Moscow and Leningrad, 1937).

Gnedich, P. P., *Kniga zhizni: Vospominaniia, 1855–1918* (Leningrad, 1929).

Golovin, A. Ia., *Vstrechi i vpechatleniia. Pis'ma. Vospominaniia o Golovine* (Leningrad and Moscow, 1960).

Gorchakov, Nikolai A., *The Theater in Soviet Russia*, translated by Edgar Lehrman (New York, 1957).

Gozenpud, A., *Russkii opernyi teatr XIX veka. 1873–1889* (Leningrad, 1973).

Grigor'ev, A. A., *Teatral'naia kritika* (Leningrad, 1985).

Grigor'ev, M., *60 let vserossiiskogo teatral'nogo obshchestva* (Moscow, 1946).

Grossman, Leonid, *Pushkin v teatral'nykh kreslakh: kartiny russkoi stseny, 1817–1820 godov* (Leningrad, 1926).

Guzovskaia, L. A. and E. Iu. Nedzvetskaia, 'Ostrovskii i moskovskie teatry (neizdannye dokumenty)', in *Literaturnoe nasledstvo*, vol. 88, book 2 (Moscow, 1974), pp. 71–99.

Haimson, Leopold, 'The Problem of Political and Social Stability in Urban Russia on the Eve of War and Revolution Revisited', *Slavic Review*, 59 (2000), no. 4, pp. 848–75.

Haimson, Leopold, 'The Problem of Social Stability in Urban Russia, 1905–1917', part 1: *Slavic Review*, 23 (1964), no. 4, pp. 619–41; part 2: *Slavic Review*, 24 (1965), no. 1, pp. 1–22.

Harding, Alfred, *The Revolt of the Actors* (New York, 1929).

Hartnoll, Phyllis (ed.), *The Oxford Companion to the Theatre*, 3rd edn (London, 1967).

Heim, Michael Henry (trans.) and Simon Karlinsky (ed.), *Letters of Anton Chekhov* (London, 1973).

Hemmings, F. W. J., *Theatre and State in France, 1760–1905* (Cambridge, 1994).

Herzen, Alexander, *My Past and Thoughts: The Memoirs of Alexander Herzen*, translated by Constance Garnett, revised by Humphrey Higgens, 4 vols. (London, 1968).

Hutchinson, John F., 'Society, Corporation or Union? Russian Physicians and the Struggle for Professional Unity (1890–1913)', *Jahrbücher für Geschichte Osteuropas*, 30 (1982), pp. 37–53.

Iablochkina, A., *75 let v teatre* (Moscow, 1960).

Iakovlev, V., *Izbrannye trudy o muzyke*, vol. 3: *Muzykal'naia kul'tura Moskvy* (Moscow, 1983).

Iankovskii, M., 'Teatral'naia obshchestvennost' Peterburga v 1905–1907 gg.', in A. Ia. Al'tshuller (ed.), *Pervaia russkaia revoliutsiia i teatr: stat'i i materialy* (Moscow, 1956), pp. 127–84.

Iazykov, D. D., *Kratkii ocherk dvadtsatipiatiletnei deialtel'nosti teatra F. A. Korsha* (Moscow, 1907).

Iazykov, D. D., '"Nedorosl'" na stsene i v literature (1782–1882 gg.)', *Istoricheskii vestnik*, 10 (1882), pp. 139–47.

Ippolitov-Ivanov, M. M., *50 let russkoi muzyki v moikh vospominaniiakh* (Moscow, 1934).

Iunisov, M. V., '"Lishnii" teatr: o liubiteliakh i ikh "gubiteliakh"', in E. V. Dukov (ed.), *Razvlekatel'naia kul'tura Rossii XVIII–XIX vv.: ocherki istorii i teorii* (St Petersburg, 2000), pp. 372–93.

Iushkov, Vl[adimir], 'Mysli o vrede i pol'ze teatrov', *Zhurnal dramaticheskii*, 1811, no. 3 (Moscow), pp. 213–24.

Jerrmann, Edward, *Pictures from St Petersburg* (London, 1852).

John Quincy Adams in Russia: Comprising Portions of the Diary of John Quincy Adams from 1809 to 1814 (New York, 1970).

Johnson, Terence J., *Professions and Power* (London, 1972).

Kallash, V. V., and N. E. Efros (eds.), *Istoriia russkogo teatra*, vol. 1 (Moscow, 1914).

Karlinsky, Simon, *Russian Drama from Its Beginnings to the Age of Pushkin* (Berkeley, Los Angeles and London, 1985).

Karpov, Evtikhii, 'A. S. Suvorin i osnovanie teatra literaturno-artisticheskogo kruzhka. Stranichki iz vospominanii "Minuvshee"' [part 1], *Istoricheskii vestnik*, 137 (August 1914), pp. 449–70.

Karpov, Evtikhii, 'A. S. Suvorin i osnovanie teatra literaturno-artisticheskogo kruzhka. Stranichki iz vospominanii "Minuvshee"' [part 2], *Istoricheskii vestnik*, 137 (September 1914), pp. 873–902.

Karsavina, Tamara, *Theatre Street: The Reminiscences of Tamara Karsavina* (London, 1950).

Katkov, M. N., *Sobranie peredovykh statei moskovskikh vedomostei. 1871 god* (Moscow, 1897).

Katkov, M. N., *Sobranie peredovykh statei moskovskikh vedomostei. 1872 god* (Moscow, 1897).

Katkov, M. N., *Sobranie peredovykh statei moskovskikh vedomostei. 1875 god* (Moscow, 1897).

Kean, Beverly Whitney, *French Painters, Russian Collectors: The Merchant Patrons of Modern Art in Pre-Revolutionary Russia* (London, 1994) (originally published as *All the Empty Palaces* (London, 1983)).

Kelly, Catriona, 'Popular, Provincial and Amateur Theatres 1820–1900', in Robert Leach and Victor Borovsky (eds.), *A History of Russian Theatre* (Cambridge, 1999), pp. 124–45.

Kelly, Catriona, and David Shepherd (eds.), *Constructing Russian Culture in the Age of Revolution: 1881–1940* (Oxford, 1998).

Kelly, Laurence, *Diplomacy and Murder in Tehran: Alexander Griboyedov and Imperial Russia's Mission to the Shah of Persia* (London and New York, 2002).

Kerzhentsev, P., *Tvorcheskii teatr: puti sotsialisticheskogo teatra*, 2nd edn (1918).

Khodotov, N. N., *Blizkoe-dalekoe* (Leningrad and Moscow, 1962).

Kholodov, E., *Dramaturg na vse vremena: Ostrovskii i ego vremia, Ostrovskii i nashe vremia* (Moscow, 1975).

Kholodov, E., 'Parter i raek: Iz istorii russkoi teatral'noi publiki', *Teatr*, 1969, no. 5 (May), pp. 79–88.

Kholodov, E. (ed.), *Istoriia russkogo dramaticheskogo teatra*, 7 vols. (Moscow, 1977–87).

Kizevetter, A. A., *Na rubezhe dvukh stoletii. Vospominaniia 1881–1914* (Moscow, 1997).

Kleberg, L., 'Vjaceslav Ivanov and the Idea of Theater', in L. Kleberg and N. A. Nilsson (eds.), *Theater and Literature in Russia, 1900–1930* (Stockholm, 1984), pp. 57–70.

Kliuchevskii, V. O., 'Nedorosl' Fonvizina', in V. O. Kliuchevskii, *Sochineniia v vos'mi tomakh*, vol. 7 (Moscow, 1959), pp. 263–87 (originally published in *Iskusstvo i nauka*, 1896, no. 1).

Kochetkova, N. D., *Fonvizin v Peterburge* (Leningrad, 1984).

Konchina Marii Gavrilovny Savinoi (Moscow, 1916).

Konechnyi, Al'bin M., 'Shows for the People: Public Amusement Parks in Nineteenth-Century St Petersburg', in Stephen P. Frank and Mark D. Steinberg (eds.), *Cultures in Flux: Lower-Class Values, Practices, and Resistance in Late Imperial Russia* (Princeton, 1994), pp. 121–30.

Konechnyi, Al'bin M. (ed.), *Peterburgskie balagany* (St Petersburg, 2000).

Koroleva, N., *Dekabristy i teatr* (Leningrad, 1975).

Koroleva, N., 'Patrioticheskaia tema na stsene peterburgskogo teatra 1805–1815 gg.', in A. Ia. Al'tshuller and N. V. Zaitsev (eds.), *Traditsii stsenicheskogo realizma. Akademicheskii teatr dramy im. A. S. Pushkina. Sbornik nauchnykh trudov* (Leningrad, 1980), pp. 88–109.

Korol'kov, K., *Zhizn' i tsarstvovanie Imperatora Aleksandra III (1881–1894 gg.)* (Kiev, 1901).

Korsh, F. A., *Kratkii ocherk desiatiletnei deiatel'nosti russkogo dramaticheskogo teatra Korsha v Moskve* (Moscow, 1892).

Kovalevskii, P. I., *Aleksandr III, tsar-natsionalist* (St Petersburg, 1912).

Kozlova, O. V., 'Russkoe teatral'noe obshchestvo, 1905–1917 g.g.' (diplomnaia rabota, Moscow, 1983).

Kruti, I., *Russkii teatr v Kazani* (Moscow, 1958).

Kugel', A., 'K tridtsatiletiiu Russkogo Teatral'nogo Obshchestva (1894–1924)' in *Vremennik Russkogo Teatral'nogo Obshchestva*, vol. 1 (Moscow, 1924), pp. 5–14.

Kumar, Krishan, 'Civil Society: An Inquiry into the Usefulness of an Historical Term', *British Journal of Sociology*, 44, no. 3 (September 1993), pp. 375–95.

Kuznetsov, Evgenii, 'The Shaping of the Bourgeois Variety Theater', *Russian Studies in History*, 31, no. 3 (winter 1992–3), pp. 11–24.

Larson, Magali Sarfatti, *The Rise of Professionalism: A Sociological Analysis* (Berkeley, 1977).

Leach, Robert, and Victor Borovsky (eds.), *A History of Russian Theatre* (Cambridge, 1999).

Leikina-Svirskaia, V. R., *Intelligentsiia v Rossii vo vtoroi polovine XIX veka* (Moscow, 1971).

Leikina-Svirskaia, V. R., *Russkaia intelligentsiia v 1900–1917 godakh* (Moscow, 1981).

Lincoln, W. Bruce, *The Great Reforms: Autocracy, Bureaucracy, and the Politics of Change in Imperial Russia* (DeKalb, Ill., 1990).

Lindenmeyr, Adele, *Poverty Is Not a Vice: Charity, Society, and the State in Imperial Russia* (Princeton, 1996).

Litvinenko, N. G., *Starinnyi russkii vodevil' (1810-e–nachalo 1830-x godov)* (Moscow, 1999).

Lowe, Charles, *Alexander III of Russia* (London, 1895).

Lukashevich, Stephen, 'The Holy Brotherhood: 1881–1883', *American Slavic and East European Review*, 18 (1959), pp. 491–509.

McCormick, John, and Claude Schumacher, 'France, 1851–1919', in Claude Schumacher (ed.), *Naturalism and Symbolism in European Theatre, 1850–1918* (Cambridge, 1996), pp. 13–108.

McKean, Robert B., *Between the Revolutions: Russia 1905 to 1917* (London, 1998).

McKean, Robert B., 'The Constitutional Monarchy in Russia, 1906–17', in Ian D. Thatcher (ed.), *Regime and Society in Twentieth-Century Russia* (Basingstoke and London, 1999), pp. 44–67.

McKean, Robert B., 'The Russian Constitutional Monarchy in Comparative Perspective', in Cathryn Brennan and Murray Frame (eds.), *Russia and the Wider World in Historical Perspective: Essays for Paul Dukes* (Basingstoke and London, 2000), pp. 109–25.

McKean, Robert B., *St Petersburg between the Revolutions: Workers and Revolutionaries, June 1907-February 1917* (New Haven and London, 1990).

MacLeod, Joseph, *The Actor's Right to Act* (London, 1981).

McReynolds, Louise, *The News under Russia's Old Regime: The Development of a Mass-Circulation Press* (Princeton, 1991).

McReynolds, Louise, *Russia at Play: Leisure Activities at the End of the Tsarist Era* (Ithaca and London, 2003).

Mally, Lynn, *Culture of the Future: The Proletkult Movement in Revolutionary Russia* (Oxford, 1990).

Mally, Lynn, *Revolutionary Acts: Amateur Theater and the Soviet State, 1917–1938* (Ithaca and London, 2000).

Malnick, Bertha, 'A. A. Shakhovskoy', *Slavonic and East European Review*, 32 (1953–4), pp. 29–51.

Malnick, Bertha, 'Mochalov and Karatygin', *Slavonic and East European Review*, 36 (1957–58), pp. 265–93.

Malnick, Bertha, 'The Origin and Early History of the Theatre in Russia', *Slavonic Year-Book (Being Volume XIX of the Slavonic and East European Review)*, 1939–40, pp. 203–27.

Malnick, Bertha, 'Russian Serf Theatres', *Slavonic and East European Review*, 30 (1951–2), pp. 393–411.

Malnick, Bertha, 'The Theory and Practice of Russian Drama in the Early 19th Century', *Slavonic and East European Review*, 34 (1955–6), pp. 10–33.

Mal'tseva, E. G., 'Akterskoe samoupravlenie v Rossii: iz istorii akterskikh tovarishchestv kontsa XIX–nachala XX veka', in Iu. M. Orlov (ed.), *Teatr mezhdu proshlym i budushchim* (Moscow, 1989), pp. 162–74.

Mamontov, V. S., *Vospominaniia o russkikh khudozhnikakh (Abramtsevskii khudozhestvennyi kruzhok)* (Moscow, 1950).

Mikhailova, R. F., 'Bor'ba peredovoi obshchestvennosti za otmenu teatral'noi monopolii i sozdanii chastnykh teatrov v 60–80 godakh XIX veka' (avtoreferat dissertatsii, Leningrad, 1962).

Mikhailova, R. F., 'K voprosu o sozdanii narodnogo teatra v Rossii v kontse 60-kh–nachale 70-kh godov XIX veka', *Vestnik leningradskogo universiteta*, 1961, no. 8 (seriia istorii, iazyka i literatury, vypusk 2), pp. 67–78.

Mikhailova, R. F., 'Vopros o teatral'noi monopolii v 1856–1858 gg.', *Nauchnye doklady vysshei shkoly. Istoricheskie nauki*, 3 (1960), pp. 76–86.

Molebnov, M. P., *Penzenskii krepostnoi teatr Gladkovykh* (Penza, 1955).

Moody, Jane, *Illegitimate Theatre in London, 1770–1840* (Cambridge, 2000).

Moore, Sonia, *The Stanislavski System: The Professional Training of an Actor* (Harmondsworth, 1976).

Morozova, T. P., and I. V. Potkina, *Savva Morozov* (Moscow, 1998).

Moser, Charles A., *Denis Fonvizin* (Boston, 1979).

Mosse, W. E., *Alexander II and the Modernization of Russia* (London, 1992).

Nelidov, V. A., *Teatral'naia Moskva (Sorok let Moskovskikh teatrov)* (Berlin and Riga, 1931).

Nemirovitch-Danchenko, Vladimir, *My Life in the Russian Theatre*, translated by John Cournos (London, 1937).

Norman, John O., 'Pavel Tretiakov and Merchant Art Patronage, 1850–1900', in Edith W. Clowes, Samuel D. Kassow and James L. West (eds.), *Between Tsar and People: Educated Society and the Quest for Public Identity in Late Imperial Russia* (Princeton, 1991), pp. 93–107.

Offord, Derek, 'Denis Fonvizin and the Concept of Nobility: An Eighteenth-Century Russian Echo of a Western Debate', *European History Quarterly*, 35 (2005), no. 1, pp. 9–38.

Olenina, A., 'Regulirovanie trudovykh otnoshenii v russkom chastnom teatre (konets XIX–nachalo XX veka)', *Ekonomika i organizatsiia teatra*, 7 (1986), pp. 163–75.

O'Malley, Lurana Donnels, *Two Comedies by Catherine the Great, Empress of Russia: 'Oh, These Times!' and 'The Siberian Shaman'* (London, 1998).

'Osobyia pravila o publichnykh zabavakh i uveseleniiakh v stolitsakh', in section 3 (razdel tret'ii) of the 'Ustav o preduprezhdenii i presechenii prestuplenii. Izdanie 1876 goda', *Svod zakonov*, 1876, vol. 14.

Ostrovskii, A. N., 'Klubnye stseny, chastnye teatry i liubitel'skie spektakli', in A. N. Ostrovskii, *Polnoe sobranie sochinenii*, 12 vols. (Moscow, 1978–80), vol. 10, pp. 114–26.

Ostrovskii, A. N., 'O prichinakh upadka dramaticheskogo teatra v Moskve', in A. N. Ostrovskii, *Polnoe sobranie sochinenii*, 12 vols. (Moscow, 1978–80), vol. 10, pp. 189–224.

Ostrovskii, A. N., *Polnoe sobranie sochinenii*, 12 vols. (Moscow, 1978–80).

Ostrovskii, A. N., 'Zapiska o polozhenii dramaticheskogo iskusstva v Rossii v nastoiashchee vremia', in A. N. Ostrovskii, *Polnoe sobranie sochinenii*, 12 vols. (Moscow, 1978–80), vol. 10, pp. 126–43.

Owen, Thomas C., *Capitalism and Politics in Russia: A Social History of the Moscow Merchants, 1855–1905* (Cambridge, 1981).

Parsons, Talcott, 'The Professions and Social Structure', in Talcott Parsons, *Essays in Sociological Theory* (New York and London, 1954), pp. 34–49.

Pavlova, T. N., 'Antrepriza Fedora Korsha', *Moskovskii nabliudatel'*, 7–8 (1992), pp. 50–3.

Pavlova, T. N., '"Davydovskie sezony" u Korsha (1886–1888 gody)', *Voprosy teatra*, 72 (1973), pp. 268–89.

Pavlova, T. N., 'Teatr F. A. Korsha (1882–1898)' (avtoreferat dissertatsii, Moscow, 1973).

Perrie, Maureen, '*Narodnost'*: Notions of National Identity', in Catriona Kelly and David Shepherd (eds.), *Constructing Russian Culture in the Age of Revolution: 1881–1940* (Oxford, 1998), pp. 28–36.

'Petr Alekseevich Plavil'shchikov', *Teatr*, 1955, no. 4 (April), pp. 190–1.

Petrovskaia, I., *Teatr i zritel' provintsial'noi Rossii: vtoraia polovina XIX veka* (Leningrad, 1979).

Petrovskaia, I., *Teatr i zritel' rossiiskikh stolits, 1895–1917* (Leningrad, 1990).

Petrovskaia, I., and V. Somina, *Teatral'nyi Peterburg: nachalo XVIII veka–oktiabr' 1917 goda* (St Petersburg, 1994).

Pogozhev, Vladimir, *Proekt zakonopolozhenii ob imperatorskikh teatrakh*, 3 vols. (St Petersburg, 1900).

Pokrovsky, B. A., and Y. N. Grigorovich, *The Bolshoi* (London, 1979).

Polenova, N. V., *Abramtsevo. Vospominaniia* (Moscow, 1922).

The Political and Legal Writings of Denis Fonvizin, translated with notes and an introduction by Walter Gleason (Ann Arbor, 1985).

'Polozhenie ob upravlenii Imperatorskimi S. Peterburgskimi Teatrami', *Polnoe sobranie zakonov Rossiiskoi Imperii (sobranie vtoroe)*, vol. 2: 1827 (St Petersburg, 1830), pp. 970–82 (statute no. 1533).

Pomeranz, William, '"Profession or Estate"? The Case of the Russian Pre-Revolutionary *Advokatura*', *Slavonic and East European Review*, 77 (1999), pp. 240–68.

Pushkin, A. S., 'Moi zamechaniia ob russkom teatre', in A. S. Pushkin, *Polnoe sobranie sochinenii v desiati tomakh*, 3rd edn., vol. 7 (Moscow, 1964), pp. 7–14.

Racin, John (ed. and trans.), *Tatyana Repina: Two Translated Texts by Alexei Suvorin and Anton Chekhov* (Jefferson, N.C., 1999).

Raeff, Marc, *Understanding Imperial Russia: State and Society in the Old Regime* (New York, 1984).

Rahman, Kate Sealey, *Ostrovsky: Reality and Illusion* (Birmingham, 1999).

Ransel, David L., *The Politics of Catherinian Russia: The Panin Party* (New Haven and London, 1975).

Rayfield, Donald, and Olga Makarova, 'Predislovie', in A. S. Suvorin, *Dnevnik A. S. Suvorina* (London and Moscow, 1999).

Reviakin, A. I., 'Ostrovskii na puti k khudozhestvennomu rukovodstvu moskovskimi teatrami', in *Literaturnoe nasledstvo*, vol. 88, book 2 (Moscow, 1974), pp. 50–70.

Rieber, Alfred J., *Merchants and Entrepreneurs in Imperial Russia* (Chapel Hill, N.C., 1982).

Rogger, Hans, *National Consciousness in Eighteenth-Century Russia* (Cambridge, Mass., 1960).

Roosevelt, Priscilla R., 'Emerald Thrones and Living Statues: Theater and Theatricality on the Russian Estate', *Russian Review*, 50 (1991), no. 2, pp. 1–23.

Rosenthal, B. G., 'Theatre As Church: The Vision of the Mystical Anarchists', *Russian History*, 4 (1977), no. 2, pp. 122–41.

Rossikhina, V. P., *Opernyi teatr S. Mamontova* (Moscow, 1985).

Rosslyn, Wendy, 'Petersburg Actresses On and Off Stage (1775–1825)', in

Anthony Cross (ed.), *St Petersburg, 1703–1825* (Basingstoke, 2003), pp. 119–47.

Rostotskii, I., 'Ostrovskii i Malyi teatr', in N. Abalkin (ed.), *Malyi Teatr, 1824–1974*, vol. 1: 1824–1917 (Moscow, 1978), pp. 203–34.

Rowell, George, *The Victorian Theatre* (London, 1956).

Rudnitsky, Konstantin, *Meyerhold the Director* (Ann Arbor, 1981).

Rudnitsky, Konstantin, *Russian and Soviet Theatre: Tradition and the Avant-Garde* (London, 1988).

Russell, Robert, 'People's Theatre and the October Revolution', *Irish Slavonic Studies*, 7 (1986), pp. 65–84.

Russkii dramaticheskii teatr. Entsiklopediia (Moscow, 2001).

Russkoe teatral'noe obshchestvo: Ustav (St Petersburg, 1903).

Sargeant, Lynn, '*Kashchei the Immortal*: Liberal Politics, Cultural Memory, and the Rimsky-Korsakov Scandal of 1905', *Russian Review*, 64 (2005), no. 1, pp. 22–43.

Schuler, Catherine A., 'The Gender of Russian Serf Theatre and Performance', in Maggie B. Gale and Viv Gardner (eds.), *Women, Theatre and Performance: New Histories, New Historiographies* (Manchester and New York, 2000), pp. 216–35.

Schuler, Catherine A., *Women in Russian Theatre: The Actress in the Silver Age* (New York, 1996).

Schumacher, Claude (ed.), *Naturalism and Symbolism in European Theatre, 1850–1918* (Cambridge, 1996).

Seligman, Adam B., *The Idea of Civil Society* (New York, 1992).

Senelick, Laurence, 'The Erotic Bondage of Serf Theatre', *Russian Review*, 50 (1991), no. 1, pp. 24–34.

Senelick, Laurence, 'Russia, 1848–1916', in Claude Schumacher (ed.), *Naturalism and Symbolism in European Theatre, 1850–1918* (Cambridge, 1996), pp. 191–257.

Senelick, Laurence, *Serf Actor: The Life and Art of Mikhail Shchepkin* (Westport, Conn., and London, 1984).

Senelick, Laurence (ed.), *National Theatre in Northern and Eastern Europe, 1746–1900* (Cambridge, 1991).

Senelick, Laurence (ed. and trans.), *Russian Dramatic Theory from Pushkin to the Symbolists* (Austin, Tex., 1981).

Shcherbatov, Prince M. M., *On the Corruption of Morals in Russia*, edited, translated and introduced by A. Lentin (Cambridge, 1969).

Shchetinin, B. A., 'F. A. Korsh i ego teatr', *Istoricheskii vestnik*, 110

(October–December 1907), pp. 168–79.

Shebuev, G., *Akterskoe schast'e. Vospominaniia* (Kuibyshev, 1964).

Shneiderman, I., *Mariia Gavrilovna Savina, 1854–1915* (Leningrad and Moscow, 1956).

Skal'kovskii, Konstantin, *V teatral'nom mire. Nabliudeniia, vospominaniia i razsuzhdeniia* (St Petersburg, 1899).

Slonim, Marc, *Russian Theater: From the Empire to the Soviets* (Cleveland and New York, 1961).

Smeliansky, Anatoly, *The Russian Theatre after Stalin*, translated by Patrick Miles (Cambridge, 1999).

Smeliansky, Anatoly, 'Russian Theatre in the Post-Communist Era', translated by Stephen Holland, in Robert Leach and Victor Borovsky (eds.), *A History of Russian Theatre* (Cambridge, 1999), pp. 382–406.

Smith, Douglas, *Working the Rough Stone: Freemasonry and Society in Eighteenth-Century Russia* (DeKalb, Ill., 1999).

Smith, Steve A., 'Popular Culture and Market Development in Late-Imperial Russia', in Geoffrey Hosking and Robert Service (eds.), *Reinterpreting Russia* (London, 1999), pp. 142–55.

Smith, Steve, and Catriona Kelly, 'Commercial Culture and Consumerism', in Catriona Kelly and David Shepherd (eds.), *Constructing Russian Culture in the Age of Revolution: 1881–1940* (Oxford, 1998), pp. 106–64.

Sollogub, V. A., *Peterburgskie stranitsy vospominanii grafa Solloguba, s portretami ego sovremennikov* (St Petersburg, 1993).

Stanislavski, Constantin [Stanislavsky], *My Life in Art*, translated by J. J. Robbins (London, 1980).

Stepanskii, A. D., *Samoderzhavie i obshchestvennye organizatsii Rossii na rubezhe XIX–XX vv.* (Moscow, 1980).

Sternin, G. Iu., et al., *Abramtsevo. Khudozhesvtennyi kruzhok. Zhivopis'. Grafika. Skul'ptura. Teatr. Masterskie* (Leningrad, 1988).

Stites, Richard, 'The Misanthrope, the Orphan, and the Magpie: Imported Melodrama in the Twilight of Serfdom', in Louise McReynolds and Joan Neuberger (eds.), *Imitations of Life: Two Centuries of Melodrama in Russia* (Durham, N.C., and London, 2002), pp. 25–54.

Stites, Richard, *Serfdom, Society, and the Arts in Imperial Russia: The Pleasure and the Power* (New Haven and London, 2005).

Suvorin, A. S., *Dnevnik A. S. Suvorina* (London and Moscow, 1999).

Suvorin, A. S., *Teatral'nye ocherki: 1866–1876* (St Petersburg, 1914).

Swift, E. Anthony, 'Fighting the Germs of Disorder: The Censorship of

Russian Popular Theater, 1888–1917', *Russian History/Histoire Russe*, 18, no. 1 (spring 1991), pp. 1–49.

Swift, E. Anthony, *Popular Theater and Society in Tsarist Russia* (Berkeley, 2002).

Taylor, S. S. B. (ed.), *The Theatre of the French and German Enlightenment* (Edinburgh and London, 1979).

Teatral'naia entsiklopediia, 5 vols. plus supplement with index (Moscow, 1961–7).

Teliakovskii, V. A., *Imperatorskie teatry i 1905 god* (Leningrad, 1926).

Thatcher, Ian D. (ed.), *Late Imperial Russia: Problems and Prospects: Essays in Honour of R. B. McKean* (Manchester, 2005).

Thurston, Gary, *The Popular Theatre Movement in Russia, 1862–1919* (Evanston, Ill., 1998).

Tikhonov, V. A., 'Teatral'nyia vospominaniia', *Istoricheskii vestnik*, June 1898, pp. 811–43.

Tolstoy, Lev, *What Is Art?*, translated by Richard Pevear and Larissa Volokhonsky (London, 1995).

Tolz, Vera, *Russia: Inventing the Nation* (London, 2001).

Troianskii, M. P., 'K stsenicheskoi istorii komedii D. I. Fonvizina "Brigadir" i "Nedorosl'" v XVIII veke', in *Teatral'noe nasledstvo* (Moscow, 1956), pp. 7–23.

Troyat, Henri, *Pushkin*, translated by Nancy Amphoux (London, 1974).

Trudy pervogo vserossiiskogo s''ezda stsenicheskikh deiatelei, 2 vols. (St Petersburg, 1898).

Tsinkovich, V. A., 'Narodnyi teatr i dramaticheskaia tsenzura', in *Teatral'noe nasledstvo* (Moscow, 1956), pp. 375–401.

Tsinkovich-Nikolaeva, V., 'Kupecheskaia tema v repertuare aleksandrinskogo teatra 1832–1842 gg.', in A. Ia. Al'tshuller and N. V. Zaitsev (eds.), *Traditsii stsenicheskogo realizma. Akademicheskii teatr dramy im. A. S. Pushkina. Sbornik nauchnykh trudov* (Leningrad, 1980), pp. 110–26.

Urusov, A. I., *Stat'i ego o teatre, o literature i ob iskusstve. Pis'ma ego. Vospominaniia o nem*, vol. 1 (Moscow, 1907).

'Ustav o preduprezhdenii i presechenii prestuplenii. Izdanie 1876 goda', *Svod zakonov*, 1876, vol. 14.

Ustav vserossiiskogo soiuza stsenicheskikh deiatelei (n.p., 1906).

Varneke, B. V., *History of the Russian Theatre: Seventeenth through Nineteenth Century*, translated by Boris Brasol (New York, 1951).

Varneke, B. V., *Istoriia russkogo teatra XVII–XIX vekov*, 3rd edn (Moscow and

Leningrad, 1939).

Vigel', F. F., *Zapiski* (Moscow, 2000).

Vitenzon, R., *Anna Brenko* (Leningrad, 1985).

Vladykin, G. I. (ed.), *A. N. Ostrovskii v russkoi kritike: sbornik statei* (Moscow, 1953).

Vol'f, A. I., *Khronika peterburgskikh teatrov s kontsa 1855 do nachala 1881 goda*, part 3 (St Petersburg, 1884).

Volkov, N., 'Teatr v epokhu krusheniia monarkhii', in *Sto let. Aleksandrinskii teatr – teatr gosdramy* (Leningrad, 1932), pp. 297–379.

Von Geldern, James, and Louise McReynolds (eds.), *Entertaining Tsarist Russia: Tales, Songs, Plays, Movies, Jokes, Ads and Images from Russian Urban Life, 1779–1917* (Bloomington and Indianapolis, 1998).

Vsevolodskii-Gerngross, V., 'Pervyia postanovki "Brigadira" i "Nedoroslia"', in V. V. Kallash and N. E. Efros (eds.), *Istoriia russkogo teatra* (Moscow, 1914), pp. 357–64.

Vsevolodskii-Gerngross, V., *Teatr v Rossii v epokhu otechestvennoi voiny* (St Petersburg, 1912).

Walkin, Jacob, *The Rise of Democracy in Pre-Revolutionary Russia: Political and Social Institutions under the Last Three Czars* (London, 1963).

Wartenweiler, David, *Civil Society and Academic Debate in Russia, 1905–1914* (Oxford, 1999).

Wiley, R. J., *Tchaikovsky's Ballets* (Oxford, 1985).

Wiley, R. J., 'The Yearbook of the Imperial Theaters', *Dance Research Journal*, 9, no. 1 (fall–winter 1976–7), pp. 30–6.

Wilmot, Martha and Catherine, *The Russian Journals of Martha and Catherine Wilmot, 1803–1808*, edited, introduced and annotated by the Marchioness of Londonderry and H. M. Hynde (London, 1934).

Wirtschafter, Elise Kimerling, 'The Common Soldier in Eighteenth-Century Russian Drama', in Joachim Klein, Simon Dixon and Maarten Fraanje (eds.), *Reflections on Russia in the Eighteenth Century* (Cologne, 2001), pp. 367–76.

Wirtschafter, Elise Kimerling, *The Play of Ideas in Russian Enlightenment Theater* (DeKalb, Ill., 2003).

Worrall, Nick, *The Moscow Art Theatre* (London and New York, 1996).

Worrall, Nick, *Nikolai Gogol and Ivan Turgenev* (London and Basingstoke, 1982).

Wortman, Richard S., *Scenarios of Power: Myth and Ceremony in Russian Monarchy*, vol. 1: *From Peter the Great to the Death of Nicholas I*

(Princeton, 1995).

Wortman, Richard S., *Scenarios of Power: Myth and Ceremony in Russian Monarchy*, vol. 2: *From Alexander II to the Abdication of Nicholas II* (Princeton, 2000).

Yastrebtsev, V. V., *Reminiscences of Rimsky-Korsakov*, edited and translated by F. Jonas (New York, 1985).

Zagorskii, M. B. (ed.), *Gogol' i teatr* (Moscow, 1952).

Zguta, Russell, *Russian Minstrels: A History of the Skomorokhi* (Oxford, 1978).

Zograf, N. G., *Malyi teatr vtoroi poloviny XIX veka* (Moscow, 1960).

NOTES

ABBREVIATIONS

GTsTM   Gosudarstvennyi tsentral'nyi teatral'nyi muzei imeni A. A. Bakhrushina.
IRDT   Kholodov, E. G. (ed.), *Istoriia russkogo dramaticheskogo teatra,* 7 vols. (Moscow, 1977–87).
RGALI   Rossiiskii gosudarstvennyi arkhiv literatury i iskusstva.
RGIA   Rossiiskii gosudarstvennyi istoricheskii arkhiv.
TE   *Teatral'naia entsiklopediia,* 5 vols., plus supplement with index (Moscow, 1961–7).
TPVSSD *Trudy pervogo vserossiiskogo s"ezda stsenicheskikh deiatelei,* 2 vols. (St Petersburg, 1898).

Introduction

1 Kallash and Efros (eds.), *Istoriia russkogo teatra,* p. v.
2 *IRDT,* vol. 1, p. 5.
3 Borovsky, 'Russian Theatre in Russian Culture', p. 10.
4 Gertsen, 'Po povodu odnoi dramy', p. 51.
5 Zagorskii (ed.), *Gogol' i teatr,* p. 386.
6 Quoted in Borovsky, 'Russian Theatre in Russian Culture', p. 11.
7 Kallash and Efros (eds.), *Istoriia russkogo teatra,* p. ix.
8 Gellner, *Conditions of Liberty,* pp. 3–4, 5. This was essentially how Alexis de Tocqueville understood the significance of associational activity in *Democracy in America* (1835–40). See also Eberly, *Essential Civil Society Reader* and Seligman, *Idea of Civil Society.* For a useful summary of the way the concept of civil society has evolved through the writings of various thinkers since the eighteenth century (including Adam Ferguson, Hegel, de Tocqueville, Marx, Gramsci and others), see Kumar, 'Civil Society'.
9 By the terms of this definition, the Russian revolutionary movement, for example, should not be considered part of civil society because it sought to dismantle the existing system rather than reform it. This is not to suggest that revolutionaries had a simple alternative to seeking the overthrow of tsarism, but merely to posit an essential distinction between two modes of action in imperial Russia.
10 Bradley, 'Subjects into Citizens'.

11 Smith, *Working the Rough Stone*, pp. 64, 69–71, 74–5, 77–8.

12 Raeff, *Understanding Imperial Russia*, pp. 129–45.

13 Lindenmeyr, *Poverty Is Not a Vice*, pp. 110, 115.

14 On the 'great reforms', see Eklof et al., *Russia's Great Reforms*; Lincoln, *Great Reforms*; Mosse, *Alexander II and the Modernization of Russia*.

15 See, for example, Owen, *Capitalism and Politics in Russia*, and Rieber, *Merchants and Entrepreneurs*.

16 Marc Raeff, for example, uses the term 'nascent' in *Understanding Imperial Russia*, p. 193. On late imperial Russia's civil society, see, for example, Balzer (ed.), *Russia's Missing Middle Class*; Bradley, 'Russia's Parliament of Public Opinion'; Bradley, 'Subjects into Citizens'; Clowes et al. (eds.), *Between Tsar and People*; Conroy, 'Civil Society in Late Imperial Russia'; Raeff, *Understanding Imperial Russia*; Walkin, *Rise of Democracy in Pre-Revolutionary Russia*; Wartenweiler, *Civil Society and Academic Debate in Russia*.

17 McKean, *Between the Revolutions*, p. 7. Of the many reasons for the lack of 'middle class' unity in Russia, one of the most important was the distrust between the entrepreneurial and intellectual classes. See Bill, *Forgotten Class*, especially chapters 7 and 8.

18 R. B. McKean, for example, has expressed doubts about the long-term prospects for the constitutional monarchy on the basis of his study of imperial Russia's social fissures and its fragile civil society. See McKean, 'Constitutional Monarchy in Russia, 1906–17'. It is interesting to note that elsewhere McKean provides a cogent argument for considering Russia after 1905 to be a 'proper constitutional monarchy' on the basis of comparisons with European equivalents: McKean, 'Russian Constitutional Monarchy in Comparative Perspective'. Moreover, he has argued that the labour unrest between 1912 and 1914 had limited revolutionary potential: McKean, *St Petersburg between the Revolutions*, especially chapters 8 and 10. Considered together, these studies – arguing that the constitutional monarchy had weak foundations but nevertheless conformed to the wider European experience and was not confronted with a revolutionary crisis on the eve of the First World War – present a challenging perspective on the period. On this issue, see also Haimson, 'Problem of Social Stability'; Haimson, 'Problem of Political and Social Stability'; Rieber, *Merchants and Entrepreneurs*; Thatcher (ed.), *Late Imperial Russia*.

19 Gellner, *Conditions of Liberty*, p. 9.

20 Ibid., p. 12.

21 Ibid., p. 100.

22 Ibid., p. 103.

23 On Russian national identities, see Tolz, *Russia*.

Chapter 1

1 Quoted in Kochetkova, *Fonvizin v Peterburge*, p. 165.

2 Petrovskaia and Somina, *Teatral'nyi Peterburg*, pp. 65–70.

3 Cross, *By the Banks of the Neva*, pp. 36–9.

4 Quoted in Petrovskaia and Somina, *Teatral'nyi Peterburg*, pp. 65–6.

5 Kochetkova, *Fonvizin v Peterburge*, p. 158.

6 Moser, *Denis Fonvizin*, especially chapter 1.

7 Quotations from the play are from Joshua Cooper's translation in Cooper,

Government Inspector and Other Russian Plays, pp. 59, 117. Cooper renders 'Nedorosl'' as 'The Infant', an alternative but less common variant.

8 Offord, 'Denis Fonvizin and the Concept of Nobility', p. 30.
9 Cross, 'English Embankment', p. 68.
10 Cooper, *Government Inspector and Other Russian Plays*, p. 113.
11 Ibid., p. 75.
12 Ransel, *Politics of Catherinian Russia*, p. 267.
13 Ibid., p. 270.
14 *Political and Legal Writings of Denis Fonvizin*, p. 11. See also Offord, 'Denis Fonvizin and the Concept of Nobility'.
15 Cooper, *Government Inspector and Other Russian Plays*, p. 72.
16 *Political and Legal Writings of Denis Fonvizin*, p. 1.
17 Cooper, *Government Inspector and Other Russian Plays*, p. 112.
18 Moser, *Denis Fonvizin*, p. 112.
19 Rogger, *National Consciousness in Eighteenth-Century Russia*, pp. 75–7.
20 Ibid., p. 277.
21 Vsevolodskii-Gerngross, 'Pervyia postanovki', p. 360.
22 Troianskii, 'K stsenicheskoi istorii', p. 8.
23 Aseev, *Russkii dramaticheskii teatr*, p. 372.
24 Women were not formally prohibited from appearing on stage in Russia, but before the nineteenth century relatively few ventured into acting and female roles were often performed by men. According to one historian, 'Even when the first contingent of actresses had been recruited with great difficulty, only young feminine parts were performed by women, while "comic old women" continued to be played by men for a long time.' Hence Shumsky in the role of Yeremeyevna. Varneke, *History of the Russian Theatre*, p. 82.
25 Quoted in Aseev, *Russkii dramaticheskii teatr*, p. 372.
26 Kochetkova, *Fonvizin v Peterburge*, p. 163.
27 Quoted in Aseev, *Russkii dramaticheskii teatr*, p. 373.
28 *Dramaticheskii slovar'*, pp. 88–9; Vsevolodskii-Gerngross, 'Pervyia postanovki', p. 361.
29 Kochetkova, *Fonvizin v Peterburge*, p. 166.
30 Aseev, *Russkii dramaticheskii teatr*, p. 375.
31 Kochetkova, *Fonvizin v Peterburge*, pp. 166–7.
32 Danilov, *Russkii dramaticheskii teatr*, p. 8.
33 Aseev, *Russkii dramaticheskii teatr*, p. 281.
34 Iazykov, '"Nedorosl'" na stsene i v literature', pp. 143–4.
35 Moser, *Denis Fonvizin*, p. 72.
36 Ibid., p. 71.
37 Quoted in Aseev, *Russkii dramaticheskii teatr*, p. 374.
38 Kliuchevskii, 'Nedorosl' Fonvizina', p. 270.
39 Moser, *Denis Fonvizin*, p. 72.
40 Slonim, *Russian Theater*, p. 34.
41 *Nevskoe vremia*, 5 April 1995, p. 4.
42 Aseev, *Russkii dramaticheskii teatr*, p. 371.
43 Troianskii, 'K stsenicheskoi istorii', p. 12.
44 Quoted in Aseev, *Russkii dramaticheskii teatr*, p. 371.
45 Pushkin, *Eugene Onegin*, stanza 18.
46 On the *skomorokhi*, see Zguta, *Russian Minstrels*.

47 Wirtschafter, *Play of Ideas*, p. 9. Wirtschafter lists several other examples from the early eighteenth century.

48 For the early history of theatre in Russia (i.e. to the mid eighteenth century), see Malnick, 'Origin and Early History of the Theatre in Russia'.

49 On Volkov, see Burgess, 'First Russian Actor-Manager'.

50 Drizen, *Stopiatidesiatiletie imperatorskikh teatrov*, p. 25.

51 Wirtschafter, *Play of Ideas*, p. 14; Burgess, 'Russian Public Theatre Audiences', p. 175.

52 Danilov, 'Materialy po istorii russkogo zakonodatel'stva o teatre', p. 177; Petrovskaia and Somina, *Teatral'nyi Peterburg*, pp. 44, 52.

53 *Arkhiv direktsii imperatorskikh teatrov*, p. 115 (Catherine II to Olsufev, 12 July 1783). The special committee existed until 1786. The entry for the directorate in the *Teatral'naia entsiklopediia* claims that the special committee replaced the directorate during those years, but other sources indicate that they coexisted. *TE*, vol. 2, column 447.

54 See Alexander, 'Catherine the Great and the Theatre', and O'Malley, *Two Comedies by Catherine the Great*. For a comparative perspective, see, for example, Taylor (ed.), *Theatre of the French and German Enlightenment*.

55 Quoted in Drizen, 'Liubitel'skii teatr pri Ekaterine II', pp. 78–9.

56 Quoted in Borovsky, 'Theatre Administration at the Court of Catherine II', p. 45.

57 Quoted in ibid. The dates of these comments are unclear.

58 Quoted in Malnick, 'A. A. Shakhovskoy', p. 33.

59 Quoted in Wirtschafter, *Play of Ideas*, p. 47.

60 *Dramaticheskii slovar'*, p. 3.

61 Shcherbatov, *On the Corruption of Morals in Russia*, p. 253.

62 Drizen, *Stopiatidesiatiletie imperatorskikh teatrov*, p. 10; Burgess, 'Russian Public Theatre Audiences', pp. 162–3.

63 Dynnik, *Krepostnoi teatr*, p. 67.

64 Quoted in Drizen, 'Liubitel'skii teatr pri Ekaterine II', pp. 83–4.

65 Quoted in Cross, 'Mr Fisher's Company of English Actors', p. 50.

66 Pushkin, 'Moi zamechaniia ob russkom teatre', pp. 8–9.

67 Borovsky, 'Theatre Administration at the Court of Catherine II', p. 45.

68 Karlinsky, *Russian Drama*, pp. 137–40.

69 In 1889–90 the building of the Bolshoi Kamenny was given to the Russian Musical Society for the St Petersburg Conservatory.

70 The Malyi Wooden Theatre in the Ekaterinsky Garden is not to be confused with references to the Free Russian Theatre as the Malyi, or Wooden Theatre, names it was given when it was taken over by the state in 1783. Tsar Paul I decreed its demolition in 1797 because it hindered parades. *IRDT*, vol. 2, p. 45.

71 Petrovskaia and Somina, *Teatral'nyi Peterburg*, p. 100; Pokrovsky and Grigorovich, *Bolshoi*, p. 7.

72 Danilov, *Russkii dramaticheskii teatr*, p. 8.

73 Simon Dixon makes a similar point with regard to Catherine II's support for the Academy of Sciences and the Academy of Fine Arts: Dixon, *Catherine the Great*, p. 103.

74 'Director', from the Russian *direktor*, here means 'manager' or 'administrator', not the stage director of a production, known in Russia as *rezhissër*, from the French *régisseur*. The use of the term *direktor* to describe managers, departmental heads and so on was common in imperial Russia. When the Ministry of the

Imperial Court was created in 1826, several of the departments it took charge of (including the directorate of Imperial Theatres) were run by *direktory*: RGIA, f. 472, op. 66, ed. khr. 468 – Proekty polozheniia ob uchrezhdenii Ministerstva imperatorskogo dvora (1881).

75 Vsevolodskii-Gerngross, *Teatr v Rossii v epokhu otechestvennoi voiny*, pp. 30, 32.
76 Danilov, 'Materialy po istorii russkogo zakonodatel'stva o teatre', p. 178.
77 Evidence suggests that Russian 'masquerades' were not identical to the masked balls familiar in other parts of Europe. In 1810, John Quincy Adams, then the United States minister to St Petersburg, attended a masquerade at the Winter Palace, later commenting, 'it is called a masquerade, but there are no masques. The imperial family and persons admitted to Court appear – the men in Venetian dominoes, the ladies in common Court dresses.' *John Quincy Adams in Russia*, p. 96. Of a ball at Peterhof in 1839 the Marquis de Custine wrote, 'it professed to be a masquerade, for the men wore a small piece of silk called a Venetian mantle, which floated in a ridiculous manner above their heads.' Custine, *Empire of the Tsar*, p. 229. For an example of a short newspaper description of a masquerade ball at the Moscow Bolshoi Theatre, see *Severnaia pchela*, 11 September 1825, p. 2.
78 *TE*, vol. 3, column 906.
79 Danilov, 'Materialy po istorii russkogo zakonodatel'stva o teatre', p. 178.
80 Danilov, *Russkii dramaticheskii teatr*, p. 12.
81 *IRDT*, vol. 2, pp. 38–40; Danilov, *Russkii dramaticheskii teatr*, p. 12.
82 Quoted in Borovsky, 'Russian Theatre in Russian Culture', p. 11.
83 Quoted in Rosslyn, 'Petersburg Actresses', p. 120.
84 Grossman, *Pushkin v teatral'nykh kreslakh*, p. 8.
85 Burgess, 'Russian Public Theatre Audiences', p. 170.
86 See Rosslyn, 'Petersburg Actresses'.
87 Iushkov, 'Mysli o vrede i pol'ze teatrov', pp. 213–24.
88 Burgess, 'Russian Public Theatre Audiences', p. 168.
89 Ibid., p. 172.
90 Quoted in ibid., pp. 172–3, 174.
91 Ibid., pp. 178–9.
92 John Carr, *A Northern Summer, or Travels around the Baltic through Denmark, Sweden, Russia, Prussia and Part of Germany in the year 1804* (London, 1805), p. 297, quoted in Burgess, 'Russian Public Theatre Audiences', p. 160.
93 Burgess, 'Russian Public Theatre Audiences', pp. 182–3.
94 For comments about the near-empty parterre at the Petrovsky, see Vigel', *Zapiski*, p. 70.
95 Grossman, *Pushkin v teatral'nykh kreslakh*, p. 14. The Russian word *kresla*, the plural of 'armchair', was used to describe approximately the first ten rows of the stalls. The rows further back were referred to as the parterre.
96 Ibid., p. 17.
97 Ibid., p. 26; Binyon, *Pushkin*, p. 78.
98 Quoted in Troyat, *Pushkin*, p. 106.
99 Quoted in ibid., p. 110.
100 Binyon, *Pushkin*, p. 66.
101 Grossman, *Pushkin v teatral'nykh kreslakh*, p. 63.
102 Rosslyn, 'Petersburg Actresses', p. 142.
103 *IRDT*, vol. 2, pp. 239–40; Danilov, *Ocherki*, p. 218.
104 Vol'f, *Khronika peterburgskikh teatrov*, p. 7.

105 Biographical information on Shakhovskoi from Malnick, 'A. A. Shakhovskoy'.
106 Grossman, *Pushkin v teatral'nykh kreslakh*, p. 36.
107 Quoted in ibid., p. 40.
108 *Repertuar i panteon*, 1843, book 1, p. 114.
109 Malnick, 'A. A. Shakhovskoy', pp. 50–1.
110 On vaudeville in Russia, see Litvinenko, *Starinnyi russkii vodevil'*.
111 Malnick, 'A. A. Shakhovskoy', p. 37.
112 Quoted in ibid., p. 43.
113 Quoted in Vsevolodskii-Gerngross, *Teatr v Rossii v epokhu otechestvennoi voiny*, p. 44.
114 Vigel', *Zapiski*, p. 137.
115 'Petr Alekseevich Plavil'shchikov', pp. 190–1; Rogger, *National Consciousness in Eighteenth-Century Russia*, pp. 148–50.
116 Vsevolodskii-Gerngross, *Teatr v Rossii v epokhu otechestvennoi voiny*, pp. 40–1.
117 Koroleva, 'Patrioticheskaia tema'.
118 Troyat, *Pushkin*, p. 65.
119 Vigel', *Zapiski*, p. 335. See also Vsevolodskii-Gerngross, *Teatr v Rossii v epokhu otechestvennoi voiny*, p. 173.
120 Quoted in ibid.
121 Ibid., pp. 176–7.
122 Ibid., p. 174.
123 Troyat, *Pushkin*, p. 64.
124 *IRDT*, vol. 2, pp. 237–8.
125 *Severnaia pchela*, 10 May 1828, pp. 1–2.
126 *IRDT*, vol. 2, p. 204; Dynnik, *Krepostnoi teatr*, p. 32.
127 Ibid., p. 36.
128 Beskin, *Krepostnoi teatr*, p. 13.
129 Malnick, 'Russian Serf Theatres', p. 395.
130 *IRDT*, vol. 2, pp. 206, 218.
131 Roosevelt, 'Emerald Thrones and Living Statues', p. 5.
132 Ibid.
133 Dynnik, *Krepostnoi teatr*, pp. 13–16.
134 Quoted in Molebnov, *Penzenskii krepostnoi teatr Gladkovykh*, p. 8.
135 Malnick, 'Russian Serf Theatres', p. 393.
136 *IRDT*, vol. 2, p. 212; Malnick, 'Russian Serf Theatres', pp. 397, 407.
137 *TE*, vol. 3, column 266.
138 Ibid., column 267.
139 Malnick, 'Russian Serf Theatres', p. 402.
140 Aseev, *Russkii dramaticheskii teatr*, p. 374.
141 Burgess, 'Nineteenth- and Early Twentieth-Century Theatre', p. 248.
142 Roosevelt, 'Emerald Thrones and Living Statues', p. 6. On Kamensky's theatre, see also Buturlin, 'Teatr grafa Kamenskogo'.
143 Senelick, 'Erotic Bondage of Serf Theatre', p. 27 (Senelick is quoting V. I. Insarskii, *Polovode*, from E. S. Kots, *Krepostnaia intelligentsiia* (Leningrad, 1926), p. 130).
144 Beskin, *Krepostnoi teatr*, p. 28.
145 Senelick, 'Erotic Bondage of Serf Theatre', p. 30.
146 Ibid., pp. 33–4.
147 Wilmot, *Russian Journals of Martha and Catherine Wilmot*, pp. 56–7.
148 *TE*, vol. 3, column 268; Malnick, 'Russian Serf Theatres', pp. 408–9.

149 The account that follows is based largely on Laurence Senelick's excellent study, *Serf Actor.*
150 *IRDT*, vol. 2, pp. 214–15; Malnick, 'Russian Serf Theatres', p. 395.
151 *IRDT*, vol. 2, pp. 219–22. It is not clear if N. G. Shakhovskoi was a relative of Alexander Shakhovskoi.
152 Ibid., p. 215.
153 Malnick, 'Russian Serf Theatres', p. 402.
154 *TE*, vol. 3, column 268.
155 *IRDT*, vol. 2, pp. 218–19.
156 Ibid., pp. 191–3.
157 Ibid., pp. 203–4, 214–15.
158 Ibid., pp. 242–3.
159 Ibid., p. 406.
160 Ibid., p. 400.
161 Stites, 'The Misanthrope, the Orphan, and the Magpie', p. 37.
162 For more on provincial troupes and strolling players, see Stites, *Serfdom, Society, and the Arts*, chapter 6.

Chapter 2

1 *Severnaia pchela*, 3 January 1825, p. 2; *Severnaia pchela*, 5 March 1825, p. 1.
2 Ibid., 21 February 1829, p. 3; Mikhailova, 'Vopros o teatral'noi monopolii', p. 82.
3 Grossman, *Pushkin v teatral'nykh kreslakh*, p. 48.
4 *Repertuar russkogo i panteon vsekh evropeiskikh teatrov na 1842 god*, no. 7, pp. 58–60.
5 *Panteon*, no. 13 (February 1854), book 2 (various pagination).
6 Borovsky, 'Russian Theatre in Russian Culture', p. 12.
7 RGIA, f. 497, op. 18, d. 12 – Vsepoddanneishei doklad ministra imperatorskogo dvora o soedinenii upravleniia imperatorskimi teatrami obeikh stolits (1 February 1842).
8 'Polozhenie ob upravlenii Imperatorskimi S. Peterburgskimi Teatrami'. See also Danilov, *Ocherki*, p. 223.
9 Pogozhev, *Proekt zakonopolozhenii*, vol. 3, p. 401.
10 Danilov, *Ocherki*, p. 222. For the argument that these regulations were designed to guard against 'seditious ideas', see also *IRDT*, vol. 3, p. 15.
11 Danilov, *Russkii dramaticheskii teatr*, p. 134.
12 *IRDT*, vol. 3, p. 9.
13 Ibid.
14 Pogozhev, *Proekt zakonopolozhenii*, vol. 3, p. 401.
15 Ibid., pp. 414–15. V. F. Adlerberg was Minister of the Imperial Court from 1853 to 1870. He was succeeded in that post by A. V. Adlerberg (1870–81), who broadly upheld his predecessor's views about private theatres.
16 *Severnaia pchela*, 23 April 1825, pp. 1–2.
17 Ibid., 10 January 1828, p. 1.
18 Ibid., 10 May 1828, p. 1.
19 Quoted in *IRDT*, vol. 3, p. 16.
20 Quoted in Danilov, *Russkii dramaticheskii teatr*, p. 134.
21 *Repertuar russkogo i panteon vsekh evropeiskikh teatrov na 1842 god*, no. 1, p. 47.
22 Jerrmann, *Pictures from St Petersburg*, p. 116. By contrast, as Jerrmann also

remarks, 'The German company is by no means the most favoured in St Petersburg' (p. 118).

23 Ibid., pp. 114–15. Jerrmann was less impressed by the repertoire, which he goes on to discuss.

24 Ibid., p. 114. See also Alekseev, *Vospominaniia aktera*, pp. 39–40, and *Teatral'nyi mirok*, 1892, no. 18, pp. 3–4.

25 *Severnaia pchela*, 18 September 1826, p. 1.

26 Koroleva, *Dekabristy i teatr*, p. 32. See also Danilov, *Russkii dramaticheskii teatr*, pp. 71–2.

27 Koroleva, *Dekabristy i teatr*, p. 21.

28 Ibid., pp. 22–4.

29 S. S. Landa, 'Vmesto predisloviia', in Koroleva, *Dekabristy i teatr*, p. 5.

30 Danilov, *Russkii dramaticheskii teatr*.

31 *TE*, vol. 1, columns 1153–5.

32 Belinsky's writings on theatre are collected in Belinskii, *O drame i teatre*.

33 *TE*, vol. 1, columns 492–6.

34 *Russkii dramaticheskii teatr. Entsiklopediia*, p. 65.

35 See, for example, Kholodov, 'Parter i raek'.

36 Falkus, *Industrialisation of Russia*, pp. 17, 34–5, 37–8.

37 *Literaturnaia gazeta*, 4 January 1845, p. 10.

38 Ibid., p. 11. For another account that indicates broad diversity in the Alexandrinsky audience, see P. Pustynnik, 'Teatral'naia publika', *Literaturnaia gazeta*, 13 November 1847, pp. 727–31.

39 Quoted in Malnick, 'Mochalov and Karatygin', p. 267.

40 Kholodov, 'Parter i raek', p. 83.

41 Ibid., pp. 83–4; *TE*, vol. 1, column 114.

42 *Severnaia pchela*, 19 May 1828, p. 3.

43 *Severnyi merkurii*, 22 June 1831, p. 299.

44 *Khudozhestvennaia gazeta*, 1 April 1840, p. 21.

45 *Literaturnaia gazeta*, 3 January 1847, pp. 9–12.

46 Perrie, '*Narodnost'*: Notions of National Identity'.

47 *Severnaia pchela*, 26 February 1836, p. 4; continued in ibid., 27 February 1836, pp. 3–4; concluded in ibid., 28 February 1836, pp. 3–4.

48 Quoted in Malnick, 'A. A. Shakhovskoy', p. 44.

49 *Repertuar i panteon*, 1843, book 1, pp. 118, 125.

50 Malnick, 'The Theory and Practice of Russian Drama', p. 30.

51 See Kelly, *Diplomacy and Murder in Tehran*.

52 Cooper, *Government Inspector and Other Russian Plays*, pp. 189–91.

53 Ibid., p. 147.

54 Ibid., pp. 148–9.

55 Ibid., p. 187.

56 Quoted in Slonim, *Russian Theater*, p. 44.

57 Kelly, *Diplomacy and Murder in Tehran*, p. 2.

58 Binyon, *Pushkin*, p. 206.

59 Herzen, *My Past and Thoughts*, vol. 1, p. 517.

60 Belinskii, *O drame i teatre*, vol. 1, p. 88.

61 For a list of all known performances of *Woe from Wit* at the Imperial Theatres, see 'Perechen' predstavlenii komedii A. S. Griboedov "Gore ot uma" na stsenakh Imperatorskikh teatrov', *Ezhegodnik imperatorskikh teatrov. Sezon 1893–1894 g.g.*

Prilozheniia, book 3 (St Petersburg, 1894), pp. 45–58.

62 *IRDT*, vol. 3, p. 21.

63 *Severnaia pchela*, 9 February 1831, pp. 1–2.

64 Ibid., 30 November 1831, p. 1.

65 Vigel', *Zapiski*, p. 440.

66 V. Filippov, 'Rannye postanovki Gore ot uma', in *A. S. Griboedov: Literaturnoe nasledstvo* (Moscow, 1946), pp. 303–4, quoted in Malnick, 'The Theory and Practice of Russian Drama', p. 14.

67 Herzen, *My Past and Thoughts*, vol. 4, pp. 1757–8.

68 Fülöp-Miller and Gregor, *Russian Theatre*, p. 38.

69 S. S. Landa, 'Vmesto predisloviia', in Koroleva, *Dekabristy i teatr*, p. 18.

70 Bertensson, 'The Premiere of "The Inspector General"', pp. 88–95.

71 Nikolai Gogol, 'Petersburg Notes for 1836', in Senelick (ed. and trans.), *Russian Dramatic Theory*, p. 24.

72 Quoted in Worrall, *Nikolai Gogol and Ivan Turgenev*, p. 25.

73 Quoted in Bertensson, 'The Premiere of "The Inspector General"', p. 94.

74 Quoted in Senelick (ed.), *National Theatre in Northern and Eastern Europe*, p. 345.

75 Quoted in Malnick, 'The Theory and Practice of Russian Drama', p. 28.

76 *Severnaia pchela*, 1 May 1836, pp. 389–92.

77 A. B. V., 'Teatral'naia khronika', in *N. V. Gogol' v russkoi kritike* (Moscow and Leningrad, 1951), pp. 165–7, quoted in Malnick, 'The Theory and Practice of Russian Drama', p. 29.

78 Tsinkovich-Nikolaeva, 'Kupecheskaia tema', pp. 111, 126.

79 Vigel', *Zapiski*, p. 552.

80 Quoted in Tsinkovich-Nikolaeva, 'Kupecheskaia tema', p. 114.

81 Ibid., pp. 112–13.

82 Danilov, *Ocherki*, p. 219.

83 *IRDT*, vol. 3, p. 19.

84 Varneke, *History of the Russian Theatre*, p. 170.

85 For more on the status and backstage tribulations of actors, see Stites, *Serfdom, Society, and the Arts*, chapter 4.

86 *IRDT*, vol. 3, p. 19.

87 *Repertuar russkogo i panteon vsekh evropeiskikh teatrov na 1842 god*, no. 1, p. 40.

88 Altschuller, 'Actors and Acting, 1820–1850', p. 104.

89 Senelick, *Serf Actor*, pp. 70–1.

90 Ibid., p. xvi.

91 Quoted in Senelick (ed.), *National Theatre in Northern and Eastern Europe*, p. 342.

92 Quoted in *IRDT*, vol. 4, pp. 13–14.

93 Quoted in Senelick, *Serf Actor*, p. 95.

94 Quoted in Senelick (ed.), *National Theatre in Northern and Eastern Europe*, pp. 337–8.

95 Quoted in Malnick, 'Mochalov and Karatygin', p. 279.

96 Quoted in ibid., p. 275.

97 Quoted in ibid., p. 278.

98 Quoted in ibid., p. 292.

99 Ibid., p. 292.

Chapter 3

1 *Russkaia stsena*, 1864, no. 1 (January), p. 1 (various pagination).
2 *IRDT*, vol. 4, p. 23; ibid., vol. 5, p. 22.
3 Kholodov, *Dramaturg na vse vremena*, pp. 98–9. For more details of performance statistics for Ostrovsky's plays, see ibid., pp. 94–124.
4 On Ostrovsky's links with the Malyi, see Rostotskii, 'Ostrovskii i Malyi teatr'.
5 Kholodov, *Dramaturg na vse vremena*, p. 15.
6 Ibid., p. 29.
7 For an alternative interpretation that stresses universal themes in Ostrovsky, see Rahman, *Ostrovsky*.
8 Quoted in Zograf, *Malyi teatr*, p. 69.
9 Vladykin (ed.), *A. N. Ostrovskii v russkoi kritike*, pp. 20–5; Dobroliubov, 'Temnoe tsarstvo'; Dobroliubov, 'Luch sveta v temnom tsarstve'; Grigor'ev, *Teatral'naia kritika*, pp. 171–204.
10 *IRDT*, vol. 5, p. 9.
11 Altschuller, 'Actors and Acting, 1820–1850', pp. 104–5.
12 Quoted in Senelick, *Serf Actor*, p. 192. For Shchepkin's difficulties with Ostrovsky's roles in general, see ibid., pp. 185–92.
13 *Russkaia stsena*, 1864, no. 6 (June), p. 81 (various pagination).
14 The committee's other members were A. M. Gedeonov (the director of Imperial Theatres), Count Shuvalov, K. V. Chevkin, Baron Meyendorf, Count Vielgorsky, Count Borkh and V. P. Panaev. Mikhailova, 'Vopros o teatral'noi monopolii', p. 77. Pogozhev gives the committee membership as Adlerberg, Gedeonov, Shuvalov, Meyendorf, Vielgorsky and Borkh. He worked from an 1863 source, whereas Mikhailova used the committee's materials. Pogozhev, *Proekt zakonopolozhenii*, vol. 3, p. 481.
15 Pogozhev, *Proekt zakonopolozhenii*, vol. 3, p. 481.
16 The committee's report is reproduced in ibid., pp. 484–93. See also Mikhailova, 'Vopros o teatral'noi monopolii', pp. 76–86; Danilov, 'Materialy po istorii russkogo zakonodatel'stva o teatre', pp. 180–1; *IRDT*, vol. 4, pp. 31–2.
17 Pogozhev, *Proekt zakonopolozhenii*, vol. 3, pp. 484–5.
18 Ibid., p. 487.
19 Ibid., p. 489.
20 Ibid., p. 490.
21 Mikhailova, 'Vopros o teatral'noi monopolii', p. 79. The German and French troupes mainly performed original drama in those languages, and the Italian troupe mainly performed opera.
22 Ibid., p. 80.
23 Pogozhev, *Proekt zakonopolozhenii*, vol. 3, p. 492.
24 Ibid.
25 Sollogub, *Peterburgskie stranitsy*, p. 307.
26 Mikhailova, 'Vopros o teatral'noi monopolii', pp. 80–1.
27 RGIA, f. 472, op. 60, d. 1942, ll. 12 ob.–14 – report from Adlerberg to the Minister of Internal Affairs, 19 May 1868, in which he reproduces his earlier report of 1858. See also Danilov, 'Materialy po istorii russkogo zakonodatel'stva o teatre', p. 181.
28 *IRDT*, vol. 4, p. 42.
29 Danilov, 'Materialy po istorii russkogo zakonodatel'stva o teatre', p. 181. The decree of 16 May 1858 nevertheless accepted some of the committee's suggestions

for financial reforms in the Imperial Theatre system. Pogozhev, *Proekt zakonopolozhenii*, vol. 3, p. 495.

30 RGIA, f. 497, op. 17, ed. khr. 101, ll. 123a–123b – Adlerberg to the director of Imperial Theatres, 2 April 1862.

31 RGIA, f. 497, op. 17, ed. khr. 101, ll. 24–24 ob. – Adlerberg to the director of Imperial Theatres, 3 April 1862.

32 RGIA, f. 497, op. 17, ed. khr. 101, ll. 141–141 ob. – Adlerberg to the director of Imperial Theatres, 29 April 1862. The first amateur performance in Passazh had taken place two years earlier. Dianina, 'Passage to Europe', p. 243, n. 21.

33 Mikhailova, 'Bor'ba peredovoi obshchestvennosti', p. 12. See also Swift, *Popular Theater*, pp. 47–53.

34 RGIA, f. 472, op. 60, d. 1942, ll. 3–4 ob. – Trepov to Alexander II, 13 April 1868.

35 RGIA, f. 472, op. 60, d. 1942, ll. 10–11 – Adlerberg to Assistant Minister of the Imperial Court, May (no day given) 1868. With the assistance of Sollogub, Trepov then submitted a more detailed version of his proposal to the Minister of Internal Affairs, A. E. Timashev. Mikhailova, 'K voprosu o sozdanii narodnogo teatra', p. 69.

36 *Balagany* (balagans) were temporary wooden theatres erected during holidays for a variety of popular entertainments, including circus and pantomime acts, magical performances, puppet shows and harlequinades.

37 RGIA, f. 472, op. 60, d. 1942, ll. 12–22 – Adlerberg to Minister of Internal Affairs, 19 May 1868.

38 Mikhailova, 'K voprosu o sozdanii narodnogo teatra', p. 70.

39 'Osobyia pravila o publichnykh zabavakh i uveseleniiakh v stolitsakh'.

40 RGIA, f. 497, op. 17, ed. khr. 109, l. 2 ob. – Sbornik deistvuiushchikh zakonopolozhenii i pravitel'stvennykh rasporiazhenii po teatral'nomu vedomstvu. Chast' I (no date, but between 1862 and 1876).

41 Petrovskaia, *Teatr i zritel' provintsial'noi Rossii*, p. 18.

42 Mikhailova, 'Vopros o teatral'noi monopolii', p. 82; Olenina, 'Regulirovanie trudovykh otnoshenii', p. 163.

43 Danilov, *Russkii dramaticheskii teatr*, p. 134.

44 Falkus, *Industrialisation of Russia*, pp. 17, 35.

45 Petrovskaia, *Teatr i zritel' provintsial'noi Rossii*, p. 28.

46 On Medvedev, see *TE*, vol. 3, column 758, and Davydov, *Rasskaz o proshlom*.

47 Petrovskaia and Somina, *Teatral'nyi Peterburg*, pp. 163–4.

48 Konechnyi, 'Shows for the People'; Konechnyi (ed.), *Peterburgskie balagany*; Donskov, *Mixail Lentovskij*; Swift, *Popular Theater*, pp. 53–8.

49 Kuznetsov, 'The Shaping of the Bourgeois Variety Theater'.

50 *Russkii dramaticheskii teatr. Entsiklopediia*, p. 32; *TE*, vol. 1, columns 311–12.

51 Vitenzon, *Anna Brenko*, p. 17.

52 'Dvadtsatipiatiletie stolichnykh chastnykh teatrov', *Teatral'naia Rossiia/ Teatral'naia gazeta*, 24 September 1905, pp. 1172–3.

53 'Pushkinskii teatr', *Russkii dramaticheskii teatr. Entsiklopediia*, p. 370.

54 Vitenzon, *Anna Brenko*, p. 23; 'Pushkinskii teatr', *Russkii dramaticheskii teatr. Entsiklopediia*, pp. 62, 370.

55 Vitenzon, *Anna Brenko*, p. 26.

56 Ibid., p. 47. One source claimed the figure was twenty thousand rubles: *Sufler*, 18 (30) September 1880, p. 1.

57 GTsTM, f. 39: 1, l. 99. – Brenko: Vospominaniia.

58 During the Pushkin's first season, from September 1880 to the end of February 1881, *Moskovskie vedomosti* publicized its performances alongside notices of the Imperial Bolshoi and Malyi repertoires, but it was always stated that only 'scenes from plays' were to be performed.

59 V. Viren, 'Podvig Anny Alekseevny', *Teatral'naia zhizn'*, 1959, no. 18, p. 26.

60 Urusov, *Stat'i ego*, vol. 1, p. 235; GTsTM, f. 39: 26, ll. 1–2/a – Dokumenty po sozdaniiu pervogo chastnogo 'Pushkinskogo' teatra A. A. Brenko (letter from Osip Levenson to the Minister of the Imperial Court, Vorontsov-Dashkov, September 1881).

61 'Material dlia istorii chastnykh teatrov v Moskve', *Teatral'nyi mirok*, 24 March 1884, p. 8; Vitenzon, *Anna Brenko*, p. 97.

62 *Sufler*, 30 January 1886, p. 3; Giliarovskii, *Moi skitaniia*, p. 216.

63 T. G., 'O pervom chastnom teatre v stolitse', *Teatral*, no. 114 (April 1897), pp. 40–56.

64 *TE*, vol. 1, columns 311–12, 693–94; *Russkii dramaticheskii teatr. Entsiklopediia*, pp. 32, 62.

65 Anon., 'Dvadtsatipiatiletie stolichnykh chastnykh teatrov', *Teatral'naia Rossiia Teatral'naia gazeta*, 24 September 1905, pp. 1172–3, based on an interview with Brenko by Giliarovsky originally published in *Rech'*, 1905; E. Beskin, 'Svetlyi put'', *Zhizn' iskusstva*, 14 October 1924, pp. 4–5.

66 *Sufler*, 18 (30) September 1880, p. 1.

67 Ibid., 2 (14) October 1880, p. 2.

68 Apart from the prominent example of Brenko's theatre, there appear to be very few recorded instances of breaches of the monopoly or of the directorate's regulations. In 1861 the second company of the Izmailovsky regiment organized theatrical performances without the permission of the directorate, and in 1862 soldiers of the Life Guard of the Moscow regiment organized an amateur performance. Mikhailova, 'Bor'ba peredovoi obshchestvennosti', p. 15.

69 Suvorin, *Teatral'nye ocherki*, pp. 52–3.

70 A. S–n [Suvorin], 'Russkaia dramaticheskaia stsena', *Vestnik Evropy*, January 1871, pp. 382–403. On Suvorin, see chapter 4.

71 Katkov, *Sobranie peredovykh statei moskovskikh vedomostei. 1875 god*, pp. 390–3.

72 Katkov, *Sobranie peredovykh statei moskovskikh vedomostei. 1871 god*, pp. 447–9.

73 Aleksandr Vol'f, 'Peterburgskie teatry i ikh sovremennoe polozhenie', *Vestnik Evropy*, March 1879, pp. 305–25. See also Vol'f, *Khronika peterburgskikh teatrov*, p. 7. From 1858 Volf had a theatre column in the Brussels-based newspaper *Le Nord* in which he demanded a series of theatrical reforms in Russia, including the legalization of private theatres.

74 Urusov, *Stat'i ego*, p. 461. See also ibid., pp. 230–6.

75 Ostrovskii, 'Klubnye stseny', pp. 114–17.

76 Skal'kovskii, *V teatral'nom mire*, pp. 8–15.

77 Ostrovskii, 'Klubnye stseny', pp. 118–19.

78 Ibid., pp. 119–26.

79 Ostrovsky to F. A. Burdin, 10 February 1881, in Ostrovskii, *Polnoe sobranie sochinenii*, vol. 12, p. 18.

80 Ostrovsky elaborated by identifying six groups that formed the theatre-less audience: tradesmen (*torgovtsy*) and salesmen (*prikazchiki*); merchants (*kupechestvo*); young people; 'educated society of middle-income' (such as scholars, professors, teachers, literary people and artists); petty traders and those

working in handicrafts (such as watchmakers, furniture makers, upholsterers, locksmiths, tailors, cobblers, etc.); and the inhabitants of the remote corners of Moscow, whose only theatre was in the very centre of the city. Such groups, claimed the playwright, did not necessarily want to go to taverns and clubs, or to get drunk on holidays, which were the only other kinds of entertainment permitted under the monopoly.

81 Ostrovskii, 'Zapiska'.

82 Ostrovskii, 'O prichinakh upadka dramaticheskogo teatra'.

83 The brief instruction was announced publicly in *Pravitel'stvennyi vestnik*, 7 (19) April 1882, p. 1.

84 Ibid., 22 August (3 September) 1881, p. 1.

85 Lukashevich, 'The Holy Brotherhood'.

86 Ostrovsky to N. Ya. Solovev, 24 August 1881, in Ostrovskii, *Polnoe sobranie sochinenii*, vol. 12, p. 35.

87 Guzovskaia and Nedzvetskaia, 'Ostrovskii i moskovskie teatry', p. 73. Shpazhinsky probably learned this from Brenko, whose theatre premiered his new play in September. In August Brenko had been promised 'full freedom' for her theatre, although no formal decision had yet been made.

88 Reviakin, 'Ostrovskii na puti', pp. 50–1.

89 GTsTM, f. 58, no. 106 – Vorontsov-Dashkov to Vsevolozhsky, 12 October 1881.

90 GTsTM, f. 58, no. 15 – Protokoly Kommissii o sostavlenii proekta polozheniia ob upravlenii Imperatorskimi Teatrami (1881–2).

91 GTsTM, f. 58, nos. 108 and 109 – Vorontsov-Dashkov to Vsevolozhsky, 25 October 1881. The existence of the commission was public knowledge. Early in November *Pravitel'stvennyi vestnik* announced that it had been created 'for the discussion of measures which could be taken with the purpose of improving theatre affairs'. The announcement also reproduced the list of questions that Vorontsov-Dashkov had asked the commission to consider. *Pravitel'stvennyi vestnik*, 3 (15) November 1881, p. 1.

92 RGIA, f. 497, op. 18, ed. khr. 15, ll. 1–5 ob. – Vsevolozhsky to Vorontsov-Dashkov, 4 January 1882.

93 RGIA, f. 497, op. 18, ed. khr. 403, ll. 11–20 ob. – *kontrol'* of the Ministry of the Imperial Court to the chancellery of the *kontrol'*, 14 March 1882; GTsTM, f. 58, no. 381 – letter from the 'Zhurnal soveta Ministra Imp. Dvora' to the directorate of Imperial Theatres, 2 (6?) March 1882. The initial proposal was to hand the troupe over to Filipp Bok, but his request was ultimately declined (the troupe was given to a certain Kartavov).

94 RGIA, f. 497, op. 14, ed. khr. 246 – Materialy po predmetu sokrashchenie raskhodov po teatral'nomu vedomstvu (1881). The report expressed ambivalence about the idea, however, claiming that competition would be harmful to Imperial Theatre revenues.

95 RGIA, f. 497, op. 18, ed. khr. 324, ll. 2–6 – Vsevolozhsky to Vorontsov-Dashkov, 20 February 1882.

96 It is worth noting that Dolgorukov had proved sympathetic to private theatrical ventures in the past, having supported the people's theatre at the 1872 Moscow Polytechnical Exposition. See Katkov, *Sobranie peredovykh statei moskovskikh vedomostei. 1872 god*, p. 160.

97 I. M. Kondratev in reply to Ostrovsky's letter of 23 June 1881, in Ostrovskii, *Polnoe sobranie sochinenii*, vol. 12, pp. 28–9.

98 The official statement on Kiester's dismissal did not mention Brenko. It simply stated that Kiester was being relieved of his duties as part of an administrative reform of the offices he held, namely the *kontrol'* and *kassa* of the Ministry of the Imperial Court. *Pravitel'stvennyi vestnik*, 26 August (7 September) 1881, p. 1.

99 Vitenzon, *Anna Brenko*, p. 96.

100 RGIA, f. 652, op. 1, d. 294, ll. 1–10 – Burdin to Vsevolozhsky, 6 September 1881. The paper that Burdin sent to Vsevolozhsky was dated 29 August, several days before the new director was appointed. It is possible that Burdin was prompted to write his paper on hearing the news of Kiester's dismissal, which was announced, for example, in *Pravitel'stvennyi vestnik* on 26 August and in *Moskovskie vedomosti* on 27 August.

101 GTsTM, f. 39: 28 – Pushkin Theatre repertoire details. Although *Moskovskie vedomosti* printed a review of a performance at Brenko's theatre of Shpazhinsky's new play *A Lie Stands Only until the Truth Is Known* in September, it did not print any notices of performances at the Pushkin for the 1881–2 season (as it had for the previous season), a fact that perhaps reflects confusion about the theatre's status. *Moskovskie vedomosti*, 8 September 1881, p. 3.

102 On 3 November 1881, an official in the Imperial Court chancellery (Kirilin) informed the manager of the directorate's Moscow branch (Begichev) that Brenko could now stage performances at the Pushkin without payment to the directorate. GTsTM, f. 39: 26, l. 2/a – Dokumenty po sozdaniiu pervogo chastnogo 'Pushkinskogo' teatra A. A. Brenko.

103 Quoted in Vitenzon, *Anna Brenko*, p. 96.

104 Ibid., pp. 96–7.

105 'Pushkinskii teatr', *Russkii dramaticheskii teatr. Entsiklopediia*, p. 370. The premises of Brenko's enterprise continued to be known as the Pushkin Theatre for some time afterwards, hosting public lectures (see, for example, *Moskovskie vedomosti*, 8 April 1882, p. 1) and providing a venue for the performances of another Russian drama troupe during the 1882–3 season (see *Moskovskii dnevnik zrelishch i ob"iavlenii*, September 1882–April 1883, *passim*). One theatrical journal referred to it as 'the theatre of Malkiel' (Pushkin)' (*Sufler*, 12 September 1885, p. 4).

106 Ostrovsky to Burdin, 10 August 1881, in Ostrovskii, *Polnoe sobranie sochinenii*, vol. 12, p. 32.

107 Ostrovskii, *Polnoe sobranie sochinenii*, vol. 12, p. 45, n. 1.

108 Reviakin, 'Ostrovskii na puti', p. 52.

109 Ostrovskii, *Polnoe sobranie sochinenii*, vol. 12, p. 50. It was not until 27 January 1882 that Ostrovsky read the paper to the commission.

110 Guzovskaia and Nedzvetskaia, 'Ostrovskii i moskovskie teatry', pp. 73–4; Ostrovskii, *Polnoe sobranie sochinenii*, vol. 12, p. 71.

111 Guzovskaia and Nedzvetskaia, 'Ostrovskii i moskovskie teatry', pp. 73–4.

112 *Pravitel'stvennyi vestnik*, 9 (21) March 1882, p. 2.

113 RGIA, f. 497, op. 2, d. 24796, l. 1 – chancellery of the Ministry of the Imperial Court to Vsevolozhsky, 21 October 1881.

114 RGIA, f. 481, op. 1 [3/1325], d. 67, ll. 26–27 ob. – Vorontsov-Dashkov to Alexander III, March (no day given) 1882.

115 See Rowell, *Victorian Theatre*. The Drury Lane and Covent Garden patents were originally granted by Charles II and reinforced by the Licensing Act of 1737.

116 See Hemmings, *Theatre and State in France*, chapter 11. The Declaration is

reproduced in Schumacher (ed.), *Naturalism and Symbolism in European Theatre*, pp. 47–8. The monopoly of the Opéra, the Comédie-Française and the Comédie-Italienne, originally established by Louis XIV, was abolished in 1791, but was effectively restored by Napoleon in 1806.

117 A good example is Sadler's Wells pleasure gardens.

118 Baker, *Rise of the Victorian Actor*, pp. 18–19. The new theatres included the Surrey (1810), the Cobury (1816), which subsequently became the Royal Victoria (1833), the Lyceum (1809?), the Olympic (1806), the Sans Pareil/Adelphi (1806), the Strand (1832) and the St James' (1835).

119 Rowell, *Victorian Theatre*, p. 13. See also Moody, *Illegitimate Theatre*, chapter 1.

120 McCormick and Schumacher, 'France, 1851–1919', p. 47.

121 In 1850 Paris had twenty-two licensed theatres, most of which were non-state.

122 Hemmings, *Theatre and State in France*, chapter 11.

123 On sending the manifesto to Grand Duke Vladimir, Alexander wrote, 'I will never suffer autocracy to be limited, as I believe autocracy to be necessary and useful to Russia.' Lowe, *Alexander III*, p. 61.

124 Danilov, *Ocherki*, p. 421.

125 See, for example, Shneiderman, *Mariia Gavrilovna Savina*, p. 130.

126 The only evidence cited by Danilov is a comment attributed by Alexander Kugel to Prince Shakhovskoi, head of the Chief Administration for Press Affairs: 'I think theatre is an ally of the government, since it diverts minds from sharp political issues.' Yet this remark was made c. 1897. See Kugel', 'K tridtsatiletiiu', pp. 5, 7.

127 RGIA, f. 497, op. 2, d. 24642, l. 56 ob. – Vedomosti o spetsial'nykh sredstv (January–December 1880).

128 See, for example, Danilov and Portugalova, *Russkii dramaticheskii teatr XIX veka*, p. 179, who claim that the government was effectively forced into the decision by 'public opinion', particularly as expressed by the 'democratic intelligentsia'. For similar emphasis on demand for theatres, see 'Monopoliia imperatorskikh teatrov', *TE*, vol. 3, columns 906–7, and Smith and Kelly, 'Commercial Culture and Consumerism', p. 124.

129 Gnedich, *Kniga zhizni*, p. 113.

130 Danilov, *Ocherki*, p. 422.

131 *Teatr i zhizn'*, 9 December 1888, pp. 2–3.

132 Rossikhina, *Opernyi teatr S. Mamontova*, pp. 31–2. For the continued popularity of amateur performances, see also Iunisov, '"Lishnii" teatr'.

133 See, for example, Tikhonov's comments on Tiflis: Tikhonov, 'Teatral'nyia vospominaniia', pp. 811–14.

134 This was despite the fact that, in 1865, Imperial Theatre artists had been prohibited from performing at other venues. Mikhailova, 'Bor'ba peredovoi obshchestvennosti', p. 15.

135 RGALI, f. 641, op. 1, ed. khr. 24, l. 122 – minutes of a meeting of the Russian Theatre Society's council, 23 October 1901.

136 RGIA, f. 497, op. 2, d. 24796, l. 6 – Vsevolozhsky's report, signed by Vsevolozhsky and Vorontsov-Dashkov, 14 November 1881.

137 See, for example, Kovalevskii, *Aleksandr III*. For a recent analysis of the shifting nature of official nationalism, see Wortman, *Scenarios of Power*, vol. 2, especially chapters 6 and 7.

138 Kizevetter, *Na rubezhe dvukh stoletii*, p. 85; Lowe, *Alexander III*, pp. 24–5, 88.

139 Kovalevskii, *Aleksandr III*, p. 13; Lowe, *Alexander III*, pp. 26–7.

140 Kovalevskii, *Aleksandr III*, pp. 17, 21–2.
141 V. G. Chernukha, 'Aleksandr III', in Chernukha (introduction) and Murav'eva (ed.), *Aleksandr Tretii*, p. 20.
142 Kovalevskii, *Aleksandr III*, p. 7.
143 Korol'kov, *Zhizn' i tsarstvovanie Imperatora Aleksandra III*, p. 149.
144 'Dnevnik naslednika', pp. 344–57. As tsarevich Alexander appears to have attended ballets, the French theatre, and musical evenings at the Admiralty.
145 Quoted in Guzovskaia and Nedzvetskaia, 'Ostrovskii i moskovskie teatry', p. 74.
146 *Teatr*, 12 March 1883, p. 4.
147 Pogozhev, *Proekt zakonopolozhenii*, vol. 1, p. 13.
148 Drizen, *Materialy*, p. 6.
149 *S.-Peterburgskiia vedomosti*, 9 (21) April 1882, p. 2.
150 *Oskolki*, 18 December 1882, front page illustration.
151 Pogozhev, *Proekt zakonopolozhenii*, vol. 1, p. 12.
152 See, for example, *IRDT*, vol. 4, p. 33; Slonim, *Russian Theater*, p. 84; Schuler, *Women in Russian Theatre*, p. 111; Senelick, 'Russia, 1848–1916', p. 193; Smith and Kelly, 'Commercial Culture and Consumerism', p. 124; Kelly, 'Popular, Provincial and Amateur Theatres 1820–1900', p. 124.

Chapter 4

1 RGALI, f. 641, op. 1, ed. khr. 2587 – list of theatres in Russia.
2 *Teatry i p'esy*, 8 May 1903, p. 3.
3 Iazykov, *Kratkii ocherk*, p. 12.
4 GTsTM, f. 123: 22–53 – Otchety po teatru Fedora Adamovicha Korsha, 1883–1915 gg.
5 Pavlova, 'Antrepriza Fedora Korsha', p. 50; *IRDT*, vol. 6, pp. 241–2.
6 GTsTM, f. 123: 22–53 – Otchety po teatru Fedora Adamovicha Korsha, 1883–1915 gg.
7 GTsTM, f. 123: 9 – Proekt organizatsii tovarishchestva na vere dlia eksploatatsii teatral'nogo predpriiatiia pod firmoiu 'Russkii dramaticheskii teatr' (no date, but approximately spring 1885). Korsh consistently subscribed to this view. See *IRDT*, vol. 6, p. 243.
8 GTsTM, f. 123: 22–53 – otchety po teatru Fedora Adamovicha Korsha, 1883–1915 gg.
9 GTsTM, f. 39: 1, l. 113 ob. – Brenko: Vospominaniia.
10 Korsh, *Kratkii ocherk*, p. 48.
11 Glama-Meshcherskaia, *Vospominaniia*, p. 206.
12 Iazykov, *Kratkii ocherk*, p. 6. The marked similarity between this book and Korsh's *Kratkii ocherk* of 1892 suggests that 'Iazykov' might be a pseudonym, but corroborative evidence remains elusive.
13 Pavlova, 'Antrepriza Fedora Korsha', p. 50.
14 Iazykov, *Kratkii ocherk*, pp. 16–17; Hartnoll (ed.), *Oxford Companion to the Theatre*, p. 567.
15 GTsTM, f. 123: 57–235 – Pozdravitel'nye telegrammy ot raznykh lits i uchrezhdenii Korshu F. A. po sluchaiu 25-ti letnego iubileia teatra (30 August 1907).
16 Arenzon, *Savva Mamontov*, p. 23.
17 Ibid., p. 5; Rossikhina, *Opernyi teatr S. Mamontova*, p. 64.

18 On Abramtsevo, see Polenova, *Abramtsevo*, and Sternin et al., *Abramtsevo*.
19 Bowlt, 'Two Russian Maecenases', pp. 447–8.
20 Ibid., p. 450.
21 Sternin et al., *Abramtsevo*, p. 45.
22 Rossikhina, *Opernyi teatr S. Mamontova*, p. 41.
23 Ibid.
24 See, for example, Ippolitov-Ivanov, *50 let russkoi muzyki*, p. 94.
25 Rossikhina, *Opernyi teatr S. Mamontova*, p. 25.
26 Gozenpud, *Russkii opernyi teatr*, p. 265.
27 Rossikhina, *Opernyi teatr S. Mamontova*, pp. 71, 90.
28 Mamontov, *Vospominaniia o russkikh khudozhnikakh*, p. 20.
29 Playbill reproduced in Bowlt, 'Two Russian Maecenases', p. 447. Bowlt explains the decision to name the theatre after Krotkov as follows: 'Mamontov felt that shareholders and fellow businessmen would be critical if his name were attached directly to such a light-hearted affair as a private opera' (p. 453, n. 15).
30 Iakovlev, *Izbrannye trudy o muzyke*, p. 223.
31 Arenzon, *Savva Mamontov*, p. 92.
32 Rossikhina, *Opernyi teatr S. Mamontova*, p. 42. Although Mamontov was acquitted – after a five-month spell in prison – his reputation was irreparably damaged and he had lost a lot of money: Kean, *French Painters, Russian Collectors*, pp. 73–5; Bowlt, 'Two Russian Maecenases', p. 450.
33 McReynolds, *News under Russia's Old Regime*, p. 74.
34 For Suvorin's career, see Rayfield and Makarova, 'Predislovie', and Ambler, *Russian Journalism and Politics*.
35 Rayfield and Makarova, 'Predislovie', p. xi.
36 See Racin (ed. and trans.), *Tatyana Repina*.
37 See Heim (trans.) and Karlinsky (ed.), *Letters of Anton Chekhov*, *passim*.
38 Karpov, 'A. S. Suvorin' [part 1], pp. 449–51.
39 Suvorin, *Dnevnik*, p. 298.
40 Karpov, 'A. S. Suvorin' [part 1], p. 452. As a youth, Karpov had spent time in 'administrative exile' for political activity: Karpov, 'A. S. Suvorin' [part 2], p. 892.
41 Karpov, 'A. S. Suvorin' [part 1], p. 452.
42 Its formal names were, from 1895, the Theatre of the Literary-Artistic Circle; from 1899, the Theatre of the Literary-Art Society; and from 1912, after Suvorin's death, the Suvorin Theatre of the Literary-Art Society. It was also known as the Malyi Theatre, however, because it used the premises of the old Malyi Theatre of Count Apraksin on the Fontanka Canal, or more commonly as the Suvorin Theatre, after its majority shareholder and effective leader.
43 Karpov, 'A. S. Suvorin' [part 1], p. 461.
44 Karpov, 'A. S. Suvorin' [part 2], p. 880.
45 On the idea of antipathy to the market in Russian culture, see, for example, Smith, 'Popular Culture and Market Development'. On the idea that theatrical activity was a form of 'spiritual compensation' for entrepreneurs, see, for example, *IRDT*, vol. 6, p. 10. On the idea that cultural activity was a 'means of gaining social approval', see, for example, Rieber, *Merchants and Entrepreneurs*, p. 166.
46 There are many more examples of new money patronizing the arts besides the ones mentioned in this chapter. Tchaikovsky, for example, was partly supported from the fortune made by the engineering and railroad magnate Karl F. von Meck (d. 1875), via his widow, Nadezhda, and the Moscow Art Theatre was bankrolled

in its early years by the wealthy tycoon Savva Morozov.

47 Petrovskaia, *Teatr i zritel' rossiiskikh stolits*, pp. 10, 68, 116.
48 Wortman, *Scenarios of Power*, vol. 2, chapter 7, and for an account of the winter ball, pp. 377–9.
49 Wortman, *Scenarios of Power*, vol. 1, pp. 380, 399.
50 Wortman, *Scenarios of Power*, vol. 2, p. 237.
51 Ibid., p. 256.
52 Iazykov, *Kratkii ocherk*, p. 24; Shchetinin, 'F. A. Korsh i ego teatr', p. 169.
53 *Moskovskie vedomosti*, 3 December 1883, p. 3.
54 *Novosti dnia*, 26 November 1883, pp. 2–3.
55 *Moskovskie vedomosti*, 3 December 1883, p. 3.
56 Iazykov, *Kratkii ocherk*, p. 24.
57 *Sovremennye izvestiia*, 1885, no. 277, cited in Gozenpud, *Russkii opernyi teatr*, p. 271.
58 *Russkii kur'er*, 11 October 1885, p. 4.
59 Ibid., 10 October 1885, p. 3.
60 *Teatr i zhizn'*, 1885, no. 178, quoted in Gozenpud, *Russkii opernyi teatr*, p. 271. For more on the Meiningen troupe, see chapter 7.
61 *Novosti dnia*, 10 October 1885, p. 3.
62 *Russkii kur'er*, 11 October 1885, p. 3.
63 Gozenpud, *Russkii opernyi teatr*, p. 270.
64 Dolgov, *Dvadtsatiletie teatra imeni A. S. Suvorina*, p. 37.
65 *Syn otechestva*, 17 (29) October 1898, p. 2.
66 *Peterburgskaia gazeta*, 13 October 1898, p. 3.
67 Ibid., 14 October 1898, p. 4.
68 *Birzhevyia vedomosti*, 13 (25) October 1898, p. 3.
69 Nemirovitch-Danchenko, *My Life*, p. 116; Schuler, *Women in Russian Theatre*, pp. 130–4.
70 The following account of Lentovsky's career is based mainly on Dmitriev, *Mikhail Lentovskii*. See also Donskov, *Mixail Lentovskij*.
71 The letter is reproduced in Donskov, *Mixail Lentovskij*, pp. 4–5.
72 Dmitriev, *Mikhail Lentovskii*, p. 117.
73 Ibid., pp. 115–16.
74 GTsTM, f. 144: 946 – Lentovskii, 'Moe upravlenie teatrami': Avtobiograficheskie zametki, 1876–1890 gg.
75 Dmitriev, *Mikhail Lentovskii*, pp. 149–50.
76 On the Skomorokh, see Swift, *Popular Theater*, pp. 61–6.
77 GTsTM, f. 144: 876 – 'Pravila dlia rasporiaditelei' narodnogo prazdnika posle koronatsiia 1883 g. mai; GTsTM, f. 144: 903 – *montirovka* of the coronation *gulian'e*.
78 GTsTM, f. 144: 492–509, ll. 2, 6–7 – Obshchaia perepiska po teatru 'Skomorokh' 1886 g. [*sic*].
79 Donskov, *Mixail Lentovskij*, pp. 66–76.
80 Dmitriev, *Mikhail Lentovskii*, pp. 31–2, 44, 155.
81 Ibid., pp. 193–4.
82 GTsTM, f. 532: 153, l. 91 – T. K. Almazova, 'M. V. Lentovskii' (dissertation, 1940s–1950s). See also Donskov, *Mixail Lentovskij*, p. 45.
83 GTsTM, f. 532: 153, l. 97 – T. K. Almazova, 'M. V. Lentovskii' (dissertation, 1940s–1950s).

84 GTsTM, f. 144: 639, ll. 5 ob.–8 – Otchet o repertuare, sostave truppy i sborakh so spektaklei v teatrakh Lentovskogo, 1886–87 teatr. sezon.
85 Donskov, *Mixail Lentovskij*, p. 3.
86 GTsTM, f. 144: 649 – Smeta mesiachnogo raskhoda po teatru 'Skomorokh', 1887–88 g.
87 Dmitriev, *Mikhail Lentovskii*, p. 223.
88 GTsTM, f. 144: 639, ll. 5 ob.–8 – Otchet o repertuare, sostave truppy i sborakh so spektaklei v teatrakh Lentovskogo, 1886–87 teatr. sezon.
89 GTsTM, f. 144: 651 – Proekt zapisi prikhoda i raskhoda i tekushchikh schetov po teatram Lentovskogo Mikh. Val., 1889 g. aprelia 3.
90 GTsTM, f. 144: 829–831 – Nekrologi o Lentovskom Mikh. Val.
91 Ibid.
92 Bakhrushin, *Vospominaniia*, pp. 254–5. Bakhrushin *fils* does not provide a date for this encounter, but it was presumably after October 1894 when the museum opened.

Chapter 5

1 On late imperial Russia's diverse commercial entertainments, see McReynolds, *Russia at Play*; Von Geldern and McReynolds (eds.), *Entertaining Tsarist Russia*, especially parts 3, 4 and 5; Kelly and Shepherd (eds.), *Constructing Russian Culture*, especially part 2.
2 Mikhailova, 'Vopros o teatral'noi monopolii', p. 82; Kruti, *Russkii teatr v Kazani*, p. 282.
3 Leikina-Svirskaia, *Russkaia intelligentsiia*, p. 186.
4 *Teatry i p'esy*, 28 January 1903, pp. 3–5.
5 *Teatral'nyia izvestiia*, 11 April 1895, p. 1.
6 Tolstoy, *What Is Art?*, p. 3.
7 *Khudozhnik*, 1 May 1892, pp. 615–16.
8 Ibid., 15 June 1892, pp. 807–8.
9 GTsTM, f. 1, op. 3: 96 – Avtobiografiia Bakhrushina (8 March 1922).
10 *TE*, vol. 1, column 467.
11 *Teatr i zhizn'*, 1 January 1890, p. 2.
12 *Teatral*, no. 33 (August 1895), pp. 126–30.
13 On Krylov see, for example, Zograf, *Malyi teatr*, pp. 280–5, 433–4.
14 *Teatr i zhizn'*, 1 January 1885, p. 1.
15 *Teatral'nyia izvestiia*, 13 August 1895, p. 1.
16 *Teatr i zhizn'*, 14 April 1889, p. 1.
17 *Sufler*, 22 September 1885, p. 1.
18 Ibid., 19 January 1886, p. 3.
19 Ibid., 4 July 1885, p. 2.
20 *Teatral'nyi mirok*, 25 April 1887, p. 1.
21 *Oskolki*, 29 September 1884, p. 7.
22 *Sufler*, 18 August 1885, p. 3.
23 *Khudozhnik*, 1 January 1892, pp. 46, 53.
24 *Sufler*, 9 February 1886, p. 1.
25 Ibid., p. 2.
26 *Teatral'nyi mirok*, 1893, no. 1, p. 4.
27 *Teatr*, 19 March 1883, p. 3.

28 *Teatral'nyi mirok*, 1 January 1884, p. 1.

29 *Teatral'nyia izvestiia*, 15 June 1895, p. 2.

30 For similar concerns and developments regarding popular literature, see Brooks, *When Russia Learned to Read*, chapter 9.

31 Swift, *Popular Theater*, p. 10; *IRDT*, vol. 6, p. 36.

32 Swift, *Popular Theater*, pp. 65, 71–2, 77.

33 Ibid., pp. 71, 81, 225.

34 For a broader view of such cultural elitism in late imperial Russia, see Brooks, *When Russia Learned to Read*, chapter 9.

35 *Teatr*, 19 February 1883, pp. 4–5.

36 *Teatr i zhizn'*, 23 November 1886, p. 1.

37 *Russkie vedomosti*, 1886, no. 350, quoted in GTsTM, f. 532: 153, l. 95 – T. K. Almazova, 'M. V. Lentovskii (dissertation, 1940s – 1950s).

38 *Teatr i zhizn'*, 1886, no. 204, quoted in GTsTM, f. 532: 153, l. 95 – T. K. Almazova, 'M. V. Lentovskii (dissertation, 1940s–1950s).

39 *Teatral*, no. 41 (October 1895), pp. 109–13.

40 Quoted in Swift, *Popular Theater*, p. 149.

41 Ibid., pp. 68, 135.

42 RGALI, f. 641, op. 1, ed. khr. 2587 – list of theatres in Russia; Swift, *Popular Theater*, p. 69; Thurston, *Popular Theatre Movement*, p. 125.

43 Swift, *Popular Theater*, pp. 67, 73.

44 Ibid., p. 38.

45 Donskov, *Mixail Lentovskij*, p. 48.

46 Swift, 'Fighting the Germs of Disorder', p. 3; Dmitriev, *Mikhail Lentovskii*, p. 233.

47 GTsTM, f. 58: 102 – undated paper on censorship by Vsevolozhsky. On late imperial Russian censorship in general, see Balmuth, *Censorship in Russia*.

48 Quoted in Swift, *Popular Theater*, p. 89.

49 Dmitriev, *Mikhail Lentovskii*, p. 239.

50 Ibid., p. 234.

51 On the way the regulation worked in practice, see Swift, *Popular Theater*, chapter 3.

52 Quoted in Tsinkovich, 'Narodnyi teatr i dramaticheskaia tsenzura', pp. 379–80.

53 Ibid., pp. 388, 391.

54 Quoted in Swift, *Popular Theater*, p. 74.

55 Quoted in Pavlova, 'Teatr F. A. Korsha', p. 20.

56 *Teatr i iskusstvo*, 18 July 1899, p. 498.

57 *Teatr*, 1 January 1883, pp. 1–2.

58 *Peterburgskaia gazeta*, 5 February 1894, p. 3.

59 Nelidov, *Teatral'naia Moskva*, p. 100. For more on the militaristic element in the Imperial Theatres, see Frame, *St Petersburg Imperial Theaters*, pp. 26–31.

60 Quoted in Pavlova, '"Davydovskie sezony"', p. 269.

61 *Teatral'nyi mirok*, 24 January 1887, pp. 6–7.

62 Nemirovitch-Danchenko, *My Life*, p. 29.

63 Varneke, *History of the Russian Theatre*, p. 375.

64 Ibid. On Ermolova, see Schuler, *Women in Russian Theatre*, chapter 4.

65 Quoted in Varneke, *History of the Russian Theatre*, p. 386.

66 Frame, *St Peterburg Imperial Theaters*, p. 71 and chapter 3 *passim*.

67 *Oskolki*, 18 February 1884, p. 2.

68 *Teatral'nyi mirok*, 17 October 1887, p. 9.

69 *Ezhegodnik imperatorskikh teatrov. Sezon 1890–91 g.g.*, introductory remarks.
70 For an overview of the history of the yearbooks, see Wiley, 'The Yearbook of the Imperial Theaters'.

Chapter 6

1 See, for instance, Carr-Saunders and Wilson, *Professions*; Johnson, *Professions and Power*; Larson, *Rise of Professionalism*.
2 Indicative of this expansion was the number of Russians with a higher education, growing from about twenty thousand in 1860 to about eighty-five thousand in 1900: Leikina-Svirskaia, *Intelligentsiia v Rossii*, p. 70. Works that discuss the late imperial Russian professions include Balzer (ed.), *Russia's Missing Middle Class*; Leikina-Svirskaia, *Intelligentsiia v Rossii*; Leikina-Svirskaia, *Russkaia intelligentsiia.*
3 Balzer, 'Introduction', p. 9; Frieden, *Russian Physicians*, p. 14; Freeze, 'The *Soslovie* (Estate) Paradigm'.
4 See, for example, Hutchinson, 'Society, Corporation or Union?', p. 42, and Pomeranz, '"Profession or Estate"?', p. 245.
5 Bailes, 'Reflections on Russian Professions', p. 45.
6 See, for example, Parsons, 'The Professions and Social Structure', and Larson, *Rise of Professionalism.*
7 Varneke, *Istoriia russkogo teatra*, p. 24.
8 Ibid., p. 25.
9 This is a very rough calculation based on two statistics for the 1870s: the dramatist A. I. Palm's calculation that there were approximately three thousand provincial actors at the end of the 1870s, and Olenina's claim that there were 102 provincial troupes at the beginning of the 1870s. Leikina-Svirskaia, *Russkaia intelligentsiia*, p. 197; Olenina, 'Regulirovanie trudovykh otnoshenii', p. 163.
10 Leikina-Svirskaia, *Russkaia intelligentsiia*, p. 203.
11 See Stites, *Serfdom, Society, and the Arts*, chapter 6.
12 *Oskolki*, 14 April 1884, p. 2. For similar sketches, see ibid., 3 March 1884, p. 1, and ibid., 9 February 1885, p. 1, the latter indicating that sometimes even Imperial Theatre artists had to resort to alternative employment during Lent, such as busking or selling fruit and vegetables.
13 Ibid., 17 March 1884, p. 5.
14 *Sufler*, 31 October 1885, p. 4
15 *TPVSSD*, vol. 1, p. 47.
16 Ibid., p. 64.
17 *Teatr i iskusstvo*, 18 March 1901, p. 243.
18 RGALI, f. 641, op. 1, ed. khr. 153a, l. 2 – Police Department, Ministry of Internal Affairs, circular to local governors (*gubernatory*), 9 January 1886.
19 Lindenmeyr, *Poverty Is Not a Vice*, p. 34.
20 Ibid., pp. 110, 115, 122, 236.
21 Stepanskii, *Samoderzhavie*, p. 27.
22 In contrast to its Soviet-era incarnation, the pre-revolutionary Russian Theatre Society has been largely neglected by historians, with the exception of a dissertation by a Moscow theatre student: Kozlova, 'Russkoe teatral'noe obshchestvo'. A few short published accounts of the society's pre-revolutionary history have appeared in memoir and anniversary literature: Grigor'ev, *60 let*;

Iablochkina, *75 let*, pp. 413–15; Kugel', 'K tridtsatiletiiu'. The following discussion is largely based on materials in the society's archive, held in Moscow at RGALI.

23 *TE*, vol. 4, column 125.

24 Kozlova, 'Russkoe teatral'noe obshchestvo', p. 19. See also *Teatral'nyia izvestiia*, 4 October 1894, p. 1.

25 RGALI, f. 641, op. 1, ed. khr. 73, l. 39 – RTO general assembly, 13–15 December 1903.

26 RGALI, f. 641, op. 1, ed. khr. 1-a, ll. 26–35 – charter of the Russian Theatre Society, approved by the Ministry of Internal Affairs on 15 May 1894.

27 Ibid.

28 RGALI, f. 641, op. 1, ed. khr. 163, l. 30 ob. – report on RTO, 17 May 1904.

29 Stepanskii, *Samoderzhavie*, p. 18.

30 RGALI, f. 641, op. 1, ed. khr. 72, ll. 47–50 ob. – provisional regulations for the issuing of loans to stage people and troupes of artists, c. October 1900.

31 RGALI, f. 641, op. 1, ed. khr. 163, l. 29 ob. – report on RTO, 17 May 1904. According to this source, these figures constitute the amount the RTO spent on its 'charitable missions', but it does not make it clear whether they represent loans alone or include expenditure on other activities that the society engaged in.

32 RGALI, f. 641, op. 1, ed. khr. 26, l. 427 – minutes of RTO council meeting, 4 May 1904 and l. 459–459 ob. – minutes of RTO council meeting, 9 June 1904.

33 RGALI, f. 641, op. 1, ed. khr. 163, l. 30 – report on RTO, 17 May 1904.

34 RGALI, f. 641, op. 1, ed. khr. 25, l. 208 – minutes of RTO council meeting, 22 October 1902.

35 *Teatr i iskusstvo*, 7 March 1901, p. 228; RGALI, f. 641, op. 1, ed. khr. 26, l. 133 – minutes of RTO council meeting, 5 June 1903.

36 GTsTM, f. 1, no. 5727 – Potekhin to Bakhrushin, 15 November 1896; *TE*, vol. 1, column 1039. For a brief account of the way the RTO's bureau functioned, see Shebuev, *Akterskoe schast'e*, pp. 63–4.

37 *Peterburgskaia gazeta*, 8 February 1894, p. 3.

38 *TE*, vol. 4, column 537; Mal'tseva, 'Akterskoe samoupravlenie', p. 164; Karpov, 'A. S. Suvorin' [part 1], p. 460.

39 RGALI, f. 641, op. 1, ed. khr. 145, ll. 11–18, 28–34 – lists of RTO agents, 1895 and n.d. but not earlier than 5 August 1899; RGALI, f. 641, op. 1, ed. khr. 163, l. 29 – report on RTO, 17 May 1904.

40 RGALI, f. 641, op. 1, ed. khr. 145, ll. 19–23.

41 RGALI, f. 641, op. 1, ed. khr. 21, ll. 7 and 7 ob. – requests from RTO agents in Simbirsk and Zhitomir regarding freedom to travel for Jewish actors, in the minutes of the RTO council meeting, 3 February 1898. The majority of Jews in the Russian empire were required to live within the so-called Pale of Settlement in the western provinces. Some Jewish merchants and those with university degrees were later allowed to live elsewhere, but they still required permission to move.

42 RGALI, f. 641, op. 1, ed. khr. 21, l. 71 ob. – minutes of RTO council meeting, 11 August 1898.

43 RGALI, f. 641, op. 1, ed. khr. 22, ll. 31 ob.–32 – minutes of RTO council meeting, 16 March 1899.

44 RGALI, f. 641, op. 1, ed. khr. 23, l. 11 ob. – minutes of RTO council meeting, 25 January 1900.

45 RGALI, f. 641, op. 1, ed. khr. 21, ll. 96 ob.–99 ob. – minutes of RTO council meeting, 27 October 1898.

46 On the Union of German Theatre People, see *Teatral'naia Rossiia/Teatral'naia gazeta*, 21 May 1905, pp. 360–3. On the Actors' Equity Association, see Harding, *Revolt of the Actors*. On the background to Equity, see MacLeod, *Actor's Right to Act*.

47 *Teatr i zhizn'*, 20 August 1889, pp. 2–3; ibid., 8 October 1889, pp. 2–3.

48 *TPVSSD*, vol. 1, p. 4.

49 Ibid., p. 9.

50 The complete proceedings of the first congress were published in two volumes in St Petersburg in 1898 as *TPVSSD*, and those of the second were extensively reported in the St Petersburg-based theatre journal *Teatr i iskusstvo* (11, 18 and 25 March 1901).

51 Balzer, 'Introduction', p. 6.

52 *TPVSSD*, vol. 1, pp. 74, 81.

53 Ibid., pp. 48–9.

54 Ibid., p. 52.

55 Ibid., pp. 56, 62.

56 Ibid., p. 98.

57 Ibid., pp. 99, 109.

58 Ibid., pp. 179–80.

59 Ibid., pp. 186–7.

60 Ibid., p. 187.

61 Ibid., p. 192.

62 Ibid., p. 208.

63 Ibid., p. 209.

64 Leikina-Svirskaia, *Russkaia intelligentsiia*, p. 204.

65 *Teatr i iskusstvo*, 11 March 1901, p. 223.

66 Shneiderman, *Mariia Gavrilovna Savina*, pp. 5, 12–29, 39–43.

67 Leikina-Svirskaia, *Russkaia intelligentsiia*, p. 194. On the 'first private drama school' in St Petersburg, see *Teatr*, 26 February 1883, pp. 14–16.

68 Stanislavski, *My Life in Art*, p. 79. On the training offered by the Imperial Theatre School in Moscow, see Schuler, *Women in Russian Theatre*, pp. 66–71. For a vivid account by a ballet pupil, see Karsavina, *Theatre Street*, chapters 5–11.

69 *TPVSSD*, vol. 1, p. 113.

70 Ibid., p. 223.

71 Ibid., p. 117.

72 Ibid., p. 229.

73 *Teatr i iskusstvo*, 18 March 1901, p. 244.

74 *TPVSSD*, vol. 1, p. 224.

75 *Teatr i iskusstvo*, 18 March 1901, p. 244.

76 Ibid.

77 Benedetti, *Stanislavski*, pp. 178–89; Moore, *Stanislavski System*, pp. 87–8; Worrall, *Moscow Art Theatre*, pp. 3, 178–98.

78 *TPVSSD*, vol. 1, pp. 127–9.

79 *Teatr i iskusstvo*, 18 March 1901, p. 247.

80 For an example of a vanishing impresario, see *Novosti dnia*, 4 February 1896, p. 4.

81 Olenina, 'Regulirovanie trudovykh otnoshenii', p. 167.

82 Ibid., pp. 165–6; *TPVSSD*, vol. 1, p. 175.

83 *TPVSSD*, vol. 1, p. 86–7.

84 Ibid., p. 142.

85 Ibid., p. 143.
86 Ibid., p. 177.
87 RGALI, f. 641, op. 1, ed. khr. 72, l. 59 ob. – council report for RTO general assembly, 23 November 1902, containing an account of what Molchanov said in March 1902.
88 Olenina, 'Regulirovanie trudovykh otnoshenii', p. 167.
89 *TPVSSD*, vol. 1, pp. 88–9.
90 RGALI, f. 641, op. 1, ed. khr. 203, ll. 24–24 ob. – impresario's declaration, 9 August 1903.
91 *TPVSSD*, vol. 1, p. 143.
92 Ibid., p. 156.
93 Olenina, 'Regulirovanie trudovykh otnoshenii', p. 167.
94 RGALI, f. 641, op. 1, ed. khr. 1-a, ll. 26–35 – charter of the Russian Theatre Society, 15 May 1894, clauses 44, 48 and 50.
95 RGALI, f. 641, op. 1, ed. khr. 148, ll. 1–1 ob. – chancellery of the Ministry of the Imperial Court to the council of the RTO, 30 October 1895; subsequent correspondence contained in this file indicates that the same sum was paid annually until the 1917 revolution.
96 RGALI, f. 641, op. 1, ed. khr. 22, l. 3 – minutes of RTO council meeting, 12 January 1899. The decision to provide the RTO with an annual subsidy was made in January 1899. The first subsidy was paid at the beginning of 1900.
97 RGALI, f. 641, op. 1, ed. khr. 18, l. 66 – minutes of RTO council meeting, 8 December 1895.
98 RGALI, f. 641, op. 1, ed. khr. 67, ll. 10–12 – protocols of RTO general assembly, 17 October 1898 and ll. 18, 20, 21, 22, 23 – letters of acceptance from the new honorary members.
99 *TPVSSD*, vol. 1, pp. 10–11.
100 RGALI, f. 641, op. 1, ed. khr. 23, l. 71 – minutes of RTO council meeting, 8 August 1900.
101 *Teatral'nyia izvestiia*, 20 April 1897, p. 3.
102 Kugel', 'K tridtsatiletiiu', pp. 5, 7.
103 RGALI, f. 641, op. 1, ed. khr. 22, ll. 15–16 – minutes of RTO council meeting, 8 February 1899.
104 RGALI, f. 641, op. 1, ed. khr. 145, l. 47 – Sergei Mikhailovich to P. N. Durnovo, 11 November 1900.
105 RGALI, f. 641, op. 1, ed. khr. 26, l. 345 – minutes of RTO council meeting, 27 January 1904; *Pravitel'stvennyi vestnik*, 9 March 1904 (cited in Kugel', 'K tridtsatiletiiu', p. 7).
106 RGALI, f. 641, op. 1, ed. khr. 163, l. 28 ob. – report on RTO, 17 May 1904; RGALI, f. 641, op. 1, ed. khr. 403, ll. 1–2 – D. S. Sipiagin to Sergei Mikhailovich, 28 January 1901.
107 Stepanskii, *Samoderzhavie*, p. 20.
108 *TPVSSD*, vol. 1, p. 108.
109 RGALI, f. 641, op. 1, ed. khr. 70, l. 14 – papers of the general assembly, 23 April 1900.
110 RGALI, f. 641, op. 1, ed. khr. 25, ll. 36–36 ob. – minutes of RTO council meeting, 15 February 1902.
111 'Ustav o preduprezhdenii i presechenii prestuplenii', clause 170.
112 *IRDT*, vol. 3, p. 19.

113 Johnson, *Professions and Power*, p. 32.
114 Bradley, 'Subjects into Citizens', p. 1123.

Chapter 7

1 Danilov, *Ocherki*, p. 477.
2 *IRDT*, vol. 7, p. 15.
3 Stanislavski, *My Life in Art*, p. 319.
4 Quoted in Worrall, *Moscow Art Theatre*, pp. 17–18.
5 Quoted in Slonim, *Russian Theater*, p. 94.
6 Nemirovitch-Danchenko, *My Life*, pp. 22–3.
7 Ibid., p. 29.
8 Ibid., p. 156.
9 *Novosti dnia*, 2 February 1896, p. 3.
10 Worrall, *Moscow Art Theatre*, p. 30.
11 Ibid., p. 36.
12 Nemirovitch-Danchenko, *My Life*, pp. 72–6.
13 Worrall, *Moscow Art Theatre*, p. 44.
14 Quoted in ibid., p. 62.
15 Nemirovitch-Danchenko, *My Life*, p. 117.
16 Benedetti (ed. and trans.), *Moscow Art Theatre Letters*, p. 9.
17 Kruti, *Russkii teatr v Kazani*, p. 282.
18 Nemirovitch-Danchenko, *My Life*, p. 118.
19 Quoted in Benedetti, *Stanislavski*, p. 68.
20 Nemirovitch-Danchenko, *My Life*, pp. 89–91.
21 Ibid., p. 98.
22 Worrall, *Moscow Art Theatre*, p. 54.
23 Frame, *St Petersburg Imperial Theaters*, p. 92; Worrall, *Moscow Art Theatre*, p. 7.
24 Worrall, *Moscow Art Theatre*, p. 86.
25 Quoted in Morozova and Potkina, *Savva Morozov*, p. 156.
26 Quoted in Nemirovitch-Danchenko, *My Life*, pp. 64–5.
27 Ibid., p. 184.
28 Ibid., p. 198.
29 Swift, *Popular Theater*, pp. 1–2; Nemirovitch-Danchenko, *My Life*, pp. 181–2.
30 Worrall, *Moscow Art Theatre*, pp. 50, 68.
31 Ibid., pp. 68–9, 70–1.
32 Ibid., p. 81.
33 Nemirovitch-Danchenko, *My Life*, pp. 257–8.
34 Quoted in Stepanskii, *Samoderzhavie*, p. 33.
35 GTsTM, f. 280: 1266 – 'Tsenzura i imperatorskie teatry', undated notes by Telyakovsky.
36 Danilov, *Ocherki*, p. 480.
37 Nemirovitch-Danchenko, *My Life*, pp. 260–3.
38 Pogozhev, *Proekt zakonopolozhenii*, vol. 1, p. 38.
39 For more details, see Frame, *St Petersburg Imperial Theaters*, p. 37.
40 Pogozhev, *Proekt zakonopolozhenii*, vol. 1, pp. 12–13.
41 On Imperial Theatre finances, see Frame, *St Petersburg Imperial Theaters*, pp. 23–5.
42 Pogozhev, *Proekt zakonopolozhenii*, vol. 1, p. 95.

43 Ibid., p. 14.
44 Ibid., p. 16.
45 Volkov, 'Teatr v epokhu krusheniia monarkhii', p. 306.
46 Slonim, *Russian Theater*, p. 133.
47 Clowes, 'Social Discourse in the Moscow Art Theater', p. 273.
48 Golovin, *Vstrechi i vpechatleniia*, p. 50.
49 Benedetti, *Stanislavski*, p. 85.
50 For an elaboration of this argument, see Frame, *St Petersburg Imperial Theaters*, chapter 2.
51 Danilov, *Ocherki*, p. 480. On Komissarzhevskaya, see Borovsky, *Triptych from the Russian Theatre*, and Schuler, *Women in Russian Theatre*, chapter 8.
52 Iankovskii, 'Teatral'naia obshchestvennost'' Peterburga', p. 139.
53 Frame, *St Petersburg Imperial Theaters*, pp. 124–5.
54 Danilov, *Ocherki*, p. 481.
55 Yastrebtsev, *Reminiscences*, pp. 352–3, 355–8.
56 GTsTM, f. 280: 1266 – 'Tsenzura i imperatorskie teatry', undated notes by Telyakovsky.
57 Sargeant, '*Kashchei the Immortal*', p. 22.
58 GTsTM, f. 280: 52 – von Bohl to Telyakovsky, 13 January 1905.
59 GTsTM, f. 280: 935 – Lopukhin (St Petersburg police chief) to Telyakovsky, 3 February 1905; Volkov, 'Teatr v epokhu krusheniia monarkhii', p. 320.
60 Khodotov, *Blizkoe-dalekoe*, p. 169.
61 Teliakovskii, *Imperatorskie teatry*, p. 50; Gnedich, *Kniga zhizni*, p. 312.
62 Danilov, *Ocherki*, p. 487.
63 *TE*, vol. 1, column 1039.
64 *Slovo*, 12 (25) February 1905, p. 7.
65 Ibid., 10 (23) March 1905, p. 8.
66 Quoted in Danilov, 'Revoliutsiia 1905–1907 godov', p. 122. For a study that plays down the extent to which artists were really concerned with politics during the 1905 revolution, see Du Quenoy, 'Harlequin's Leap'.
67 RGALI, f. 641, op. 1, ed. khr. 74, ll. 53 ob.–54 ob. – general assembly, meetings held on 28 February, 3 March and 6 March 1905.
68 RGALI, f. 641, op. 1, ed. khr. 27, l. 230 ob. – minutes of RTO council meeting, 13 July 1905.
69 RGALI, f. 641, op. 1, ed. khr. 28, ll. 50–51 – minutes of RTO council meeting, 29 September 1905.
70 RGALI, f. 641, op. 1, ed. khr. 28, l. 2 ob. – minutes of RTO council meeting, 24 August 1905.
71 Balzer, 'Introduction', p. 10.
72 Galai, *Liberation Movement in Russia*, pp. 223, 234–6, 245–50.
73 Kugel', 'K tridtsatiletiiu', p. 7.
74 RGALI, f. 641, op. 1, ed. khr. 74, ll. 57, 67 – general assembly, meetings held on 28 February, 3 March and 6 March 1905.
75 RGALI, f. 641, op. 1, ed. khr. 74, l. 68 ob. – general assembly, meetings held on 28 February, 3 March and 6 March 1905.
76 Kugel', 'K tridtsatiletiiu', p. 7.
77 Sargeant, '*Kashchei the Immortal*', p. 38.
78 *TPVSSD*, vol. 1, p. 153.
79 RGALI, f. 641, op. 1, ed. khr. 74, ll. 7 ob.–8 – report of the RTO auditing

commission, 2 February 1905.

80 *Russkoe teatral'noe obshchestvo*, p. 5.

81 *Ustav vserossiiskogo soiuza stsenicheskikh deiatelei.*

82 According to Kugel, the Union of Theatre People 'began to acquire in many people's eyes the characteristics of a workers' union [*rabochii soiuz*]'. Kugel', 'K tridtsatiletiiu', p. 8.

83 This is the essential distinction between a trade union and a professional association offered by Carr-Saunders and Wilson: 'Though the protective motive [predominant in trade unions] is present [in professional associations], it is only one among many and by no means always the most important. In particular the desire to hall-mark the competent and to foster the study of the [professional] technique give to the technique such an importance that boundaries are clearly defined and stable.' Carr-Saunders and Wilson, *Professions*, p. 319.

84 The Russian term that came to be used for 'trade union' is *profsoiuz*, 'professional union'. Consequently, while the RTO was clearly a professional association and not a trade union according to the English-language understanding of these terms, the distinction appears to be less clear-cut in Russian. More research is needed on the pre-revolutionary meanings of these terms.

85 Teliakovskii, *Imperatorskie teatry*, p. 24.

86 *IRDT*, vol. 7, p. 314.

87 Teliakovskii, *Imperatorskie teatry*, p. 33.

88 Ibid., p. 42.

89 Ibid., p. 52.

90 Gnedich, *Kniga zhizni*, p. 313.

91 Frame, *St Petersburg Imperial Theaters*, pp. 131–2.

Epilogue

1 *Teatral'nyia izvestiia*, 18 September 1901, p. 2.

2 Briusov, 'Nenuzhnaia pravda'. For the symbolists' ideas about theatre, see also Rosenthal, 'Theatre As Church'.

3 Kleberg, 'Vjaceslav Ivanov and the Idea of Theater'; Rudnitsky, *Russian and Soviet Theatre*, pp. 9–10.

4 Gauss, *Lear's Daughters.*

5 Frame, *St Petersburg Imperial Theaters*, chapter 7.

6 Russell, 'People's Theatre', p. 69. On amateur theatre, see Mally, *Revolutionary Acts.*

7 Kerzhentsev, *Tvorcheskii teatr*; Rudnitsky, *Meyerhold*, chapter 6.

8 On Proletkult, see Mally, *Culture of the Future.*

9 Carter, *New Spirit in the Russian Theatre*, p. 15.

10 Gorchakov, *Theater in Soviet Russia*, p. vii.

INDEX